For Phillip

The EU, US and China Tackling Climate Change

The feeling of optimism that followed the COP 21 Paris Conference on Climate Change requires concrete action and steadfast commitment to a process that raises a number of crucial challenges: technological, political, social and economic. As climate change worsens, new robust leadership is imperative.

The EU, US and China Tackling Climate Change examines why a close collaboration between the EU and China may result in the necessary impetus to solidify a vision and a roadmap for our common future in the Anthropocene. Kalantzakos introduces a novel perspective and narrative on climate action leadership through an analysis of international relations. She argues that a close EU–China collaboration, which does not carry the baggage of an imbedded competition for supremacy, may best help the global community move towards a low carbon future and navigate the new challenges of the Anthropocene. Overall, Kalantzakos demonstrates how Europe and China, already strategic partners, can exercise global leadership in an area of crucial common interest through their web of relations, substantial development aid, and the use of soft power tools throughout the developing world.

This book will be of great interest to students and scholars of environmental politics, international relations, climate change and energy law and policy.

Sophia Kalantzakos is Global Distinguished Professor in Environmental Studies and Public Policy at New York University, USA/Abu Dhabi.

Routledge Studies in Environmental Policy

The EU, US and China Tackling Climate Change

Policies and Alliances for the Anthropocene

Sophia Kalantzakos

Routledge
Taylor & Francis Group

LONDON AND NEW YORK

First published 2017 by Routledge

2 Park Square, Milton Park, Abingdon, Oxfordshire OX14 4RN
52 Vanderbilt Avenue, New York, NY 10017

Routledge is an imprint of the Taylor & Francis Group, an informa business

First issued in paperback 2018

British Library Cataloguing-in-Publication Data
A catalogue record for this book is available from the British Library

Library of Congress Cataloging-in-Publication Data
Names: Kalantzakos, Sophia, author.
Title: The EU, US and China tackling climate change:
policies and alliances for the anthropocene / Sophia Kalantzakos.
Description: Milton Park, Abingdon, Oxon; New York, NY:
Routledge/Earthscan, 2017. | Series: Routledge studies in
environmental policy
Identifiers: LCCN 2016058685 | ISBN 9781138237858 (hbk) |
ISBN 9781315298870 (ebk)
Subjects: LCSH: Climatic changes–Prevention–International
cooperation. | Climatic changes–Government policy–European
Union countries. | Climatic changes–Government policy–United
States. | Climatic changes–Government policy–China.
Classification: LCC QC903 .K193 2017 | DDC 363.738/74561–dc23
LC record available at https://lccn.loc.gov/2016058685

ISBN: 978-1-138-23785-8 (hbk)
ISBN: 978-0-367-17929-8 (pbk)

Typeset in Goudy
by Deanta Global Publishing Services, Chennai, India

Contents

Acknowledgments

My oldest debt of gratitude is to my father, Aristides, who from the cradle cultivated my curiosity in the ways of both local and global politics. Asteris Huliaras has been a careful and helpful critic of this book and I wish to thank him not only for his unstinting encouragement and guidance, but also for his warm friendship. Beth Daniel Lindsay of the NYUAD Library has been an invaluable resource and I wish to thank as well Mohan Vasanth, Otto Kakhidze and my student Paula Monserrat Estrada Tun for help along the way.

A fellowship at the Rachel Carson Center enabled me to write this manuscript in idyllic conditions and I am deeply grateful to its directors, Christof Mausch and Helmut Trischler, as well as to my cohort of fellows, for making my time in Munich so stimulating and pleasant. NYU and NYUAD have offered wonderful environments in which to teach and do research over the years and I'm grateful to the many colleagues and students who have made life in a university setting so stimulating. I would be remiss, however, if I did not single out Jonathan Lipman for all manner of help through the years, Dick Foley, Hilary Ballon, and finally Carol Brandt, who has helped make NYUAD such an extraordinary experience. I would like to take this opportunity to thank both institutions for providing both time and funds in support of my research. By a nice irony, my former Dean at SIPA, Lisa Anderson, was visiting at NYUAD during the final stages of the book and I want to thank her for some fun and stimulating luncheon discussions on the US, the EU, China, and beyond.

I am pleased to thank Margaret Farrelly for assisting with the editing process and I owe a further debt of thanks to Routledge's anonymous readers for exceptionally helpful and detailed criticism. Finally, I would like to dedicate this book to my husband Phillip who has been a pillar of support and a vital sounding board. I would also like to let my daughter Alexandra know that I fully credit her for being a good sport throughout.

Introduction
EU and China: An alliance for the Anthropocene

We are in a race against time … Together, let us turn the aspirations of Paris into action … so that the spirit of solidarity of Paris lives again.

UN General Secretary Ban Ki-moon
New York, April 22, 2016

This book is about leadership. Leadership in the time of the Anthropocene and after the Conference of the Parties (COP) 21. The kind of leadership that can galvanize the world community to take the hope born in Paris and transform it into a movement that will push beyond promises. Leadership that will drive bold and unprecedented action before the damage to the earth's systems surpasses our capacity to repair. What possible partnerships can guide us best through the unchartered waters that we are now seeking to cross? Conditioned to accept the outcome of doing nothing—what we call business as usual—the world has difficulty imagining a future where the covenants on which human "civilization" has been built will need to be re-examined.

Simon Dalby poignantly noted that,

> politics is not now just a matter of institutions, sovereignties, governance, arrangements, parties, movements, leaders, and states. It is now unavoidably a matter of cities, pipelines, technological innovations, and discussions about the future configurations of the planet … The new material circumstances wherein humanity has become effectively a geological force requires a much more fundamental rethinking of the geo in geopolitics than most analysts have so far contemplated.[1]

In this quest for leadership in the Anthropocene, I propose that a strategic, full-fledged partnership between the European Union (EU) and China could become our best hope to confront both the climate crisis and the wider challenges that lie beyond.

Why these two actors?

Am I ignoring the United States (US) by design?

Why wouldn't a joint US–China leadership model be more appropriate and more effective? Aren't they the new superpowers of the twenty-first century?

Why not a tripartite partnership between the US, the EU, and China?

These are all valid questions, of course, and furthermore the entire world community needs to partake in the effort to confront the climate crisis. The Paris Agreement that went into effect on November 4, 2016[2] required the ratification of a combination of 55 countries representing 55 percent of global emissions. Inevitably, the list of possible actors always boiled down to all or some combination that included the EU, the US, and China.[3] These actors all have the economic weight, the political clout and a wide network of global relationships that can provide the momentum for moving forward.

As Paris itself proved, the world is not yet fully prepared to bindingly legislate its way out of this crisis (strictly speaking Parties are still not legally bound at the international level to achieve their targets).[4] Nor has the certainty of science proven enough of an incentive for nations to spring to action. The renowned American attorney Ken Feinberg, who specializes in mediation and alternative dispute resolution, during a talk in Germany outlined the problem: "We ask too much from the courts. We expect too much from Science. They can only say and do so much. The rest, meaning most everything, is politics."[5] Politics is not about the math; it is about perceptions; it is about rivalries, stories, suspicions, common history. It is also about people, their personalities, their strengths, their visions and how they impact their time. Politics matter though they remain both volatile and highly unpredictable.

First things first: Shouldn't the US and China lead the way? Are they not after all the biggest emitters? There is no doubt that these two countries are a big part of the problem and need to be part of the solution. However, that does not mean that they can jointly lead by example and provide a credible path forward. To begin with, while the US government under President Obama began to project renewed energy in dealing with the climate crisis, the political realities in the US have not sufficiently changed, thus warning us not to become overly optimistic by official declarations. Up until very recently the US had hindered the possibility of reaching a meaningful international agreement on the reduction of carbon emissions. The climate debate remains highly polarized in the US and Congress has consistently rejected any attempts to set targets or standards or taxes on fossil fuels. Even the Paris Agreement had to be ratified by executive order under President Obama because it would not have passed if put to a Congressional vote.[6] More tellingly, the 2016 electoral upset that brought Donald Trump to power is expected to, at the very least, upend the Obama presidency's positive momentum in international climate talks. The comfortable Republican majority in the US Congress may also derail domestic efforts to decarbonize the economy.

The fierce opposition of special interests, the reigning mantra of energy independence, traditional exceptionalism and isolationism form the unique American narrative. The mixture of denial and foot-dragging for years spilled over into the way the world perceived the global prospects for dealing with climate change at the international level. It was what gave other countries the perfect excuse to posture and delay. Moreover, the US–China relationship is tainted by an underlying simmering rivalry that is only strengthening as the PRC gains superpower status. As far back as the Nixon administration in 1968, the US government had argued that an isolated China was a more dangerous opponent than one that engaged in global institutions. Nixon did not want to see China operate as a destabilizing force in international affairs and this was his principal motivation for opening up relations with China in 1972. Engaging China, however, does not preclude an enduring spirit of competition and an underlying suspicion of these interactions.

While engagement takes place at multiple levels, the US–China rivalry is often alluded to for domestic and international audiences. In his state of the Union Speech in 2013,[7] for example, President Barack Obama, without mentioning Europe at all, pushed for renewables in the US energy mix by challenging China's investment in the production of clean technology.

> Four years ago, other countries dominated the clean energy market and the jobs that came with it. We've begun to change that. Last year, wind energy added nearly half of all new power capacity in America. So let's generate even more. Solar energy gets cheaper by the year – so let's drive costs down even further. As long as countries like China keep going all-in on clean energy, so must we.

In the State of the Union speech in 2014, he again drew competitive comparisons to China by declaring that "… for the first time in over a decade, business leaders around the world have declared that China is no longer the world's number one place to invest; America is."[8] On the question of human rights, furthermore, the US has been vocal about political dissidents, religious freedom and the status of Tibet. US rhetoric on these topics is an irritant and a source of friction in US–China relations.

The emerging US–China rivalry in both the economy and geopolitics is the buzzword in Washington, D.C. and is echoed in Beijing. While the US has officially declared its pivot toward Asia, (both militarily and financially) China too, under Xi Jinping, has not remained idle. The PRC is counteracting the American pivot through a variety of bold new initiatives that are catching the world's attention. China's recent initiatives to build a new Asian Infrastructure Investment Bank (AIIB)[9]—seen as a rival to the World Bank, the IMF and the Asian Development Bank—and to reimagine and rebuild the Silk Road,[10] give expression to a "Chinese dream" in Central Asia and beyond,[11] fanning geopolitical tensions.

In a surprising move, however, in November 2014, Presidents Obama and Xi Jinping addressed the problem of climate change during their Summit in Beijing. Though their respective team of experts had been negotiating for some time prior to this announcement, the move captured the attention of the international community. It signaled a possible important shift by two of the world's largest emitters, indicating that they had perhaps now stepped up their commitment to jointly lead in this historic undertaking.

The statement that the two presidents issued declared their intent to take on responsibility for their nations' part in the climate crisis. What was more telling, however, was how the declaration was presented to the international community because it revealed more about the US intent to revive the past bipolar power structure while simultaneously aiming to contain the growing rivalry with the PRC through peripheral collaboration. This kind of strategizing does not bode well for the future of the climate or the planet. Although from its actions, the Chinese government has shown a preference for a multipolar world, it did not object to sharing the limelight with the US. It has subscribed to a relationship with the US that features bilateral cooperation on select items. The released statement that perhaps focused more narrowly on mitigation, technological research and development, and the deployment of renewables emphasized the importance of working bilaterally. In spite of the optimism it provoked, however, the communiqué read more like a list of emission reduction schemes and invest-ment opportunities and lacked a much-desired transformational narrative. What was likewise strikingly absent in the joint communiqué was any acknowledgment of the work of others, most notably the EU. Therefore, while the challenge of climate change and the environment may seem to be an important and attractive area for US–China cooperation, it is inevitably plagued by the overall geopoliti-cal rivalry that has increasingly become the framework in which cooperation and engagement take place. It is also pegged as an "area of cooperation," i.e. a theme that should not raise red flags, a peripheral issue where rivals can perhaps meet without jeopardizing their "core interests." This may, at least, best reflect the American mindset.

At the surface, and from the Chinese perspective, the climate crisis may have provided some opportunity for meaningful and "painless" talks with the US. Given China's rapid ecosystem deterioration and public outcry against the ram-pant pollution, the topic helps set the stage for engagement, especially since the parameters of the collaboration remain narrow. There are those in China, how-ever, who remain suspicious of American intentions. It is not surprising therefore that, in the view of some Chinese experts, in pushing for cooperation on climate change, the US has in fact been attempting to contain China's rise before the PRC's economy surpasses its own. This pervasive suspicion[12] is not uncommon in China, especially given America's previous record in climate change negotia-tions and its own rhetoric on how a binding agreement would negatively impact its own economic growth. Finally, China itself is undergoing significant transfor-mation, growing increasingly assertive, flexing its muscles in its own neighbor-hood, and looking to showcase its achievements in order to take its rightful place among the most powerful nations. These underlying debates are but a preview of why it would be unwise to sacrifice the push for far-reaching climate action on the pyre of US–China rivalry.

Why would the EU be a better fit? Here, the reasons are manifold, starting with the most obvious. Despite President Obama's heartfelt pronouncements, it is the EU, not the US, which has a proven record of commitment in greening its economy, paving the way to a low carbon future and protecting biodiversity. Europe's involvement with climate change policy has evolved over four distinct periods: the formation and formulation phase from the late 1980s–1992, the

Kyoto Protocol negotiation phase from 1992–2001, the Kyoto Protocol rescue phase 2001–2005 after President Bush announced he would not be ratifying the protocol, and the current period that included the push to reach a new international binding agreement[13] in Paris.

Certainly, the EU has defended its commitment to a legally binding and rules-based approach to international action on climate change while implementing an ambitious action plan to diversify its energy mix, promote emission reductions and resource efficiency in its own territory. It has used regulations, taxation, outreach programs, standards, policies, laws, directives, media and politics to create a narrative of economic opportunity while continuing to protect the ecosystem. In fact, it is clear that in the time after Kyoto, the EU has starkly differentiated itself from the US in policy ambition, stringency and scope and has legislated broadly *vis-à-vis* climate change.

Already in March 2007, the European Council embarked on a binding plan to reduce greenhouse gas (GHG) emissions. Known as the 20 – 20 – 20 targets,[14] the plan mandated a 20 percent reduction of GHG emissions below 1990 levels by 2020. It also set a target of a 20 percent increase in the share of renewable energies in overall energy consumption, including a 10 percent binding minimum target for transport fuels and a 20 percent cut in primary energy consumption compared to projected levels through energy–efficiency improvements. These goals were backed by legislation across the Union. The EU also launched and supported the EU emissions trading system (EUETS), adopted regulations on emission performance for new cars, and encouraged and facilitated new technologies in renewables.[15]

Nothing similar happened in the US over that same period. In fact, President Obama had to resort to his executive powers to effect change through the Clean Air Act for stricter emission standards for transport and stationary emission sources.[16] Right after the Paris Agreement, moreover, in February 2016, the US Supreme Court in a highly unusual move decided to temporarily suspend the implementation of the Clean Power Plan, which required coal- and gas-fired power plants to cut their emissions for the first time. This meant that the Obama administration's signature legislation to help reduce emissions was put on hold while the court battle over its legality continued. Moreover, in June 2015, the high court ruled against efforts to regulate mercury and other toxic air pollutants. While the US government deals with push back on efforts to maintain its Paris commitments, Europe continues to forge ahead, having now mapped out its even more ambitious 2030 goals[17] for the Union as a whole, while countries like Germany are aiming for a broader energy transformation known as *Energiewende*.[18] In fact, Germany proceeded to make climate action a key focus of its G20 Presidency that runs through 2017.[19] What is more, the EU continues to demonstrate that its commitment to climate action is backed by a larger philosophy of development and life in the Anthropocene.

There are a number of reasons why EU–China leadership in the Anthropocene could prove to be effective. The EU, in describing its own foreign policy objectives, supports a multipolar world, the importance of cooperation through international institutions and adherence to the rule of law. China, as an emerging power, shares Europe's views on multipolarity and working through international institutions to help sustain stability and cooperation worldwide. Until now, China has maintained a stance of non-interference in the internal affairs of other states and has strategically avoided antagonizing other industrial powers to focus on its domestic development. Nonetheless, it has already begun to re-assert itself in Asia and abroad through strong development aid programs in Africa and elsewhere, much like the EU that is in fact the largest donor of development aid in the world.

According to those closely monitoring Chinese politics, President Xi Jinping is personally invested in matters of foreign policy. He has not only travelled extensively, but has also received many foreign visitors in his own country.[20] Yet, Xi Jinping has also to come to terms with pressing domestic realities. China today is already the world's second largest economy and the largest consumer of oil on the planet. In just under fifty years, China has radically transformed itself into a global economic powerhouse. This transformation begun by Deng Xiaoping has come at an astonishing cost to the environment and the wellbeing of its citizens, a fact that can no longer be ignored. Rhetorically, the Chinese government acknowledged the problem about four decades ago, establishing the first Environmental Protection Law in 1979[21] and the State Environmental Protection Committee in 1984.[22] After the United Nations Conference on Environment and Development in 1992, China was one of the first countries to formulate and carry out a strategy of sustainable development.[23] Since the 10th Five-Year plan (FYP) (2001–2005) the government increased its emphasis and goals *vis-à-vis* environmental protection and energy use in its planning process. Yet, little changed. A decade ago, the government once again pledged to tackle air pollution, access to clean water, and food safety. Today, pressure to deliver on these commitments is mounting and rhetoric must turn into action.[24] This is why in November 2012, the 18th National Congress of the Central Committee of the Communist Party adopted the grand vision of "ecological civilization" which meant that ecological goals were now given equally high-priority status along with economic, social, cultural and political development.

As the world's largest energy consumer and carbon emitter, China can no longer encourage unbridled growth at the expense of its environment. Tackling this issue, especially in a time when the pace of economic growth is slowing, will be one of the greatest challenges for President Xi Jinping. Bringing millions of people into the middle class each year will not be enough to maintain political legitimacy. The health risk to citizens by the heavy smog, unsafe water, and problems in the food supply are only growing[25] and so is the realization that this kind of environmental degradation has gone far enough and must now be reversed. What is clear today is that the state of China's environment is poisoning the country's economy, and this will adversely impact investment that continues to play a central role in the nation's growth.[26]

There are a number of areas where the government has room in which to dynamically intervene. First, environmental regulations already existing on the books can be tightened and enforced. Monitoring enforcement in the regions has been a continuous challenge for the central government. Second, the government has announced a decision to rein in the polluting industries as well as coal-fired plants.[27] The results of these decisions, however, need to be carefully monitored to measure their ultimate effectiveness. Third, there is a growing need to address sustainable urban planning for the continuing urbanization of the country. The rapid growth of cities puts pressure on their infrastructure and the quality of life of their citizens. Nonetheless, urbanization inevitably represents an opportunity to create more sustainable models of city planning which aim at the creation of smart green cities, where changes can be made on the existing infrastructure and technologies can be woven in to help create a new kind of urbanity. This not only would allow for close cooperation with the EU, whose expertise is unrivaled, but also for the implementation of new green technologies and sustainable practices, taking advantage of China's centralized planning structure.

In terms of governance, the members of the EU may be mature democracies and free market economies, but the Union does provide its European partners with a level of central planning that allows for coordination of its 28 states.[28] China's unique model of centralized planning and one–party governance is coupled with a continually liberalizing economy. In China, while political demonstrations may not be condoned, there has been civil outcry over environmental issues and there the government has allowed society more leeway to express its frustration and to voice its demands for change. Increasingly segments of Chinese society are asking more vocally for the enforcement of existing environmental regulations and for cleanup efforts to reverse the damage already done. In addition to these commonalities, both Europe and China share long historical exchanges that go back to the time of the creation of the Silk Road.

The EU and China represent formidable international actors, with a combined population of over 1.8 billion, increasing economic interdependence, and shared interests. Xi Jinping's trip to Europe in the spring of 2014 and his high profile visit to EU headquarters underscores both a strengthening relationship and the desire to build upon and expand ties beyond trade agreements. There is already an ongoing dialogue in place *vis-à-vis* the climate crisis with the EU sharing its best practices and strategies with its Chinese counterparts, thus providing the platform for further collaboration on this front. The EU and China formed a Strategic Partnership in 2003 that has built on the initial 1985 EU China trade and cooperation agreement. The ground is already set for the promotion of an ambitious agenda to fight climate change[29]. The EU and the PRC have introduced three pillars of high level exchanges: the High-Level Strategic Dialogue (2010), the High-Level Economic and Trade Dialogue (2008) and the High-Level People-to-People Dialogue (2012).[30] The two powers underscore collaboration opportunities in the document describing the nature of their 2020 Agenda for Strategic Cooperation highlighting the emerging green sectors. The EU has also undertaken to facilitate the building of China's emission trading market which after being piloted will launch nationally in 2017 and work together for the building of both EU and China low-carbon cities, communities and industrial parks thus controlling GHG emissions.

Although, the building blocks for such a partnership are already there, much needs to be done for both entities to fully realize the potential of such collaborative leadership. As China asserts itself on the world stage expanding ties across the globe, it still remains caught up in affairs of its own neighborhood and in the narrative of simmering rivalry with the US, especially after the latter's declared strategic pivot toward Asia. For the PRC, US rivalry not only poses a security threat in military terms and an aggressive economic competitor, but also a deeper political threat to the regime, offering the lure of the democratic process to an increasingly robust middle class that is clearly on the rise.

These realities could be an additional reason for China to meaningfully deepen its relationship with the EU, which expresses its views and projects its power in a very different manner from the US's more heavy-handed insistence on exporting liberal democratic values and principles. Working closely with Europe on the climate crisis may be just what China needs to escape the push and pull of the self-fulfilling prophesy of its inevitable clash with the US. Working closely with the EU will not limit either actor from tapping into its network of "friends" across the globe. By drawing them in and including them as part of a transformation project, such a soft power approach would lead to deeper power realignments. This kind of leadership paradigm sits well with both Europe and China and the multipolarity they wish to see shaping global relations for the twenty-first century. It will also allow the PRC the opportunity to retrace its steps and find how to more efficiently and sustainably provide for its citizens, without plundering the planet's resources.

This kind of initiative would be a godsend for the EU as well. Although the Union has done much to move toward the decarbonization of its economy, to weave sustainability throughout its policies and laws, and to champion a binding international agreement to deal with the climate crisis, it has lost the opportunity to make all these initiatives become its central vision for the future. It has been bogged down in an internal dispute within the Eurozone that will not be resolved by pinching pennies and institutionalizing austerity as the new norm. Moreover, the increasing flows of migration toward the EU from Africa, the Middle East and Asia because of war, climate and economic disparity, are testing European solidarity. The explosion in the rates of migration has also served as a warning about how climate change has already impacted developing regions of the world. The EU urgently needs a dream, an optimistic vision for the future and a quintessentially European one in order to once again project "civilian power"[31] and international relevance. Climate action, the protection of the environment and the quest for a meaningful narrative for the Anthropocene provide a perfect fresh story line for Europe, one that it believes in, one that it can champion in earnest. Working together with another major power to achieve this kind of transformation would only add more value and purpose to the venture.

There are a number of hurdles that need to be overcome, however. Forging a bolder and deeper EU–China alliance requires rethinking on both sides for a number of reasons: first, because of the way they view each other, and second, because of the possibility of a strong negative response toward this new partnership by the US. With respect to the latter, there is no doubt that the EU–US bond has been among the strongest and deepest of international relationships. Their ties are both socio-economic and security oriented. However, relations have become increasingly strained though the bond has not yet been broken. Still, Europe is now a mature power of 500 million people, a prosperous Union that despite its current difficulties maintains an enviable record of achievements. It cannot, therefore, afford to make its decisions based solely on pushback from the US. The EU would surely tread lightly, building its ties with China while making sure to extend an open invitation to the US to partake in the wider conversation for the Anthropocene. This is after all part of the multilateral diplomacy that the EU espouses.

For China too, maintaining friendly, cooperative relations with the US is preferable to outright hostility and rivalry. Yet, whether or not it partners more closely with Europe may have no bearing on its relationship with the US moving forward. This may particularly be true under President Trump, whose modus operandi has thus far been the use of skillful disruption of the existing status quo with the aim of ad hoc bilateral deal-making. Moreover, China has already arrived, and while it may not seek to become a global player according to the rules and prescriptions dictated by the US, it too has been seeking a more attractive international narrative given that a sole focus on trade is at the moment less appealing.

Could a solution to this quandary be some form of tripartite cooperation? Though the cooperation of all three powers may initially appear plausible, it remains highly improbable for a number of reasons. The following list is by no means exhaustive but points to some possible constraints and obstacles that such an arrangement might face. The US for example has demonstrated a preference for bilateral agreements; it has, moreover, been seeking to revive a bipolar power relationship with China, which it views as its main rival, in order to better control and preserve the current divisions and structure of the international security system. Furthermore, a tripartite partnership would diminish the symbolic impact of the American Pacific Power narrative that accompanies the US pivot toward Asia.[32] For the most part, and even under the Obama presidency, the climate crisis, while one of the major global challenges facing the international community, was not viewed as being the overarching one. With the change of guard in Washington, D.C., the climate crisis will drop in policy importance and will be replaced by issues of economic growth and security as the top priorities on the American agenda. By the same token, a tripartite partnership would not be an ideal solution for China either. Such an arrangement might re-awaken a sense of encirclement and attempt to limit China's outreach and influence, flexibility and independence in its dealings, especially with the developing world. For the EU as well, such an arrangement would probably require inordinate strategic and political maneuvering between the two other powers, thus impeding progress on game-changing climate action.

With respect to how the EU and China see each other, there are a number of possible challenges that need to be overcome. While China views the

EU as a powerhouse of technology and innovation as well as a critical trading partner, for example, it does not perceive it as a geostrategic competitor. The ongoing EU debt crisis in the eyes of some policy makers in China serves as an indicator of EU political weakness and perhaps even decline. While Europe was once thought of as a rising alternative to US dominance, this belief has lost its momentum.[33] Europe's hesitation or inability to create a stronger political Union doesn't allow it to be seen as a unitary global player with a clear voice in international relations. Nonetheless, Europe has successfully learned to act within these constraints sometimes deliberately as a whole, other times on a national level, depending on what the situation demands. Europeans as well have mixed feelings about China. They share historic ties and a strong trade relationship. China's financial liquidity, moreover, was wooed especially after the 2008 global financial crisis, but though its investments in Europe were welcome, there has been growing unease about its rapid expansion into the European economy. Increasingly, European fears have grown that Chinese investment may be more of a response to a fire sale rather than a healthy investment strategy that will benefit both sides.

Despite these constraints, opportunities remain plentiful and the possibilities of further exploring this burgeoning relationship still abound. As there are no competing strategic and military interests or territorial claims to divide them, a complementary symbiosis that moves beyond the limits of purely economic and trade interests is possible and will help to articulate a more cohesive policy between them.[34] These possibilities have, furthermore, sparked a growing interest in academic and policy circles for new research to understand EU–China diplomacy, both traditional and soft, and in the assessment of the effectiveness of the current strategic partnership.[35]

Former EU Commissioner for Climate Action Connie Hedegaard saw the potential of a close alliance between the EU and China. During an April 2014 visit, she emphasized how impressed she was by the action the PRC was taking to cut emissions: "I would hope that this domestic strong focus can be translated into a strong position internationally, because that would be a game changer in the international talks."[36]

It has not been my intention to overlook the input of the network of domestic actors both private and public that are actively contributing to the discussions of climate and environmental governance. Numerous stakeholders that include business, the media, NGOs, local communities, mayors and governors and civil society are all weighing-in on the challenges ahead. They are not all on the same page and they too often compete, driven by their perceived interests. Many scholars, moreover, have been focusing on the potential of their transformational input and the ways that they are driving climate action and planning possible responses to the Anthropocene. Yet, in this book, I argue that at both a national and international level, states remain the entities that render structure to politics and the economy, provide the legal framework, and maintain economic and administrative instruments at their disposal. Moreover, at a global level, state actors ultimately negotiate treaties and agreements. This book argues that though there are no guarantees of success, the hope sparked by COP 21 in Paris points to an extraordinary opportunity for the EU and China to work together, using their strengths, addressing their weaknesses, and forging a new era of vision, stewardship, and leadership in the Anthropocene.

Notes

1 Simon Dalby, "Environmental Geopolitics in the Twenty-First Century," *Alternatives: Global, Local, Political* 39, no. 1 (February 1, 2014): 3–16.
2 "Paris Agreement – Status of Ratification," accessed December 7, 2016, http://unfccc.int/paris_agreement/items/9444.php.
3 The US, China, and the EU all ratified the Agreement.
4 "All Parties have a legally binding obligation to prepare, communicate and maintain a nationally determined mitigation contribution. This ends the old division of countries in the United Nations Framework Convention on Climate Change (UNFCCC) and the Kyoto Protocol, under which only some countries have mitigation commitments. While strictly speaking, Parties are not legally bound at the international level to achieve their targets, each Party is legally bound to pursue domestic mitigation measures, with the aim of achieving the objectives of their contributions. This, combined with robust transparency and accountability provisions, provides a solid basis for an inclusive regime." European Commission-Climate Action, "Questions and Answers on the Paris Agreement," accessed December 7, 2016, https://ec.europa.eu/clima/sites/clima/files/international/negotiations/paris/docs/qa_paris_agreement_en.pdf.
5 "Toxic Legacies – Agent Orange as a Challenge", *Agent Orange Conference*, Evangelische Akademie Tutzing, Germany, 28.06.2015 – 30.06.2015. Feinberg was appointed Special Master of the US government's September 11th Victim Compensation Fund and served as the Special Master for Troubled Asset Relief Program (TARP) Executive Compensation. Additionally, Feinberg served as the government-appointed administrator of the BP Deepwater Horizon Disaster Victim Compensation Fund. Feinberg was appointed by the Commonwealth of Massachusetts to administer the One Fund—the victim assistance fund established in the wake of the 2013 Boston Marathon bombings. Most recently, Feinberg was retained by General Motors to assist in their recall response and by Volkswagen to oversee their US compensation of VW diesel owners affected by the Volkswagen emissions scandal.
6 "Obama, Chinese President Ratify Climate-Change Agreement," *The Washington Times*, accessed December 7, 2016, http://www.washingtontimes.com/news/2016/sep/3/obama-xi-ratify-climate-change-agreement/.
7 Barack Obama, "State of the Union 2013," *The White House*, accessed December 17, 2016, https://www.whitehouse.gov/node/196281.
8 Barack Obama, "President Barack Obama's State of the Union Address," *Whitehouse.gov*, January 28, 2014, https://www.whitehouse.gov/the-press-office/2014/01/28/president-barack-obamas-state-union-address.
9 The AIIB initiative was launched by President Xi Jinping in late 2013.
10 Cary Huang, "57 Nations Approved as Founder Members of China-Led AIIB," *South China Morning Post*, accessed October 15, 2016, http://www.scmp.com/news/china/diplomacy-defence/article/1766970/57-nations-approved-founder-members-china-led-aiib."UK Support for China-Backed Asia Bank Prompts US Concern," *BBC News*, March 13, 2015, sec. Business, http://www.bbc.com/news/world-australia-31864877.
11 Neil Thompson, "China's Growing Presence in Russia's Backyard," *The Diplomat*, March 25, 2015, accessed August 1, 2016, http://thediplomat.com/2015/03/chinas-growing-presence-in-russias-backyard/.

12 Yu Hogyuan, "The Process of the Copenhagen Negotiations and the Development of US-China Carbon Diplomacy," *Asia Pacific Studies*, no. 3 (2010): 98.
13 Rüdiger Wurzel and James Connelly, eds., *The European Union as a Leader in International Climate Change Politics*, (London: Routledge, 2012).
14 "Europe 2020 – EU-Wide Headline Targets for Economic Growth," *European Commission*, accessed December 7, 2016, http://ec.europa.eu/europe2020/targets/eu-targets/index_en.htm.
15 Jon Birger Skjærseth, Guri Bang, and Miranda A. Schreurs, "Explaining Growing Climate Policy Differences Between the European Union and the United States," *Global Environmental Politics* 13, no. 4 (September 17, 2013): 61–80, doi:10.1162/GLEP_a_00198.
16 Lawrence Hurley and Valerie Volcovici, "U.S. Supreme Court Blocks Obama's Clean Power Plan," *Scientific American*, February 9, 2016, accessed October 15, 2016, https://www.scientificamerican.com/article/u-s-supreme-court-blocks-obama-s-clean-power-plan/.
17 "A 2030 Framework for Climate and Energy Policies," *European Commission*, 27 March 2013, http://cor.europa.eu/en/activities/stakeholders/Documents/comm169-2013final.pdf.
18 Thomas L. Friedman, "Germany, the Green Superpower," *The New York Times*, May 6, 2015, accessed September 10, 2016, http://www.nytimes.com/2015/05/06/opinion/thomas-friedman-germany-the-green-superpower.html.
19 "Germany Makes Climate Action a Key Focus of G20 Presidency," *UNFCCC*, accessed December 7, 2016, http://newsroom.unfccc.int/unfccc-newsroom/germany-makes-climate-action-key-focus-of-g20-presidency/.
20 Tim Summers, "Chinese Foreign Policy: What to Expect in 2015," *Chatham House*, 13 January 2015, accessed October 15, 2016, https://www.chathamhouse.org//node/16637.
21 The Environmental Protection Law was adopted in 1979 but continued to be revised in 1989 and 2014. See Zhilin Mu, Shuchun Bu, and Bing Xue, "Environmental Legislation in China: Achievements, Challenges and Trends," *Sustainability* 6, no. 12 (December 5, 2014): 8967–79; Shi-qiu Zhang, "Environmental Regulatory and Policy Framework in China: An Overview," *Journal of Environmental Sciences* 13, no. 1 (2001): 122–28.
22 Chinese Academy for Environmental Planning," accessed March 15, 2017, http://www.caep.org.cn:8080/english/ReadNewsen.asp?NewsID=1517.
23 "Earth_Summit," accessed March 15, 2017, http://www.un.org/geninfo/bp/enviro.html.
24 Qi Ye, "China's Commitment to a Green Agenda," *McKinsey & Company*, accessed October 15, 2016, http://www.mckinsey.com/global-themes/asia-pacific/chinas-commitment-to-a-green-agenda.
25 Rebecca Nadin, Sarah Opitz-Stapleton, and Xu Yinlong, eds., *Climate Risk and Resilience in China* (London; New York: Routledge, 2015).
26 Mun S. Ho and Chris P. Nielsen, *Clearing the Air: The Health and Economic Damages of Air Pollution in China* (Cambridge, MA: MIT Press, 2007). Dongyong Zhang, Junjuan Liu, and Bingjun Li, "Tackling Air Pollution in China—What Do We Learn from the Great Smog of 1950s in LONDON," *Sustainability* 6, no. 8 (August 18, 2014): 5322–38, doi:10.3390/su6085322.
27 "China currently has over 900,000MW of coal-fired capacity, the equivalent of about 1,300 large coal-fired units." See Lauri Myllyvirta, "China Keeps Building Coal Plants despite New Overcapacity Policy," *Energydesk*, July 13, 2016, http://energydesk.greenpeace.org/2016/07/13/china-keeps-building-coal-plants-despite-new-overcapacity-policy/; "China to Halt Construction on Coal-Fired Power Plants in 15 Regions," *Scientific American*, accessed December 7, 2016, https://www.scientificamerican.com/article/china-to-halt-construction-on-coal-fired-power-plants-in-15-regions/.

28 Neill Nugent, *The Government and Politics of the European Union* (New York: Palgrave Macmillan, 2010).After the Brexit vote of 2016, the UK will be leaving the EU and the member-states will once again be 27.

29 "EU-China 2020 Strategic Agenda for Cooperation," *European Union – EEAS (European External Action Service) Delegation of the European Union to China,* accessed October 15, 2016, http://eeas.europa.eu/delegations/china/index_en.htm.

30 Jing Men, "Is there A Strategic Partnership between the EU and China?" *European Foreign Affairs Review* 19, no. 3 (81/01 2014): 5–17.

31 Although European states maintain strong military capabilities and partake in the North Atlantic Treaty Organization (NATO) and the Common Security and Defense Policy, Europe seeks to project power through the building of cooperative and stable relations with other nations and by promoting multilateral solutions to common problems. Recently, and perhaps because of the election of Donald Trump to the presidency of the US, Europe has begun to more openly discuss the creation of an EU defense budget in order to pool resources. Note that a number of EU member states have had a tradition of neutrality or semi-neutrality and have been reluctant to overdevelop security and defense policies. Furthermore, these policies also raise issues of sovereignty for member-states and also over both ends and means, as was seen in the EU member split over the 2003 US invasion of Iraq. "Wolfgang Schäuble Calls for Joint EU Defense Budget," *Financial Times,* accessed December 7, 2016, https://www.ft.com/content/a20e8ade-9554-11e6-a1dc-bdf38d484582.Nugent, *The Government and Politics of the European Union,* 386.

32 For decades the US had been highly focused on the Middle East and embroiled in ongoing conflicts wreaking havoc in the region. China's rise, security concerns, and the high growth rates of Asian economies led to an intentional shift of strategic focus back to the Asia-Pacific region after 911 and particularly under the Obama administration. See Foreign Policy Initiative, "The Obama Administration's Pivot to Asia" accessed March 15, 2017, http://www.foreignpolicyi.org/content/obama-administration-pivot-asia.

33 Kerry Brown, *The EU-China Relationship : European Perspectives: A Manual for Policy Makers* (Hackensack, N.J: World Scientific Publishing Company, 2015).

34 Roland Vogt, *Europe and China: Strategic Partners or Rivals?* (Hong Kong: Hong Kong University Press, 2012).

35 Jing Men, "EU-China Relations and Diplomacy: Introductory Note," *European Foreign Affairs Review* 19, no.3 (2014): 1–3.

36 Stian Reklev, "EU Climate Chief Urges China to Show International Commitment," *Reuters,* April 23, 2014, accessed May 1, 2015, http://www.reuters.com/article/us-china-eu-climatechange-idUSBREA3M0F320140423.

Bibliography

BBC News. "UK Support for China-Backed Asia Bank Prompts US Concern." *BBC News,* March 13, 2015, sec. Business. http://www.bbc.com/news/world-australia-31864877.

Boyer, Dave. "Obama, Chinese President Ratify Climate-Change Agreement." *The Washington Times.* Accessed December 7, 2016. http://www.washingtontimes.com/news/2016/sep/3/obama-xi-ratify-climate-change-agreement/.

Brown, Kerry. *The EU-China Relationship : European Perspectives: A Manual for Policy Makers.* Hackensack, N.J: World Scientific Publishing Company, 2015.

Chen, Kathy and Stanway, David. "China to Halt Construction on Coal-Fired Power Plants in 15 Regions." *Scientific American.* Accessed December 7, 2016. https://www.scientificamerican.com/article/china-to-halt-construction-on-coal-fired-power-plants-in-15-regions/.

Dalby, Simon. "Environmental Geopolitics in the Twenty-First Century." *Alternatives: Global, Local, Political* 39, no. 1 (February 1, 2014): 3–16.

European Commission. "A 2030 Framework for Climate and Energy Policies," 2013. http://cor.europa.eu/en/activities/stakeholders/Documents/comm169-2013final.pdf.

European Commission. "Europe 2020 – EU-Wide Headline Targets for Economic Growth." Accessed December 7, 2016. http://ec.europa.eu/europe2020/targets/eu-targets/index_en.htm.

European Commission-Climate Action. "Questions and Answers on the Paris Agreement." Accessed December 7, 2016. https://ec.europa.eu/clima/sites/clima/files/international/negotiations/paris/docs/qa_paris_agreement_en.pdf.

European Union. "European Union – EEAS (European External Action Service) | Delegation of the European Union to China." Accessed October 15, 2016. http://eeas.europa.eu/delegations/china/index_en.htm.

Friedman, Thomas L. "Germany, the Green Superpower." *The New York Times*, May 6, 2015. http://www.nytimes.com/2015/05/06/opinion/thomas-friedman-germany-the-green-superpower.html.

"Germany Makes Climate Action a Key Focus of G20 Presidency." *UNFCCC.* Accessed December 7, 2016. http://newsroom.unfccc.int/unfccc-newsroom/germany-makes-climate-action-key-focus-of-g20-presidency/.

Huang, Cary. "57 Nations Approved as Founder Members of China-Led AIIB." *South China Morning Post.* Accessed October 15, 2016. http://www.scmp.com/news/china/diplomacy-defence/article/1766970/57-nations-approved-founder-members-china-led-aiib.

Ho, Mun S., and Chris P. Nielsen. *Clearing the Air: The Health and Economic Damages of Air Pollution in China.* Cambridge, MA: MIT Press, 2007.

Hogyuan, Yu. "The Process of the Copenhagen Negotiations and the Development of US-China Carbon Diplomacy". *Asia Pacific Studies*, no. 3 (2010): 98.

Hurley, Lawrence and Volcovici, Valerie. "U.S. Supreme Court Blocks Obama's Clean Power Plan." *Scientific American.* Accessed October 15, 2016. https://www.scientificamerican.com/article/u-s-supreme-court-blocks-obama-s-clean-power-plan/.

Men, Jing. "EU-China Relations and Diplomacy: Introductory Note." *European Foreign Affairs Review* 19, no. 3 (81/01 2014): 1–3.

Men, Jing. "Is There A Strategic Partnership between the EU and China?" *European Foreign Affairs Review* 19, no. 3 (81/01 2014): 5 – 17.

Mu, Zhilin, Shuchun Bu, and Bing Xue. "Environmental Legislation in China: Achievements, Challenges and Trends." *Sustainability* 6, no. 12 (December 5, 2014): 8967–79, doi:10.3390/su6128967.

Myllyvirta, Lauri. "China Keeps Building Coal Plants despite New Overcapacity Policy." *Energydesk*, July 13, 2016. http://energydesk.greenpeace.org/2016/07/13/china-keeps-building-coal-plants-despite-new-overcapacity-policy/.

Nadin, Rebecca, Sarah Opitz-Stapleton, and Xu Yinlong, eds. *Climate Risk and Resilience in China.* London, New York: Routledge, 2015.

Nugent, Neill. *The Government and Politics of the European Union.* Basingstoke England; New York: Palgrave Macmillan, 2010.

Obama, Barak. "State of the Union 2013." *The White House.* Accessed December 17, 2016. https://www.whitehouse.gov/node/196281.

Reklev, Stian. "EU Climate Chief Urges China to Show International Commitment." *Reuters*, April 23, 2014. http://www.reuters.com/article/us-china-eu-climatechange-idUSBREA3M0F320140423.

Skjærseth, Jon Birger, Guri Bang, and Miranda A. Schreurs. "Explaining Growing Climate Policy Differences Between the European Union and the United States." *Global Environmental Politics* 13, no. 4 (September 17, 2013): 61–80. doi:10.1162/GLEP_a_00198.

Summers, Tim. "Chinese Foreign Policy: What to Expect in 2015." *Chatham House.* Accessed October 15, 2016. https://www.chathamhouse.org//node/16637.

Thompson, Neil. "China's Growing Presence in Russia's Backyard." *The Diplomat.* Accessed September 25, 2016. http://thediplomat.com/2015/03/chinas-growing-presence-in-russias-backyard/.

"Toxic Legacies – Agent Orange as a Challenge," *Agent Orange Conference.* Germany: Evangelische Akademie Tutzing, 28.06.2015 - 30.06.2015.

United Nations Framework Convention on Climate Change. "Paris Agreement - Status of Ratification." Accessed December 7, 2016. http://unfccc.int/paris_agreement/items/9444.php.

Vogt, Roland. *Europe and China: Strategic Partners or Rivals?* Hong Kong: Hong Kong University Press, 2012.

Wagstyl, Stefan. "Wolfgang Schäuble Calls for Joint EU Defence Budget." *Financial Times.* Accessed December 7, 2016. https://www.ft.com/content/a20e8ade-9554-11e6-a1dc-bdf38d484582.

The White House, Office of the Press Secretary. "President Barack Obama's State of the Union Address." *Whitehouse.gov*, January 28, 2014. https://www.whitehouse.gov/the-press-office/2014/01/28/president-barack-obamas-state-union-address.

Wurzel, Rüdiger, and James Connelly, eds. *The European Union as a Leader in International Climate Change Politics.* London: Routledge, 2012.

Ye, Qi. "China's Commitment to a Green Agenda | McKinsey & Company." Accessed October 15, 2016. http://www.mckinsey.com/global-themes/asia-pacific/chinas-commitment-to-a-green-agenda.

Zhang, Dongyong, Junjuan Liu, and Bingjun Li. "Tackling Air Pollution in China—What Do We Learn from the Great Smog of 1950s in LONDON." *Sustainability* 6, no. 8 (August 18, 2014).

Zhang, Shi-qiu. "Environmental Regulatory and Policy Framework in China: An Overview." *Journal of Environmental Sciences* 13, no. 1 (2001): 122–28.

1   The US

Still reluctant and unreliable

There was a time when the United States (US) had an environmental awakening that took the country by storm. Between 1968 and 1972 and through the better part of the 1970s, public opinion rallied for environmental action. Years of accumulating evidence had alerted Americans to a wide range of growing environmental problems. Rachel Carson's *Silent Spring* (1962), for example, presented a scathing critique of the indiscriminant use of chemicals. While employed to exterminate a limited and arbitrary array of pests, they were in fact poisoning the natural world, including humans. All across the nation there was increasing concern over acute air and water pollution and their impact on public health. Nuclear fall-out from bomb testing in the atmosphere, strip mining in regions like Appalachia and the destruction of ancient forests worried the public, as species after species, which carried with them a symbolism of America's identity, seemed to be threatened with extinction. Population explosion,[1] especially in the developing world and its repercussions on industrialized nations, captured the public's imagination, echoing fears of ensuing resource competition and unrest. News of droughts and famine happening across the world added to these worries. Reports of shocking environmental catastrophes due to oil spills off of Cornwall and Santa Barbara and news of an insecticide spill in the Rhine River, decimating fish populations in Germany and the Netherlands, all added fuel to the flames. Populations worldwide, but principally in developed nations, began to question civilization's accomplishments. They wondered about the fate of the planet itself.[2] United Nations (UN) Secretary General U Thant's warning that "the future of life on earth could be endangered,"[3] helped crystallize a wide range of concerns into concrete demands for both new legislation and policies that would address environmental issues in the US. Registering public concerns, policy makers pledged to deal with a wide range of important environmental challenges that in turn led to unprecedented action undertaken by the US government.

In a speech which might today seem surprising, it was a Republican president, Richard Nixon, who acknowledged a worried nation's concerns and stood up for concrete action. In his January 22, 1970 State of the Union Address which marked the beginning of a decade full of possibility, he wondered:

The great question of the seventies is, shall we surrender to our surroundings, or shall we make our peace with nature and begin to make reparations for the damage we have done to our air, to our land and to our water?

Restoring nature to its natural state is a cause beyond party and beyond factions … .

Clean air, clean water, open spaces-these should once again be the birth-right of every American. If we act now, they can be … . The program I shall propose to Congress will be the most comprehensive and costly program in this field in America's history … It is not a program for just one year … but 5 years or 10 years—whatever time is required to do the job … . The answer is not to abandon growth, but to redirect it.[4]

Nixon's speech reaffirmed commitment to growth and prosperity but simultaneously acknowledged what today seems almost improbable to suggest, that is, that the US government would take concerted action to rectify environmental damage. He freely admitted that it would be an ongoing, long-term, and expensive project that Americans needed to pay for to make "peace with nature." He proposed this comprehensive plan of action to benefit humanity and "enrich life itself and enhance our planet as a place hospitable to man."

Scholars argue that the level of Nixon's determination was short-lived, his rhetoric misleading once push-back to his efforts by the automobile industry, for instance, became more apparent. David Zwick's criticism is biting, "The President climbed aboard the environmental bandwagon in 1970 when the fare was cheap, but quickly jumped off again as soon as the stakes began to rise."[5] Nixon's political instincts told him that this was an issue that united a nation which was conflicted over the war in Vietnam and upheaval for the attainment of "new" social rights. He saw the possibility of putting forth a message that resonated to all Americans and took it.[6] The credit for the bills passed during this period belongs to Congressional mobilization, perseverance, and leaders like Edmund Muskie (Democratic senator from Maine) who had adroitly won much bipartisan support for his bill on air pollution, for instance.[7] Reactions from industry were to be expected given the extent of the proposed actions to deal with pollution and environmental degradation. They did not passively sit back to watch the tide change against their interests. Nonetheless, even if Nixon was in fact opportunistic, his words, as they were spoken at that historic moment, reflected the spirit of the wider public's determination to rally to action that has not since been repeated in quite the same way.

Even President Obama who, as we will see later on, brought the US back to the climate "table" in his second term, spoke almost sheepishly as he tried to explain that, although people understand that climate change poses a problem, getting them to act is another matter. In fact, in an interview to journalists Julie Hirschfeld Davis, Mark Landler and Coral Davenport of the *New York Times* in 2016, President Obama discussed climate action during his term in office and how it needed to be framed for the wider public.

During the course of my presidency, we've solidified that climate is real, it's important, and we need to do something about it … but … translating concern into action is the challenge … what makes climate change difficult is that it is not an instantaneous catastrophic event … . So part of our goal has been to raise awareness … create frameworks, structures, rules … create economic opportunity and improve people's well being.[8]

In contrast, Nixon's 1970 speech exuded confidence and faith in the government and the people. He projected determination and the belief that America would not stay idle and that government could set its detailed plan in motion. Nixon was fortunate in that he had the help and willingness of a forward thinking Congress that pushed him to put forth a robust environmental agenda into action. Among the most important federal laws on the environment enacted during the 1970s (during Nixon's administration and beyond) were the following: National Environmental Policy Act of 1969, the Resources Recovery Act of 1970, the Clean Air Act Amendments of 1970, the Federal Water Pollution Control Act (Clean Water Act) Amendments of 1972, the Federal Environmental Pesticides Control Act of 1972, the Marine Protection Act of 1972, the Coastal Zone Management Act of 1972, the Endangered Species Act of 1973, the Safe Drinking Water Act of 1974, the Toxic Substances Control Act of 1976, the Federal Land Policy and Management Act of 1976, the Resource Conservation and Recovery Act of 1976, the National Forest Management Act of 1976, the Surface mining Control and Reclamation Act of 1977.[9] While Nixon's speech marks a turning point in US environmental legislation, the first Earth Day celebration in the US that took place in the spring of 1970 served as a catalyst for the rise of the environmental movement as environmental issues soared to the top of the priorities list on the nation's policy agenda.

Senator Gaylord Nelson from Wisconsin held the strong belief rooted in liberalism that government could serve people's needs. In the 1950s as governor of Wisconsin, he actively supported policies by which a more affluent America could invest both in society and in the future. Although he didn't start out as a politician with an environmental agenda, his interest was first triggered by the growing sprawl of metropolitan Milwaukee and Chicago that led to a mass exodus of urban dwellers looking for opportunities to commune with nature. As a result, Nelson found the green spaces of his childhood overrun by people. In response he created the Outdoor Recreation Act Program to preserve state lakes and woods and marshes. By the time he became a senator in 1962, Nelson was a transformed conservation advocate. He worked tirelessly, and increasingly his interest revolved around issues of water pollution and extended to the wider environmental crisis he was increasingly witnessing. Nelson was inspired by the strategies of the anti-war movement and vowed to organize a nation-wide environmental teach-in in the spring of 1970.

Nelson's call to action resulted in thousands of events taking place across the US. Adam Rome in *The Genius of Earth Day* (2014) attributed the birth of the first green generation of Americans to Nelson's initiative because "roughly 1,500 colleges and 10,000 schools held teach-ins. Earth Day activities took place in hundreds of churches and temples, in city parks and in front of corporate and government buildings."[10] Thousands of people were involved in something that had never happened before. To organize it required out-of-the-box thinking, creating the first eco-infrastructure model that went on to become the kernel for lobbying efforts, environmental programs, eco-literature, environmental desks in media publications, etc. Until then, the environmental movement had been severely fragmented. Earth Day galvanized the efforts of activists and breathed real life into their endeavors. It was a time of empowerment that stayed with many of them for decades, shaping their careers and their life choices.

This was a time when the US was transitioning into a new period of political history. The New Deal that had brought the country out of the depression had served its purpose, and in the post-Second World War period of increasing affluence it gave way to a new liberalism that now included a "qualitative element." Government was now seen as having a new and expanded role in improving the quality of peoples' lives and protecting the environment. This was a time when Americans were comfortable enough financially to start wondering about the quality of the milk they drank, the suburban sprawl that was devouring open spaces, the smog over its cities, the repercussions of chemicals in all areas of life, the nuclear fall-out, the overcrowded schools, the growing urban waste and the pollution of the rivers and streams. They dared to question their nation's direction and pondered whether they would prefer to pay for quality of life rather than additional consumption. In the 60s and 70s these questions (which remain pertinent today) were deeply and seriously debated, and while choices were never consistent or straightforward, at that time conditions made action possible, even at substantial financial cost.

In 1964, President Lyndon Johnson spoke about the "Great Society" that he described in ways that continue to sound fresh and relevant.

> It is a place where man can renew contact with nature … It is a place where men are more concerned with the quality of their goals than the quantity of their goods … We have always prided ourselves on being not only America the strong and America the free, but America the beautiful … Today that beauty is in danger. The water we drink, the food we eat, the very air that we breathe, are threatened with pollution. Our parks are overcrowded, our seashores overburdened. Green fields and dense forests are disappearing.[11]

While far-reaching legislation on environmental issues happened principally in the 1970s, the 1960s brought to the fore that environmental problems fell under the purview and responsibility of the federal government.

The most chilling and thought provoking intervention, however, that profoundly changed the outlook of her generation and subsequent ones as well was Rachel Carson's book, *A Silent Spring* (1962). It was now a scientist who was speaking about how human power to alter nature had now become very dangerous.

The most alarming of all man's assaults upon the environment is the contamination of air, earth, rivers, and sea with dangerous and even lethal materials. This pollution is for the most part irrecoverable; the chain of evil it initiates not only in the world that must support life but in living tissues is for the most part irreversible. In this now universal contamination of the environment, chemicals are the sinister and little recognized partners of radiation in changing the very nature of the world – the very nature of its life … As Albert Schweitzer has said, "Man can hardly even recognize the devils of his own creation."[12]

The book was a controversial bestseller that sparked an intense discussion amongst the public and scientists alike. Paul Ehrlich, inspired by Rachel Carson, took up the mantle of holding scientists accountable for the consequences of their activities. He argued that they needed to leave their ivory towers and join society in the debates that were ever more important. Ehrlich himself produced a book that defined his generation and sold close to a million copies. Half a century after its publication, *The Population Bomb* (1968),[13] which appeared in paperback in 1968, continues to be discussed, and Ehrlich's ideas debated even if the kind of Armageddon he had predicted has not yet transpired.[14] Ehrlich sketched a dystopian world in which too many people scrambled for limited resources. He claimed that because of the growth in population the planet would no longer be able to feed its inhabitants, having surpassed its capacity to provide for everyone. Today, while the population has passed the seven billion mark, his worst fears have thankfully not come to pass. Ehrlich, however, faces staunch criticism for not amending his ideas to reflect this reality. He remains unapologetic, defending his predictions because a combination of an overcrowded planet and the over-use of natural resources and climate change continue to support his doomsday scenarios even if they come to pass at a later date. At the time, however, this controversial book stirred both academia and a public that increasingly wanted to understand the challenges ahead.

It was, therefore, not surprising that on Earth Day, thousands of people spoke. Professors from all fields of academia had a prominent voice in the teach-ins. Politicians enthusiastically participated and grabbed the media headlines. In Philadelphia, Democratic Senator Edmund Muskie, said that Earth Day indicated a need for an "environmental revolution."[15] Congress took the day off so its members could partake and speak around the country and two-thirds of them did just that.[16] Union leaders, businessmen, religious leaders, activists took a stand on a variety of issues often quite controversial for the day. Most press coverage gave Earth Day its due, though there were some journalists that portrayed it as "pure rhetoric." They were a minority voice in the media. Luckily, today's funders of the widespread and effective "campaigns of doubt" that have questioned the scientific validity of climate change had not yet unleashed their divisive rhetoric to oppose public mobilization.

In his speech on Earth Day, Gaylord Nelson, whose tireless efforts along with thousands of others across the nation, led to this historical occasion, stressed that,

Earth Day is dramatic evidence of a broad new national concern that cuts across generations and ideologies … Pull together a new national coalition whose objective is to put Gross National Quality on a par with Gross National Product. Campaign nationwide to elect an "Ecology Congress" as the 92nd Congress.[17]

Nelson and others from the political world showed that they were able to connect the dots into a comprehensive platform, a blue print of how to build "bridges between human and nature's systems,"[18] in order to respond to the growing challenges of their time.

While government rallied alongside the public, theologians also came out on Earth Day to respond to the critique raised by Lynn White Jr. that Christianity had driven a wedge between the human and the nonhuman world when it advocated that, "nature has no reason for existence save to serve man."[19] His critique unleashed a fierce debate and forced religious circles to reflect about the environment. Religious leaders like Reverend John Claypool approached environmental issues in a way that reflected the growing concern about what society was doing and how faith could reframe the message. He told members of the Louisville Crescent Hill Baptist Church that

Two years ago I am not even sure I had heard the word "ecology", and I certainly did not realize the gigantic proportion of the problems this word stands for. Since then, however, we have all been inundated about what may happen very shortly to this planet Earth; and whether we like it or not, we have to make some kind of response to all of this.[20]

Claypool also argued that,

The Good Life – however vaguely it may be defined – has most of us securely in its clutches … and this glut of affluence is one of the main culprits of our environment … are we willing to undergo the radical alteration of life style that will be called for if the balance of man and air and earth and water is to be restored? Nothing less than this will really touch the depths of the problem.[21]

Professors like Kenneth Boulding, from the University of Colorado who had been speaking about the relationship between economics and the environment captured the movement's imagination with his "Earth as Spaceship" analogy that on Earth Day and beyond gained tremendous traction. Boulding emphasized the notion that humans thought of themselves as living on an illimitable planet because for thousands of years there had been new frontiers to discover, where people could escape and get a second chance. Boulding set out to challenge this false perception by comparing the Earth to a single spaceship in order to invoke limits and fixed boundaries in the popular imagination.

> The closed economy of the future might … be called the 'spacemen' economy, in which the earth has become a single spaceship, without unlimited reservoirs of anything, either for extraction or for pollution, and in which, therefore, man must find his place in a cyclical ecological system.[22]

He did not stop there, however, adding a new concept to drive home the linearity of economic analysis as it was expressed through GNP as a measurement of economic progress, which would not work if "the earth is a closed system, a spaceship." The GNP, he argued, roughly measured the total throughout. He described it as a linear process that does not loop. The GNP did not account for natural capital depletion. It measured production and consumption. And while it gave us the false sense of being able to quantify our economic achievements, it had its limitations and could not address the needs of how the planet truly operated. "Economic development is the process by which the evil day is brought closer when everything will be gone …"[23]

It seemed that America took pleasure in taking action as people asked challenging questions in search of information. Newspaper articles of that time describe the apprehension ahead of Earth Day. Nobody was sure what to expect, but in the end people of all ages filled the streets of cities like New York, taking part in activities that inspired policy makers in particular who grew hopeful that perhaps they could now rally support for their clean-up efforts and to fight pollution.[24] Combining frameworks of alarm and hope, Earth Day indicated that American society had reached a level of economic abundance and security and was now seeking to rethink the future. It also gave Americans an issue that they felt they could do something about. As James Reston put it in a *New York Times* article on April 26, 1970,

> The American people finally have a personal and political issue they can do something about – if they're really serious … The environment issue is as close as the local dump, and can be influenced by anybody who can smell, hear or breathe.[25]

Although, the deep hope that America would embark on a deep social and political transformation did not come to fruition, what followed was an unprecedented decade of new initiatives, new institutions, new legislation and a new ethos.

Kraft and Vig argue that

> most of the new social regulation of the 1970s, that is, federal programs that used regulatory techniques to achieve broad social goals, reflected strong pressures from environmental and consumer organizations backed by a massive shift in public opinion favoring vigorous protection of public health, safety, and the environment. Moreover, such legislation was developed through bipartisan coalitions in the key House and Senate committees that sought consensus on the major environmental issues.[26]

They were seen as necessary in light of perceived market failures to control pollution, prompting Congress to conclude that national policy was the best recourse available to respond to the demands on the public agenda. Environmental policy making also reflected the wide belief of the time that environmental fixes were readily available and through technological innovation, many problems would be remedied quickly. By acting swiftly, government also proved to the public that it was capable of effectively responding to new challenges when called to step in.

While American mobilization was particularly robust, environmental awakening was also taking place in other countries around the same time, particularly in Western Europe,[27] translating into policy action by governments, increased public awareness and the rise of political expressions of environmentalism. In the US, environmental issues continued to have a prominent place on the agenda under Jimmy Carter. In his message to the Congress in 1977, Carter called for the use of executive action.

> Intelligent stewardship of the environment on behalf of all Americans is a prime responsibility of government. Congress has in the past carried out its share of this duty well – so well, in fact, that the primary need today is not for new comprehensive statutes but for sensitive administration and energetic enforcement of the ones we have. Environmental protection is no longer just a legislative job, but one that requires – and will now receive-firm and unsparing support from the Executive Branch.[28]

He went on to detail all the areas where he would focus the executive branch's attention: pollution and public health, assuring environmentally sound energy development, measures to improve the urban environment, protecting natural resources, preserving national heritage, protecting wildlife, affirming concern for the global environment, and improving the implementation of environmental laws. With regard to global environmental policies, the administration's priorities focused on supporting further research on global environmental changes and their impact on the US. Moreover, the government would offer international assistance on population problems, extend support for international environmental agreements and prohibit commercial whaling.[29]

In the 60s and 70s there were two main areas in which environmental policy was focused: efforts revolving around air and water pollution control and the limitation of exposure to toxic chemicals. Policy-making continued also to reflect conservation efforts that included the protection of public lands, waters and wildlife that were considered part of the country's national heritage. In time, however, a backlash to the cost of regulation in different areas of the American economy became apparent and grew stronger. To reduce the cost of regulatory compliance, economists advocated market incentives as an alternative. In the case of the environment, the options that were under consideration included taxes on pollution discharged as, well as permits to discharge pollution that are fixed in number and exchangeable among polluters.[30] Congress did not immediately gravitate toward these kinds of mechanisms, but persistent pressure by the business community led to increased support for the introduction of methods of cost-benefit and risk-benefit analysis as ways of improving efficiency in environmental administration. Gradually, environmental policy went from being an area of consensus to a battleground of different schools of thought.

When Ronald Reagan was elected he came to power determined to tackle what he saw as over-regulation. In the early years of the administration, the government slashed budgets, reduced environmental enforcement and opened public lands for mining, drilling, grazing and other private uses. Attacks were launched on grounds of efficiency and equity of environmental policies. The Reagan White House marked the beginning of a substantial change in the prioritization of environmental issues. In fact, Reagan's objective was to reverse the cycle that began in the 60s and 70s and had contributed so much to building environmental rules and policies. By the same token, the environment was squarely incorporated into the battleground for de-regulation. While the Reagan administration did not manage to roll back environmental regulations[31] the budget cuts he made took a significant toll, resulting in a slow-down of programs and a loss of experienced personnel. The impetus that characterized the previous period fizzled out and eventually came to a halt. The environment remained a battleground in the coming years, even while the threat of climate change and its impact on natural systems became a global concern. Fears and reports on global warming multiplied during the 1980s. Eventually they piqued Congressional interest and led to a number of hearings responding to the latest international scientific report by World Climate Program presented in Villach, Austria. According to this report, since "the understanding of the greenhouse question is sufficiently developed, scientists and policy makers should begin an active collaboration to explore the effectiveness of alternative policies and adjustments."[32]

Scientific warnings of the growing threat to the global climate raised an alarm in the Office of Management and Budget (OMB). Their concern was that the dire messages regarding the climate crisis, if true, might require policy responses that would impact the economy. The government's dilemma was whether to agree to research the issue further (thereby delaying action) or comply with calls for immediate measures that in their view would certainty harm business interests and the economy. The administration opted to invest in research to inform future policy action. It enacted the Global Climate Protection Act of 1987 (P.L. 100-204) that was a culmination of numerous Congressional hearings on this matter. The Act gave the Environmental Protection Agency (EPA) and the State Department authority to develop climate change policy. Though the president signed off, he was not on board with this legislation, the argument being that there was already an authority responsible for interagency coordination of science issues.[33]

Nonetheless, it was difficult to desist from action because this was also the time when the "ozone hole" was discovered and the Brundtland Commission Report, *Our Common Future*, was published, with the result that discussions about the climate and the environment were reaching new heights. Dealing with the stratospheric "ozone hole" was an urgent challenge but the US encouraged the passing of the Montreal Protocol which was finalized in 1987 and ratified it in 1988.[34] In order to explain the ratification of the Montreal Protocol, some scholars argue that American chemical companies (that were directly affected by this agreement) had already produced alternatives and it therefore made business sense for them not to fight the Protocol but to show their support, fearing a wider pushback on the industry if they stood in opposition.

Cost-benefit analysis, nevertheless, maintained its momentum in public discourse over the Bush administration and into the Clinton years, and for the environment that meant a preference for market-based instruments. George Bush Sr., for instance, carried on in much the same vein as his predecessor, but in a tribute to his presidency, amended the Clean Air Act in 1990. Air pollution was still on the public's mind and Bush Sr. was committed to addressing this issue as it reflected a priority for urban dwellers. His record on environmental policy was otherwise mixed.

American emissions had been growing throughout the 1980s, but when the recession hit, it became even harder to overcome the fears of the economic implications of reducing emissions. Furthermore, it is also important to underscore that in the beginning of the environmental movement and during this period of recession, the international debates had mostly focused on the nature of the problem and the kinds of norms that would govern the international response.[35] It was only from 1992 onwards, that it became increasingly clear that domestic reforms would also be required to respond effectively to the global climate crisis.

There was an initial expectation that the Clinton administration would champion the climate and other environmental items given that Vice-President Al Gore had a strong record with respect to the climate. No radical shift took place, however, and the administration's proposals largely resembled those of previous ones. Much resistance to environmental and natural resource policies came from the 104th US congress (1995–1997). After 40 years, Republicans returned victorious to hold the majority in both the House and the Senate. The political shift in Congress brought with it a strong backlash on a wide range of government activities including policies pertaining to the environment. Once again the economy became the top priority of the policy agenda because it had taken a downturn in the previous years. Clinton used his executive authority to strengthen the EPA and adopted measures to protect public land and endangered species. Addressing the climate problem, however, posed the greatest difficulty, particularly with so much Congressional push back. The administration resorted to extensive internal maneuvering and negotiations to achieve some progress on this front. Congress consistently opposed them. Clinton agreed to support an international protocol that would set binding targets and emission reductions over a particular timeframe but did not commit to do this before 1997 when the Kyoto Protocol negotiations were to take place. In the interim he sought to reach consensus with Congress but it was proving impossible.

Then Clinton identified a political opportunity. The Republican Congress was under attack for pushing back on the environment in a time when the entire world was pushing for international action. In a particularly bold move, Clinton indicated that the US would support legally binding emission targets (though the administration remained vague on the details) and confirmed support for reaching an agreement at Kyoto, calculating that this decision might also help his re-election in 1996.[36] The president must have known that the policy window on such an agreement had long expired, and he would face staunch opposition by Congress. He could not engineer the momentous change in policy that he had envisioned because there was no possibility of achieving consensus on possible solutions. Moreover, the issue was not drawing as much public engagement as was needed to keep up the pressure, particularly when Congress was projecting a high cost on job growth and the economy.

As the years went by, the divide between Republican and Democratic policy makers continued to widen. According to the League of Conservation Voters (LCV), it appears that Senate Democrats averaged about 85 percent of support of the positions of the LCV and the environmentalists, while Senate Republicans averaged only 8 percent.[37] Environmental policy also took a hit under George W. Bush, who famously rejected the Kyoto Protocol in 2001, describing it as "fatally flawed," and "in many ways, unrealistic." In his address about climate change on June 11, 2001, he stated that,

> Many countries cannot meet their Kyoto targets. The targets themselves were arbitrary and not based upon science. For America, complying with those mandates would have a negative economic impact, with layoffs of workers and price increases for consumers. And when you evaluate all these flaws, most reasonable people will understand that it's not sound public policy. That's why 95 members of the United States Senate expressed a reluctance to endorse such an approach.[38]

The American decision was followed by international uproar because it dealt a strong blow to global climate action. He insisted that the Kyoto Protocol, by exempting the developing nations around the world, was not in the US's best interests. When he, moreover, pointed out the shared obligations of China and India to address climate change he faced heated opposition.[39] This was in line with the determined belief among developing countries that the developed world had primarily caused the climate debacle and should do their share to reverse the damage.

Throughout his presidency, George W. Bush, moreover, sided with what he viewed as his party's business base and in particular mining, agriculture, oil and timber interests. To do so he used his executive authority to push for deregulation and voluntary, flexible and cooperative programs. He pushed for further budget cuts, but now he, in turn, found congressional pushback. His focus was on increasing energy supplies to secure cheap energy for the American economy (especially given the high fossil fuel prices at the time). Vice-President Dick Cheney was assigned this task. A bill was passed in 2005 that gave energy producing companies "massive subsidies."[40] Bush also sought to give even more responsibility to the states instead of the federal government for environmental issues.

Since that Golden Era of the 60s and 70s, the US went from a leader in enacting forward thinking environmental policies and legislation, to displaying avoidance and obstructionism in light of growing international efforts to coordinate responses to the growing climate crisis and mounting environmental degradation. Already in Rio in 1992, the American stance on global negotiations would start to crystallize. The US refused to ratify the Convention on Biological Diversity[41] although it signed it. As we have seen, while agreeing to sign and ratify the UN Framework Convention on Climate Change, the US ended up rejecting the Kyoto Protocol that accompanied it. The US, moreover, has signed but not ratified the Biosafety Protocol.[42] Overall, the US has not been in favor of binding international commitments to reduce carbon emissions.

Its preference has been that each nation be allowed to set its own targets for emission reductions. It has also supported technological innovation, alternative fuels and energy efficiency as ways to reduce emissions. The US took the position that its own compliance was linked to the developing world also taking action with the support of wealthier countries,[43] knowing this would sidetrack negotiations which in that period drew a clear distinction between the obligations of developed and developing nations. American posturing stalled meaningful decisions early on. It soured the prospects of global action to stop temperatures from rising beyond 2°C, and it helped to spread malaise across the globe and fears that humanity had embarked on a voyage of no return. If the US was not supporting the world's efforts, why should other industrial nations, let alone developing ones chose to decarbonize and sacrifice the kind of growth and modernity that America already had?

What accounts for this change in both behavior and outlook, especially after such a strong social awakening in the 1960s and 1970s that culminated in calls for social change and an end to the Vietnam War? First and foremost, the US's lack of action has been linked to its declared strategic interest for uninterrupted access to cheap energy, particularly fossil fuels. America's insatiable desire for cheap energy to power its economic growth has given the fossil fuel industry inordinate power and influence over policy decisions. It is opposed to taxation and regulation. It stands against attempts at reducing carbon emissions or placing any kind of restrictions that it considers an economic burden. Moreover, the fossil fuel industry remains a recipient of US subsidies even while it continues to grow and thrive. Because climate change negotiations are so closely linked to energy options to achieve a reduction in CO2 emissions, the fossil fuel industry in the US has aggressively lobbied against any binding limits.

In 1988 the problem of global warming resurfaced with a vengeance. James Hansen testified in front of a Senate Committee that it was 99 percent probable that global warming had begun. His testimony triggered a renewed worldwide discussion on the greenhouse effect and what kind of threat it represented to the planet's future. That year, the UN General Assembly passed Resolution 43/53 on the "Conservation of climate as part of the common heritage of mankind." It gave both the go ahead for the creation of the Intergovernmental Panel on Climate Change (IPCC) and a timeframe in which to submit its report. Interest in climate change rose further, leading scientists to speak out, legislators to propose bills, the IPCC to prepare its first report and prompting the world to consider moving toward some form of international agreement on emission reductions.

These developments directly impacted major fossil fuel companies. They decided to strike back while the iron was hot and invested in a far-reaching campaign of distraction and denial that took many forms over the years. They launched attacks against climate science and climate policy. First, through the Global Climate Coalition and then with the help of the George C. Marshall Institute, they successfully created public confusion over the validity of scientific findings concerning climate change and, furthermore, generated the false impression that the scientific community had not even reached a consensus over whether climate change was happening and whether it was the result of human activity. The "denialist" camp exploited public ignorance enlisting a few select scientists willing to question and disrupt the consensus. Where the public wanted certainty, scientists could only speak in probabilities when discussing their findings.

Furthermore, unlike Europe which widely accepted the scientific findings about climate change and boasted a wide political consensus on the issue, the climate crisis became highly politicized in Washington, D.C. Taking a closer look at US public opinion data based on a nationally representative survey published by the Yale Project on Climate Change Communication in March 2015, Americans continue to appear substantially removed from the topic even though gradually they are accepting that global warming is in fact happening.[44]

Seventy-four percent of Americans answered that they "rarely" or "never" discuss global warming, a number that increased from 60 percent in 2008. Americans also say they hear about global warming in the media once a month (21 percent) and once a week (19-percent). Twenty-five-percent say they never hear their acquaintances talk about global warming.[45] Furthermore, according to the same report, about 52 percent think that global warming, if it is happening, is mostly human caused, while three in ten (32-percent) say they believe it is due mostly to natural changes in the environment. Finally, one in ten Americans understands that more than 90 percent of climate scientists agree global warming is human caused.[46]

Political divisions, with respect to climate change related issues, as the latest PEW report (May-June 2016) indicates, continue unabated.[47] These differences also impact the way Americans evaluate actions that can be taken to respond to the climate crisis. Some of the findings are particularly telling in the extent of the differences between Republicans and Democrats. For example, with respect to power plant emission restrictions, 76 percent of liberal Democrats versus 29 percent of conservative Republicans say this makes a big difference. By the same token, 71 percent of liberal Democrats versus 27 percent of conservative Republicans think an international agreement to limit carbon emissions would make a difference. Similarly, 67 percent of liberal Democrats versus 27 percent of conservative Republicans find that tougher fuel efficiency standards for cars and trucks make a big difference. Finally, 67 percent of liberal Democrats versus

23 percent of conservative Republicans agree that corporate tax incentives to encourage businesses to reduce the "carbon footprint" from their activities would make a difference.[48]

There are many reasons that have been set forth as explanations of why the US took such a reactionary position with regard to the climate crisis. There are those who maintain that science was not enough. People could not understand it, and the threat seemed too intangible and removed. If Armageddon were to happen, it wasn't happening in the here and now. Activists and a number of scholars and analysts, as we have seen, blame industry interests for sponsoring the campaign of denial and of continually influencing the political process to achieve gridlock in Washington, D.C, The power of the fossil fuel industry has undoubtedly played a prominent role in the story as well by pushing for energy security, energy independence and cheap uninterrupted access to energy at all costs.

Yet there are other reasons that have contributed to the US exhibiting such unique behavior compared to other industrial nations. In the US, government itself has been under attack. It has been undermined and often discredited. Government mandates, regulations and increased taxation (especially of industry and the rich) are looked upon with suspicion. Some critics attribute the staunch opposition of industry to the heavy regulatory framework initiated in the 1970s when government action became so robust. Environmental policies meant to fight pollution, for instance, were seen as imposing 'excessive' new burdens and costs on industry. This led business interests to actively reframe the discourse into a message that big government was adversely impacting entrepreneurship and business. As economic growth remains the yardstick by which success is measured, industry contended that this cannot be achieved under a strong regulatory framework (the European model disputes this claim).

In recent years, moreover, the US has witnessed a growth of staunchly religious and politically conservative and populist political movements that have ruptured social unity, testing not only national cohesion, but also the narrative of what America now stands for. Although still active in international affairs, the US is demonstrating an appetite for growing isolation and a tendency to securitize all aspects of life. To an outsider, the US seems to operate under the presumption of a constant threat from external and domestic foes, from economic and trade competitors, cyber attackers, rising powers, migrants and terrorists, all of which help create a climate of domestic angst and uncertainty. These kinds of fears do not then translate into support for genuine and comprehensive international cooperation but instead provoke retrenchment and recoiling from taking on new obligations and responsibilities.

In 2007 a ray of hope appeared on the horizon. Al Gore released a movie that would re-invigorate the debate over climate change. *An Inconvenient Truth* was a documentary that told the story of how the climate crisis was evident and that Americans (and the rest of the world) could no longer afford to ignore it. Al Gore did not just produce a movie. He personally took it on a national and international tour which is how it reached a critical mass of people generating responses that environmentalists hoped would last. The IPCC report that same year confirmed that climate change was happening and that it enjoyed scientific consensus. For a moment, it seemed that the US could and would once again take the lead. CEOs from major companies pushed for emission ceilings, and 36 US states developed "climate action plans." Five hundred and twenty-two US cities agreed to adhere to the Kyoto standards even though the US refused to ratify the agreement.

The momentum did not last. Moreover, the pendulum swung in the opposite direction. The 2008 global financial crisis constituted the kiss of death for climate discourse. America now scrambled to save the banks, the economy overall and American jobs. Savings of a lifetime were wiped out overnight. There was fear that the global financial system was melting down and that it wouldn't recover. Contagion spread all across the nation and the world economy. Any measure that would remotely appear to be hampering a speedy return to growth was shelved and moreover cast down by opposition. Gridlock in Washington, D.C. combined with an even more polarized debate over the scientific validity of climate change and a demonization of any emission cutting schemes or policies aimed at reducing American fossil fuel dependency took hold of the discourse, leading environmentalists, scientists and those of the public who were concerned about this issue to lose heart that the US would ever be able to be part of a global solution.

The Obama administration was the last vestige of hope. In 2009, the US House of Representatives approved a cap and trade scheme in response to the growing threat of climate change. During the election campaign Obama himself had expressed the ambition to reduce carbon emissions by 80 percent by 2050 with the assistance of a cap and trade scheme.[49] The partisan conflict that ensued over the bill, however, along with aggressive lobbying efforts on the part of industry interests prevented the Senate from acting on the bill through the 111th Congress, sealing its death in 2011.[50] Instead of becoming a rallying cry for unity and action, the climate crisis had now officially become one of the most politicized topics in the US. Congress also objected when the European Union (EU) attempted to require all flights within, to, or from the European Economic Area to be covered by the EU's cap-and-trade system from 2012. The Senate in fact voted unanimously in favor of legislation that would protect US airlines from taking part in the EU Emissions Trading System (EU ETS).[51]

Indicative of the kind of leverage American pushback has had was that it forced the Europeans to hold off. According to the Commission, the decision to include aviation in the EU ETS was found to be the "most cost-efficient and environmentally effective option for controlling aviation emissions."[52] According to EU data, aviation accounts for 3-percent of the EU's total greenhouse gas (GHG) emissions, and the large majority comes from international flights. Aviation emissions are projected to continue to grow and according to ICAO forecasts, they could grow an additional 300 to 700 percent by 2050. As things stand now, the International Civil Aviation Organization (ICAO) has been tasked to develop a global market-based mechanism to address international aviation emissions by 2016 and apply it by 2020. This agreement followed years of pressure from the EU for global action.[53]

The demonstration of this kind of unrelenting Congressional pushback was a turning point for the Obama administration. The president sought an alternative route since it did not seem possible to reach any kind of consensus through Congress. Obama opted to press forward using administrative decisions that did not require Congressional approval. The vehicle that worked best was the EPA, through which new rules could be made. By 2012, he finalized the new vehicle fuel efficiency regulations managing to gain the cooperation of the automobile industry. The administration took extensive action on the energy front promoting research and development for energy efficiency technologies and renewables. This decision, especially with respect to renewables, was heavily criticized but it did encourage the diversification of the country's energy mix. Still, the president's overall record remained mixed. Under his watch, oil production surged 82 percent and natural gas production was up nearly 25 percent.[54] In fact, Obama supported fracking, for which he received much criticism. Though it has allowed the US to use a cleaner fuel to power its economy at low cost, increasingly replacing coal as a result, hydrofracking itself poses many environmental risks in its extraction. It still produces emissions, and given its low price, contributes to a slow-down of the transition to renewables. During the Obama presidency, a series of events fueled the ongoing debate over how to satisfy US energy needs while tackling the impacts of pollution and emissions. The BP Deep Water Horizon Oil Spill of 2010, for instance, heightened debate about the safety of deep sea drilling. The conflict was over the kind of standards necessary to use these techniques of extraction. Pipelines were also under increased scrutiny and one project, the Keystone XL pipeline, designed to bring Canadian tar sands to US oil refineries, after much heated debate and public demonstrations was vetoed by President Obama, causing Congressional uproar.

The administration did try to regulate the fracking industry through a series of new stringent regulations issued by the US Bureau of Land Management. After years of deliberation these stipulated, for instance, that companies drilling for oil and natural gas would need to disclose the chemicals they use in the fracking process. Key provisions of the new rules included the requirement of strong cement barriers between the well and any water zones it passes through, public disclosure of chemicals that companies used in fracking, stricter storage protocols for recovered waste-water and measures to lower the risk of cross-contamination from fracking chemicals.[55] The rules drew heated criticism from the oil and gas industries. On June 22, 2016, a federal judge in Wyoming struck down the new regulations, ruling that Congress had not granted such authority to the Bureau of Land Management.[56]

Another area that left Obama open to criticism was his granting permission to drill in the Arctic Ocean, a decision that drew the wrath of environmentalists. He furthermore agreed (with reservations) to lift the 40-year-old ban on the export of most US crude. In 2013, President Obama went ahead to set a new goal to regulate carbon emissions from coal-fired electric power plants using the authority of the Clean Air Act. This measure was deemed particularly significant because the 600 existing coal-fired plants in operation emit approximately

40 percent of energy-related GHG. It also meant that coal was now the principal fuel under "attack." Unfortunately, these regulations have been contested robustly in court, and the entire plan is currently stalled. Climate change still remains low in the public's list of domestic priorities. According to a list produced by PEW Research Center, priorities rank as follows: economy, terrorism, education, jobs, social security, health care costs, Medicare, reducing crime, budget deficit, poor and needy, immigration, military, environment, tax reform, criminal justice reform, climate change, gun policy and global trade.[57] It appears, therefore, that climate change continues to be regarded as a problem of the future.[58]

Nonetheless, while the federal government is caught in a political battle over the climate, state and local governments are carving out their own responses to the climate threat. California's cap-and-trade scheme, for instance, went into effect on January 1, 2013. Although this is not a federal scheme, California does represent the ninth largest economy in the world, and the level of its success, as well as the knowledge it will generate, may influence other states to use this market tool to price carbon and reduce emissions. At present the scheme covers nearly 85 percent of the state's total GHG emissions and extends to large electric power plants and large industrial plants. In January 2014, California and Quebec linked up in this program. The target for California is to reduce emissions to 1990 levels by 2020 and achieve the 80 percent reduction of GHG emissions by 2050.[59] Because action on climate change has been primarily linked to the reduction of energy emissions, the emphasis has been in finding ways to reduce dependence on fossil fuels, reducing their use through energy efficiency applications and developing new technologies for carbon capture. Cities across the US have taken independent action and have mobilized to embrace a variety of programs to green urban centers, encourage the deployment of renewables, make changes in transport, promote recycling and energy efficiency measures and revisit waste management, setting concrete targets not only to reduce carbon emissions, but also to improve the overall quality of life.

Nonetheless, the media and scholarly literature for the most part focus on how the US government failed to produce a comprehensive and targeted response to climate change domestically and project an ambitious and constructive leading role in international negotiations. Even though domestically certain policies that supported further scientific research were better received, in the end, the US response to the climate crisis was incremental and piecemeal. In the future, and as the climate crisis worsens, environmental policy in the US will inevitably need to become linked to the sustainable development model of growth as demonstrated, for instance, in Europe and increasingly in China as reflected in its 13th Five-Year Plan (FYP).

This will affect policy-making design over a wide range of areas from energy use, transportation, urban planning and design, agriculture, food production, health and safety, to population growth and the protection of ecosystems. Still, attempts at taking a more comprehensive approach to climate policy became more evident over the course of President Obama's second term. He gradually became more vocal in speaking about the climate crisis, and it began to feature significantly in his speeches. He took a stand and gave it priority status on both his domestic and international agendas. In COP 21 in Paris the US submitted its Intended Nationally Determined Contributions (INDCs) by which, "The United States intends to achieve an economy-wide target of reducing its greenhouse gas emissions by 26-28 percent below its 2005 level in 2025 and to make best efforts to reduce its emissions by 28%." While the base year of emissions is not the highest in the US history of emissions, it continues to be one of the highest (contrasted to the 1990 base year chosen by the EU).[60] "This target is consistent with a straight line emission reduction pathway from 2020 to deep, economy-wide emission reductions of 80% or more by 2050."[61]

Most notably, however, President Obama underscored the shift in government policy on the issue of climate change by actively seeking and obtaining the cooperation of Chinese President Xi to announce to the world that the two "superpowers" could and would cooperate to do something about this grave threat to the earth's system. Obama's move to internationalize his domestic agenda in order to deal with the climate crisis was aimed at different audiences. He came out "boldly" to tell the American people that scientists agreed that this was a real threat to life itself, that his countrymen had an obligation to the next generation of Americans to protect the planet and that the economy would not suffer but grow instead. His rhetoric was in line with the image that the US opts to globally project, that is, that if an issue is important enough then the US will never merely follow, but will take on a leadership role. Furthermore, Obama was openly declaring that the world had once again returned to a bipolar power arrangement. As befits a superpower, the US would take the lead by working together with their archrival, setting aside all differences to nobly cooperate on saving the planet for future generations. The two largest emitters were now poised to demonstrate that they would lead by example. This created much hope for COP 21 that did—almost miraculously—deliver a positive outcome, even though just a few days before a terrorist attack on Paris had thrown the country and the world into renewed turmoil with France declaring a state of emergency.

The problem of course with Obama's approach was that he clearly showed a preference for bipolar relations which accounts for the fact that the European Union, which had been the leading advocate for binding emission reductions and had set forth a plan proving in practice that emissions could be reduced without undermining the economy, was not invited to share the spotlight on that particular day, nor in subsequent announcements. There were, of course, a number of problems with Obama's approach to climate negotiations. First, his international position was vulnerable because it did not have Congressional support, and in the US the executive cannot get very far by ignoring the legislative and judicial branches of government. Indeed, Obama's domestic policies have already been pushed back most notably by the courts. Second, Obama singled out the climate crisis as one of the only areas in which the US and China could hope to cooperate without having to compromise on any of their core interests. While this may not be a problem per se, US-China core interests are often in conflict, which makes the climate an easy victim when other heated disputes that are now rearing their heads disrupt the willingness or mere feasibility of working together in the future.

There is of course no denying that having the US onboard is vital for any global climate agreement or even for a global effort to produce measurable results. Yet it proved both premature and even shortsighted to put the fate of battling the climate crisis into the hands of American leadership. Domestic conditions in the US are such that they do not support such a choice. The result of the November 2016 elections proved just that. President Obama shone a lantern on the climate crisis, by raising awareness and seeking to reduce the voices of doubt over whether or not climate change was taking place. He used his executive authority to try to pass measures that would allow the US to reduce emissions and to show responsibility in the face of such a grave global crisis. He may have restored some of the international faith that was lost during the previous years with respect to the position of the US and in international climate negotiations. Following the November 2016 election however, the Obama administration was succeeded by Republican Donald Trump in an unprecedented electoral upset.[62] In contrast to Barack Obama, Trump has publicly stated that he does not believe in climate change and that he continues to back the production and reliance on fossil fuels as the energy of choice.[63] This change in power does not bode well either for climate negotiations or for the numerous measures that Obama legislated so that the US could honor its obligations in Paris and to the world.

Notes

1 Paul Ehrlich, *The Population Bomb* (New York: Ballantine Books, 1968).
2 William Cronon, *The Environmental Moment: 1968–1972*, ed. David Stradling (Seattle: University of Washington Press, 2012), 1968–72.
3 "The Deteriorating Environment," *The New York Times*, June 25, 1969, accessed June 14, 2015.
4 "Annual Message to the Congress on the State of the Union, Richard Nixon, XXXVII President of the United States: 1969-1974," January 22, 1970,http://www.presidency.ucsb.edu/ws/index.php?pid=2921&st=&st1=.
5 David Zwick, "Water Pollution" in *Nixon and the Environment: The Politics of Devastation*, (New York: Village Voice, 1972), 30.
6 J. Brooks Flippen, *Nixon and the Environment* (Albuquerque: University of New Mexico Press, 2000), 50–56.
7 James Miller, "Air Pollution," in *Nixon and the Environment: The Politics of Devastation* (New York: Village Voice, 1972), 14.
8 Julie Hirschfeld Davis, Mark Landler, and Coral Davenport, "Obama on Climate Change: The Trends Are 'Terrifying,'" *The New York Times*, September 8, 2016, http://www.nytimes.com/2016/09/08/us/politics/obama-climate-change.html.
9 US Environmental Protection Agency, "Laws & Regulations," accessed November 6, 2016, https://www.epa.gov/laws-regulations.
10 Adam Rome, *The Genius of Earth Day: How a 1970 Teach-In Unexpectedly Made the First Green Generation* (New York: Hill and Wang, 2014), x–xi.
11 Lyndon B. Johnson, "Remarks at the University of Michigan, May 22, 1964," Public Papers of the Presidents of the United States: Lyndon B. Johnson, 1963–1964 (2 volumes) (Washington, D.C.: U.S. Government Printing Office, 1965) I, 704–705.

12   Rachel Carson, *Silent Spring* (Boston: Houghton Mifflin Company, 1962), 6.
13   Ehrlich, *The Population Bomb.*
14   Clyde Haberman, "The Unrealized Horrors of Population Explosion," *The New York Times*, May 31, 2015, http://www.nytimes.com/2015/06/01/us/the-unrealized-horrors-of-population-explosion.html.
15   Gladwin Hill, "Activity Ranges From Oratory to Legislation; Oratory and Legislation Mark Drive on Pollution", *The New York Times*, April 23, 1970, accessed June 15, 2015.
16   Rome, *The Genius of Earth Day*, 166–167.
17   David Stradling, *The Environmental Moment: 1968–1972* (Washington, D.C.: University of Washington Press, 2013), 85.
18   Stradling, *The Environmental Moment: 1968–1972*, 85.
19   Lynn White, "The Historical Roots of Our Ecological Crisis," *This Sacred Earth: Religion, Nature, Environment*, (1967): 184–193.
20   The text of Claypool's sermon is printed in: Henlee H. Barnette, *The Church and the Ecological Crisis* (Grand Rapids, MI: William B. Eerdmans, 1972), 98–107.
21   Barnette, *The Church and the Ecological Crisis*, 98–107.
22   Kenneth E. Boulding, "The Economics of the Coming Spaceship Earth," in the *Environmental Quality in a Growing Economy: Essays from the Sixth RFF Forum*, edited by Henry Jarrett, (Baltimore, MD: Johns Hopkins University Press, 1966), 4, 9.
23   Kenneth E. Boulding, "Fun and Games with Gross National Product-The Role of Misleading Indicators in Social Policy," in *The Environmental Crisis: Man's Struggle to live with Himself*, edited by Harold W. Helfich Jr. (New Haven: Yale University Press, 1970), 169.
24   David Bird, "In the Aftermath of Earth Day: City Gains New Leverage," *The New York Times*, April 24, 1970, accessed June 15, 2015. http://query.nytimes.com/gst/abstract.html?res=9E0DE6DA1131E236A05757C2A9629C946190D6CF.
25   James Reston, "Washington: The Politics of Pollution," *The New York Times*, April 26, 1970, http://www.nytimes.com/1970/04/26/archives/washington-the-politics-of-pollution.html. In contrast to how the public viewed issues of pollution and the environment the climate crisis has been perceived by the American public as something very remote and overwhelming for individual engagement.
26   Michael E. Kraft and Norman J. Vig, "Environmental Policy in the Reagan Presidency," *Political Science Quarterly* 99, no. 3 (1984): 415–39.
27   Chris Rootes, *Environmental Protest in Western Europe* (Oxford: Oxford University Press, 2007).
28   Jimmy Carter, "The Environment Message to the Congress," accessed November 9, 2016, http://www.presidency.ucsb.edu/ws/?pid=7561.
29   Jimmy Carter, "The Environment Message to the Congress."
30   Kraft and Vig, "Environmental Policy in the Reagan Presidency."
31   Philip Shabecoff, "Reagan and Environment: To Many, a Stalemate," *The New York Times*, January 2, 1989, sec. U.S., http://www.nytimes.com/1989/01/02/us/reagan-and-environment-to-many-a-stalemate.html.
32   Loren R. Cass, *The Failures of American and European Climate Policy: International Norms, Domestic Politics, and Unachievable Commitments* (Albany: State University of New York Press, 2006), 21.
33   Roger A. Pielke, "Policy History of the US Global Change Research Program: Part I. Administrative Development," *Global Environmental Change* 10, no. 1 (2000): 9–25.
34   Bureau of Public Affairs Department Of State, "The Montreal Protocol on Substances That Deplete the Ozone Layer," *U.S. Department of State*, April 12, 2007, http://www.state.gov/e/oes/eqt/chemicalpollution/83007.htm.
35   Cass, *The Failures of American and European Climate Policy*, 20.
36   Christopher J. Bailey, *US Climate Change Policy* (Farnham, Surrey: Ashgate Publishing, Ltd., 2015), 76–78.

37   Michael E. Kraft, ed., *Public Policy; Politics, Analysis, and Alternatives*, 5th Revised ed. edition (Los Angeles: CQ Press, 2014).

38   Office of the Press Secretary, "President Bush Discusses Global Climate Change," accessed November 10, 2016, https://georgewbush-whitehouse.archives.gov/news/releases/2001/06/20010611-2.html.

39   Bailey, *US Climate Change Policy*, 96.

40   Norman J. Vig and Michael E. Kraft, *Environmental Policy: New Directions for the Twenty-First Century 8th Edition* (Thousand Oaks, CA: CQ Press, 2012), 96.

41   "List of Parties," *Convention on Biological Diversity*, accessed November 6, 2016, https://www.cbd.int/information/parties.shtml.

42   Bureau of Public Affairs, Department of State. "Frequently Asked Questions on the Cartagena Protocol on Biosafety (CPB)," accessed November 6, 2016, https://2001-2009.state.gov/g/oes/rls/or/2004/29751.htm.

43   Bailey, *US Climate Change Policy*, 61.

44   About two in three (63 percent) Americans think global warming is happening. By contrast, only about one in five Americans (18-percent) thinks global warming is not happening. "Climate Change in the American Mind," *Yale Project on Climate Change Communication*, March 2015, http://environment.yale.edu/climate-communication-OFF/files/Global-Warming-CCAM-March-2015.pdf.

45   "Climate Change in the American Mind."

46   "Climate Change in the American Mind."

47   Cary Funk and Brian Kennedy, "The Politics of Climate," *Pew Research Center: Internet, Science & Tech*, October 4, 2016, http://www.pewinternet.org/2016/10/04/the-politics-of-climate/.

48   Funk and Kennedy, "The Politics of Climate."

49   John Carey, "Obama's Cap-and-Trade Plan," *Bloomberg.com*, March 5, 2009, http://www.bloomberg.com/news/articles/2009-03-04/obamas-cap-and-trade-plan.

50   Henry Waxman, "H.R.2454 – 111th Congress (2009–2010): American Clean Energy and Security Act of 2009," legislation, (July 7, 2009), https://www.congress.gov/bill/111th-congress/house-bill/2454. Bryan Walsh, "Why the Climate Bill Died," *Time*, accessed November 7, 2016, http://science.time.com/2010/07/26/why-the-climate-bill-died/."As the World Burns," *The New Yorker*, accessed November 7, 2016, http://www.newyorker.com/magazine/2010/10/11/as-the-world-burns.

51   International Centre for Trade and Sustainable Development, "EU Airline Emissions Rule Under Fire by US Senate," accessed November 7, 2016, http://www.ictsd.org/bridges-news/bridges/news/eu-airline-emissions-rule-under-fire-by-us-senate.

52   European Commission, "Reducing Emissions from Aviation," accessed November 7, 2016, https://ec.europa.eu/clima/policies/transport/aviation/index_en.htm.

53   European Commission, "Reducing Emissions from Aviation."

54   Jennifer A. Dlouhy, "Despite Protests, Oil Industry Thrives Under Obama Agenda," *Bloomberg.com*, January 5, 2016, http://www.bloomberg.com/news/articles/2016-01-05/despite-protests-oil-industry-thrives-under-obama-energy-agenda.

55   Scott Neuman, "Interior Department Issues New Fracking Rules for Federal Lands," *NPR.org*, accessed November 7, 2016, http://www.npr.org/sections/thetwo-way/2015/03/20/394282086/interior-dept-issues-new-fracking-rules-for-federal-lands.

56   Camila Domonoske, "Federal Judge Strikes Down Obama Administration's Fracking Rules," *NPR.org*, accessed November 7, 2016, http://www.npr.org/sections/thetwo-way/2016/06/22/483061014/federal-judge-strikes-down-obama-administrations-fracking-rules.

57   Pew Research Center for the People and the Press, "The Public's Policy Priorities for 2016," January 21, 2016, http://www.people-press.org/2016/01/22/budget-deficit-slips-as-public-priority/1-21-2016_06/.

58   For more information, see Bailey, who gives a wider policy perspective on US action with respect to the climate: Bailey, *US Climate Change Policy*.

59   Center for Climate and Energy Solutions, "California Cap and Trade," accessed
      November 2, 2016, http://www.c2es.org/us-states-regions/key-legislation/california-
      cap-trade.
60   Intended Nationally Determined Contributions (INDC), *United States of America*,
      http://www4.unfccc.int/submissions/INDC/Published%20Documents/United%20
      States%20of%20America/1/U.S.%20Cover%20Note%20INDC%20and%20
      Accompanying%20Information.pdf
61   To understand the level of US commitment it is worthwhile comparing with that of
      the European Union: "The EU and its Member States wish to communicate the fol-
      lowing INDC. The EU and its Member States are committed to a binding target of
      an at least 40% domestic reduction in greenhouse gas emissions by 2030 compared
      to 1990, to be fulfilled jointly, as set out in the conclusions by the European Council
      of October 2014." "Intended Nationally Determined Contribution of the EU and its
      Member States," *European Union*, March 6, 2015, http://www4.unfccc.int/submis-
      sions/INDC/Published%20Documents/Latvia/1/LV-03-06-EU%20INDC.pdf
          Finally, China's INDC targets are as follows:
      "Based on its national circumstances, development stage, sustainable development
      strategy and international responsibility, China has nationally determined its actions
      by 2030 as follows: To achieve the peaking of carbon dioxide emissions around 2030
      and making best efforts to peak early; to lower carbon dioxide emissions per unit of
      GDP by 60% to 65% from the 2005 level; to increase the share of non-fossil fuels in
      primary energy consumption to around 20%; and to increase the forest stock volume
      by around 4.5 billion cubic meters on the 2005 level."
          "Enhanced Actions on Climate Change: China's Intended Nationally Determined
      Contributions(unofficial translation)," June 30, 2015, http://www4.unfccc.int/
      Submissions/INDC/Published%20Documents/China/1/China's%20INDC%20-%20
      on%2030%20June%202015.pdf.
62   Matt Flegenheimer and Michael Barbaro, "Donald Trump Is Elected President in
      Stunning Repudiation of the Establishment," *The New York Times*, November 9,
      2016, http://www.nytimes.com/2016/11/09/us/politics/hillary-clinton-donald-trump-
      president.html.
63   Adam Withnall, "Why President Trump Is an Even Bigger Disaster than You
      Realised," *The Independent*, November 9, 2016, http://www.independent.co.uk/news/
      world/americas/us-elections/president-donald-trump-disaster-paris-climate-change-
      agreement-cop-22-un-climate-summit-a7406366.html.

Bibliography

Bailey, Christopher J. *US Climate Change Policy*. Farnham, Surrey: Ashgate Publishing,
      Ltd., 2015.
Barnett, Henlee H. *The Church and the Ecological Crisis*. Grand Rapids, MI: William B.
      Eerdmans, 1972.
Bird, David. "In the Aftermath of Earth Day: City Gains New Leverage." *The New York
      Times*. April, 24, 1970. Accessed June 15, 2015. http://query.nytimes.com/gst/abstract.
      html?res=9E0DE6DA1131E236A05757C2A9629C946190D6CG.
Carey, John. "Obama's Cap-and-Trade Plan." *Bloomberg.com*. March 5, 2009. http://www.
      bloomberg.com/news/articles/2009-03-04/obamas-cap-and-trade-plan.
Carson, Rachel. *Silent Spring*. Boston: Houghton Mifflin Company, 1962.
Carter, Jimmy. "The Environment Message to the Congress." Accessed November 9,
      2016. http://www.presidency.ucsb.edu/ws/?pid=7561.
Cass, Loren R. *The Failures of American and European Climate Policy International Norms,
      Domestic Politics, and Unachievable Commitments*. Albany: State University of New
      York Press, 2006.

Center for Climate and Energy Solutions. "California Cap and Trade." Accessed November 2, 2016. http://www.c2es.org/us-states-regions/key-legislation/california-cap-trade.

Convention on Biological Diversity. "List of Parties." Accessed November 6, 2016. https://www.cbd.int/information/parties.shtml.

Cronon, William. *The Environmental Moment: 1968–1972.* Edited by David Stradling. Seattle: University of Washington Press, 2012.

Department Of State. Bureau of Public Affairs. "The Montreal Protocol on Substances That Deplete the Ozone Layer." *U.S. Department of State.* April 12, 2007. http://www.state.gov/e/oes/eqt/chemicalpollution/83007.htm.

Department Of State. The Office of Electronic Information, Bureau of Public Affairs. "Frequently Asked Questions on the Cartagena Protocol on Biosafety (CPB)." Accessed November 6, 2016. https://2001-2009.state.gov/g/oes/rls/or/2004/29751.htm.

Dlouhy, Jennifer. "Despite Protests, Oil Industry Thrives Under Obama Agenda." *Bloomberg.com.* January 5, 2016. http://www.bloomberg.com/news/articles/2016-01-05/despite-protests-oil-industry-thrives-under-obama-energy-agenda.

Domonoske, Camila. "Federal Judge Strikes Down Obama Administration's Fracking Rules." *NPR.org.* Accessed November 7, 2016. http://www.npr.org/sections/thetwo-way/2016/06/22/483061014/federal-judge-strikes-down-obama-administrations-fracking-rules.

Ehrlich, Paul. *The Population Bomb.* New York: Ballantine Books, 1968.

European Commission. "Reducing Emissions from Aviation." Accessed November 7, 2016. https://ec.europa.eu/clima/policies/transport/aviation/index_en.htm.

Flegenheimer, Matt, and Michael Barbaro. "Donald Trump Is Elected President in Stunning Repudiation of the Establishment." *The New York Times.* November 9, 2016. http://www.nytimes.com/2016/11/09/us/politics/hillary-clinton-donald-trump-president.html.

Flippen, J. Brooks. *Nixon and the Environment.* Albuquerque: University of New Mexico Press, 2000.

Funk, Cary and Kennedy, Brian. "The Politics of Climate." *Pew Research Center: Internet, Science & Tech.* October 4, 2016, http://www.pewinternet.org/2016/10/04/the-politics-of-climate/.

Gore, Al (writer), and Davis Guggenheim (director). *An Inconvenient Truth.* Accessed March 15, 2017. https://www.algore.com/library/an-inconvenient-truth-dvd.

Haberman, Clyde. "The Unrealized Horrors of Population Explosion." *The New York Times.* May 31, 2015, http://www.nytimes.com/2015/06/01/us/the-unrealized-horrors-of-population-explosion.html.

Helfich, Harold W, Jr. ed. *The Environmental Crisis: Man's Struggle to live with Himself.* New Haven: Yale University Press, 1970.

Hill, Gladwin, "Activity Ranges From Oratory to Legislation; Oratory and Legislation Mark Drive on Pollution", *The New York Times.* April 23, 1970. Accessed June 15, 2015.

Hirschfeld Davis, Julie, Mark Landler, and Coral Davenport. "Obama on Climate Change: The Trends Are 'Terrifying.'" *The New York Times.* September 8, 2016. http://www.nytimes.com/2016/09/08/us/politics/obama-climate-change.html.

International Centre for Trade and Sustainable Development. "EU Airline Emissions Rule Under Fire by US Senate." Accessed November 7, 2016. http://www.ictsd.org/bridges-news/bridges/news/eu-airline-emissions-rule-under-fire-by-us-senate.

Jarret, Henry, ed. *Environmental Quality in a Growing Economy: Essays from the Sixth RFF Forum.* Baltimore, MD: Johns Hopkins University Press, 1966.

Johnson, Lyndon. B. "Remarks at the University of Michigan, May 22, 1964." Public Papers of the Presidents of the United States: Lyndon B. Johnson, 1963–1964 (2 volumes). Washington, D.C.: U.S. Government Printing Office, 1965.

Kraft, Michael E., ed. *Public Policy; Politics, Analysis, and Alternatives.* 5th Revised edition. Los Angeles: CQ Press, 2014.

Kraft, Michael E., and Norman J. Vig. "Environmental Policy in the Reagan Presidency." *Political Science Quarterly* 99, no. 3 (1984).

Lizza, Ryan. "As the World Burns." *The New Yorker.* Accessed November 7, 2016. http://www.newyorker.com/magazine/2010/10/11/as-the-world-burns.

Neuman, Scott. "Interior Department Issues New Fracking Rules For Federal Lands." *NPR. org.* Accessed November 7, 2016. http://www.npr.org/sections/thetwo-way/2015/03/20/394282086/interior-dept-issues-new-fracking-rules-for-federal-lands.

Office of the Press Secretary. "President Bush Discusses Global Climate Change." Accessed November 10, 2016. https://georgewbush-whitehouse.archives.gov/news/releases/2001/06/20010611-2.html.Pew Research Center for the People and the Press. "The Public's Policy Priorities for 2016.". Accessed January 21, 2016. http://www.people-press.org/2016/01/22/budget-deficit-slips-as-public-priority/1-21-2016_06/.

Pielke, Roger A. "Policy History of the US Global Change Research Program: Part I. Administrative Development." *Global Environmental Change* 10, no. 1 (2000): 9–25.

Reston, James. "Washington: The Politics of Pollution." *The New York Times.* April 26, 1970. http://www.nytimes.com/1970/04/26/archives/washington-the-politics-of-pollution.html.

Rome, Adam. *The Genius of Earth Day: How a 1970 Teach-In Unexpectedly Made the First Green Generation.* New York: Hill and Wang, 2014.

Rootes, Chris. *Environmental Protest in Western Europe.* Oxford: Oxford University Press, 2007.

Shabecoff, Philip. "Reagan and Environment: To Many, a Stalemate." *The New York Times.* January 2, 1989, sec. U.S. http://www.nytimes.com/1989/01/02/us/reagan-and-environment-to-many-a-stalemate.html.

Stradling, David. *The Environmental Moment: 1968–1972.* University of Washington Press, 2013.

UN Secretary General U Thant. "The Deteriorating Environment." *The New York Times,* June 25, 1969.

US EPA, OA. "Laws & Regulations." Collections and Lists. Accessed November 6, 2016. https://www.epa.gov/laws-regulations.

Vig, Norman J., and Michael E. Kraft. *Environmental Policy: New Directions for the Twenty-First Century* 8th Edition. Thousand Oaks, CA: CQ Press, 2012.

Walsh, Bryan. "Why the Climate Bill Died." *Time.* Accessed November 7, 2016. http://science.time.com/2010/07/26/why-the-climate-bill-died/.

Waxman, Henry. "H.R.2454 – 111th Congress (2009–2010): American Clean Energy and Security Act of 2009." Legislation, July 7, 2009. https://www.congress.gov/bill/111th-congress/house-bill/2454.

White, Lynn. "The Historical Roots of Our Ecological Crisis." *This Sacred Earth: Religion, Nature, Environment,* (1967): 184–193.

Withnall, Adam. "Why President Trump Is an Even Bigger Disaster than You Realised." *The Independent.* Accessed November 9, 2016. http://www.independent.co.uk/news/world/americas/us-elections/president-donald-trump-disaster-paris-climate-change-agreement-cop-22-un-climate-summit-a7406366.html.

Yale Project on Climate Change Communication. "Climate Change in the American Mind." Accessed March 2015. http://environment.yale.edu/climate-communication-OFF/files/Global-Warming-CCAM-March-2015.pdf.

2   The European Union
A hopeful paradigm

In July 2016, the European Commission presented a new set of measures by which it planned to accelerate the pace of emission reductions across economic sectors. This announcement was largely anticipated as it constituted the next logical step after the "success" of the Conference of the Parties (COP) 21 in Paris, in which the European Union (EU) had played a pivotal role. The European Commission's proposals were designed to assist member–states in staying competitive. They also sought to build a resilient energy union, taking into account the growing significance of climate policy. Although such announcements may no longer make headlines in a way that they might have a few years back, it reflected how far Europe had come in its implementation of emission reduction schemes. Most importantly, it showcased Europe's systemic understanding of the new emerging challenges in the Anthropocene.[1]

Today climate action plans from around the world show a growing convergence. Their main targets often include: a diversification of the energy mix, a pre-occupation with energy security, the strengthening of resilience and an engagement in international negotiations. The EU, however, has also been among the first and certainly among the most dedicated actors in the developed world to place its climate action plan at the center of a more integrated approach to challenges ushered in by the Anthropocene.

Environmental policy was not originally a core area for European politics at the birth of the European experiment. The Treaty of Rome in 1957 created a European Economic Community (EEC).[2] Free trade among member states to achieve economic integration was the key area of cooperation, especially at a time when environmental considerations had not captured the imagination and attention of mainstream political parties and the wider public. As a consequence, European institutions had not been granted any authority by which to make environmental decisions. At the time, and although lacking a legal basis for pushing the environmental policy agenda, legislation was based on a "dynamic" interpretation of the treaty itself. While a sound and clear legal basis to tie in environmental action to Community goals was being sought, the stipulations in Articles 94 (ex-Article 100) and 308 (ex-Article 235) of the Treaty on European Union (TEU), served initially as the basis of authority. Article 94, for instance, allowed for the harmonization between member states, especially with regard to production-related environmental regulations. However, as time went by the use of this authority would prove limiting, especially in the event that member states would either seek to block the adaptation of stricter policies or when policies were not sufficiently taking into account the variation of ecological conditions between the different countries. Article 308 of the TEU enabled the Community "to pass suitable measures in such cases in which action on behalf of the EU appears necessary to achieve its objectives, even if the Treaty does not explicitly include the authority necessary for doing so." This Article again covered economic-related environmental issues.[3]

Since that limited beginning, Europe has come a long way to create a vast web of policies, regulations and legislation that have been extended to all areas of environmental protection. It was an ingenious first step to link environmental considerations directly to issues of trade and the lowering of trade barriers between member states. This allowed for the environment, previously a mere by-product of economic thinking, to rise in significance as environmental crises reared their head and prompted the international community to begin thinking about human interactions with the environment. A UN Conference on the Human Environment was organized in Stockholm in 1972, and as a result environmental issues were gradually seen as critical for the European integration process. There were, of course, serious reasons for concern. Acid rain and cross-border air pollution showed politicians and policy makers that environmental problems do not stop at national borders. Pollution was a global issue regardless of where it originated. In response to these problems, the EU environmental action program was put into effect in 1973 (OJ C 112/1 from 20.12.1973) supported by the European Court of Justice[4] that provided it legitimacy. Moreover, the action program of 1973 underscored the interdependence of environmental protection, economic development and prosperity and emphasized the prevention of environmental damage, the conservation of ecological equilibrium and the use of resources in a rational manner. The novelty, at the time, was that this set of policies emphasized the importance of assessing other areas of policy concurrently to discern whether or not they would generate harmful impacts on the environment, thus ushering in the first notions of sustainable development in Europe.

Although the first program focused on water protection and waste, it made special reference to: agriculture, spatial planning and emissions control issues. The protection of nature was emphasized in the next program, while the third and fourth action programs focused on the harmonization of environmental standards across an internal market.[5] Popular concerns over a variety of issues including clean air, noise, and risk management for industrial sites led to calls for emission limits, among other demands. This reflected a particular German concern, having sprung from the growing power of the Green Party that pressed for a harmonized emissions control policy, especially of vehicles and high polluting industries. Other northern states such as the Netherlands, but also the Scandinavian nations, became sources of environmental policy inspiration and set a higher bar for the rest of the members. Furthermore, this era witnessed the emergence of Europe's modern environmental movement from the late 1960s onwards as part of a New Left agenda that pushed for robust policy action. Students kept the political class keenly aware of calls for change by staging large protests on social and environmental issues.

Public expressions of environmentalism took the form of street demonstrations, non-violent direct action and boycotts. The larger objectives were for government and corporations to turn their attention to growing environmental challenges and to pressure them to alter their policies, practices and behavior in response to protesters' demands. In the 1970s, Greenpeace stood out in this regard, by masterfully refining the tactics of symbolic protest and galvanizing the public imagination to put pressure on perpetrators of environmental degradation. Both their message and the manner by which they brought it to the public's attention transformed Greenpeace into one of the fastest growing organizations of the environmental movement in the 1980s. European concern over the environment reached new heights in both the 1980s and 1990s, especially with regards to pollution. As a result, political parties all across the spectrum began to incorporate environmental agendas into their platforms in order to mainstream the issue and to prevent the left from monopolizing public concerns. In this way, the environment found its "institutional" voice. Environmental agencies were set-up to deal with problems that the public had identified. Environmental Ministries were created. Across Western Europe new green political parties were formed and grew in strength. This dynamic government response to pollution reduction dampened the protests and made many environmental concerns more routine, although debates over the use of nuclear power continued, especially in countries where nuclear power plants were in operation.[6] The nuclear accident in Chernobyl in 1986, for instance, surprised most national governments in both its magnitude and severity. Radioactive contamination was widespread and the Soviet Union's secrecy over events and their repercussions made matters even worse. The public, at the time, received conflicting information about how to respond to its aftermath. The lack of transparency fueled widespread anger and prompted thousands in cities like Rome and West Berlin to take to the streets in protest of nuclear weapons and nuclear power.[7] The revival of the nuclear arms race between the West and the Soviet Bloc had also triggered the fear of nuclear war, provoking riots and protests throughout the West.

As a result, the environmental agenda in Europe continued to grow over three decades. Moreover, the adaptation of the Single European Act in 1987 that expanded the original Treaty, resulted in environmental policy becoming a declared task of the Community.[8] In the 1990s, environmental policy took on the wider sustainability framework and melded into a paradigm for sustainable development. While this approach continued to embrace a utilitarian view of nature, sustainable development was considered a useful tool to improve the state of the environment with an eye to resource efficiency and the needs of future generations.

On a more global level, alarm over climate change increased dramatically in the 1980s and 1990s making it clear that action would inevitably require international mobilization. The EU was particularly well suited to contribute to the global climate discussions, having extensive experience in global regime building and a deep-rooted conviction on the benefits of multilateral diplomacy and cooperation. Within the EU, proposed policies reflected a preference for the use of economic instruments in the form of environmental taxes, for instance, designed to complement the regulatory framework and promote behavioral change by supporting energy efficiency measures and fuel substitution. To ensure success of its strategy, the EU embraced a combination of carrots and sticks and was assisted by the continued positive reinforcement of a strong environmental social movement.

That is not to say that the commission's ambitious and progressive environmental agenda did not find resistance at a national level. There was, in fact, considerable pushback that underscored the limits of European integration with respect to the environment. What started as a push for comprehensive change by example became watered down by national reactions and the rise of other more immediate concerns that suddenly came into play. The 1990s constituted a period of dramatic shifts on the European continent. The Cold War ended abruptly, leading to regime shifts all across Central and Eastern Europe. The fall of the Iron Curtain revived the dream of a united continent and made enlargement plans, which included the re-unification of Germany, a top EU priority. These types of concerns weakened some of the earlier appetite for environmental agenda setting. Of course, plans did not entirely come to a standstill. Policy action grew in another direction to focus on the inclusion of stakeholders, bringing in social forces and NGOs to weigh in on priorities, strategies and recommendations for environmental policy and action. Sectoral fears over the potentially high costs that the European Commission's increasingly ambitious environmental agenda might incur led particular interest groups but also member–states—concerned with new harder economic realities—to vocalize their reluctance. The commission responded by turning toward sectoral self–responsibility and voluntary action by transport, agriculture or economic ministries to help push forward necessary changes. This approach produced mixed results. Nonetheless, new complex and holistic framework legislation was introduced in the late 90s. The Ambient Air Quality Directive (96/62), the Water Framework Directive (2000/60) and the IPPC–Directive (1996/61), formulated an ambitious work program for the next several decades, but most importantly "delegated a number of decisions and tasks to member–states, bureaucratic networks or to civil society and business."[9] After that wave of new regulations, the 6th Environmental Action Program shifted its attention to concentrate principally on thematic issues that included pesticides, the use of resources, recycling practices, soils, the urban and marine environment and clean air.[10]

Despite the ups and downs, the temporary delays and setbacks, the die had been cast. The aims of European policy on the environment described in Articles 11 and 191 of the Treaty on the Functioning of the European Union (TFEU) stipulated that "environmental protection requirements must be integrated into the definition and implementation of the Union policies and activities, in particular with a view of promoting sustainable development" (Article 11). Furthermore, some of the objectives listed in Article 191 emphasized the preservation, protection and improvement of the quality of the environment, the protection of human health and the importance of making prudent and rational use of natural resources and underscored a particular focus on combating climate change (Article 191). Moreover, environmental policy in the EU was now based on the precautionary principle and principles of preventative action, adapting the polluter pay principle.[11] Sustainability, preventative action, the polluter pays, shared responsibilities of different levels of government and integration of environmental concerns into other policy areas – all became part of not only the EU's operating principles, but were also given treaty status and incorporated in EU legislation when and where appropriate.[12]

All the work that Europe has done in this regard is particularly important in the Anthropocene. Today, the EU is a mature power of 500 million people representing the largest and perhaps wealthiest trading bloc in the world.[13] According to March 2016 Eurostat statistics, currently the EU–28 accounts for approximately 15 percent of the world's trade in goods. While its companies maintain a strong showing among the world's Fortune 500, the EU itself has sought ways to provide socioeconomic benefits and services for its population. Europe's members have reallocated funds from military spending, for example, to social policies to provide healthcare, sick leave, childcare and work training and job creation for its families. The EU has defended its democratic principles, the rule of law and championed the creation of new institutions both within the EU and globally that foster inclusiveness, participation, responsibility and peace. It seeks to build consensus through multilateralism, regional networks and targeted investments. More importantly, the EU has shown an understanding that the climate crisis is not only about emissions, but that it involves a number of cross-cutting issues that represent some of the most pressing challenges and areas where new policy initiatives are sorely needed. These include issues such as the circular economy, sustainability of cities, eco-innovation, etc.

Recognizing that the climate crisis radically influences growth models, development, poverty, international politics and leadership models, the EU has positioned itself as the international agenda setter for climate action. Not only has it sought a leadership role in climate negotiations, but it also has focused on delivering concrete results at home. Its aim is to lead by example and to provide an alternative scenario to a growth and energy intensive model that leaves the planet with no future. Europe's leadership role has not been static and has displayed different approaches and styles which reflect its key strengths: its large economy, its bargaining skills and its diplomatic agility in fostering agreements. Europe has been able to redefine interests for a global audience by conceptualizing notions of sustainability along with narratives of ecological modernization and a transition to a low–carbon economic model for growth. Although it has not always been able to speak with one voice, the EU has managed, with respect to climate negotiations, to project a position of long-term commitment to the process and has maintained coordination among its member–states to display its strong political will at critical junctures. Through perseverance and by setting an example, it has contributed to keeping the climate negotiations alive when they seemed to be unraveling, and it has successfully made the case for an energy mix diversification and the weaving of sustainability across policy areas.

EU climate policy went through distinct stages. The 1980s until 1992 were the time of formulation and the beginnings of an articulated position toward the climate crisis. From 1992 until 2001, negotiations revolved around the Kyoto Protocol and Europe began to vocalize the need for a more concrete strategy and emission reduction targets. Next came the period of 2001 to 2005 where efforts were concentrated on rescuing the progress achieved in Kyoto after the US refusal to ratify the Protocol. Not only was the Bush administration's move highly contested and criticized, but its subsequent moves served to obstruct progress on climate for the rest of the international community. The US, for example, continued to attend COP meetings with smaller delegations and pursued other forums for climate discussions, such as the Asia–Pacific Partnership on Clean Development and Climate and the Major Emitter Forum.[14] In response to what could have been a fatal blow to a global accord on climate emission reductions, the EU strongly criticized the position and decision of the United States (US) to withdraw from the Protocol. Furthermore, it insisted that the Kyoto Protocol be ratified by other nations, even though the US had pulled out. After overwhelming support by the European Parliament, the EU itself ratified the Protocol in May 2002. Moreover, Europe used its lobbying skills to robustly seek the cooperation of both Japan and Russia, asking them to ratify the Kyoto Protocol so that it could take effect in 2005.[15] At that juncture, the EU put itself in the forefront of negotiations to keep the Kyoto Protocol alive. This focused effort led to major changes within the EU itself and gave it a leadership role at the climate discussions. Through its efforts, the EU salvaged the Kyoto Protocol and paved the way for Copenhagen, although it seemed clear that an agreement in Copenhagen would be extremely difficult to achieve.

Following this rollercoaster-like period, EU leadership intensified both domestically and internationally. Starting in 2005, it took a bold step to draw the market into the decarbonization of the economy by establishing the European Union Emissions Trading System (EU ETS) which became the world's first international carbon trading system, modeled largely on the US sulfur dioxide emissions trading system that was established under the 1990 Clean Air Act Amendments. The EU ETS aimed at providing a market tool that would incentivize companies to reduce their emissions and cap EU emissions in order to reverse emission increases. Thirty-one countries including Iceland, Liechtenstein and Norway are under this scheme that limits emissions from more than 11,000 heavy energy-using installations and airlines operating between these countries. Currently, the EU ETS covers approximately 45 percent of the EU's greenhouse gas (GHG) emissions.[16]

In 2006,[17] the Stern review became public which helped to solidify European resolve to mobilize against the climate threat. Commissioned by the Chancellor of the Exchequer, in the UK, the Stern Review intended to assess the evidence and help build understanding about the economics of climate change. It was perhaps the first time that a document focused so clearly on spelling-out the potential cost of disruption and its impact on GDP. While there are many who criticized Stern's figures,[18] the work raised awareness about the impacts of climate change among the business community that before had been largely unconvinced and unengaged. By labeling the climate crisis as the "greatest and widest market failure," the Stern Review informed the world about the need to now factor in the economics of risk and uncertainty with respect to the climate. It also pointed out that climate change was not a short-term issue with a quick fix, but that it required long-term planning. Moreover, it highlighted the importance of taking strong and early action by demonstrating in numbers how the benefits would considerably outweigh the costs. The Review focused on mitigation and adaptation and made it clear that while developing poorer nations would suffer first, the impact of climate change on advanced industrialized nations would also be severe.

It is not that this information was not available prior to this report. It was just that the timing, the clear economic perspective that it offered and the concrete solutions it proposed helped to cement European resolve to tackle the climate crisis simultaneously on all fronts with a comprehensive narrative to build its case. In fact, Europe has framed its call to arms as an opportunity to fulfill its wider holistic agenda of job creation, innovation, greater energy autonomy, a boost for the knowledge economy, energy savings and the protection of the planet's fragile ecosystem. Turning the crisis into an opportunity helped rally and maintain citizen support for the EU plan to decarbonize its economy and weave sustainability through all the policies of the EU. Two other important developments took place around the same time, bringing climate change to the top of the political agenda. The Intergovernmental Panel on Climate Change (IPCC) report of 2007 and Al Gore's *Inconvenient Truth* documentary made it clear that the crisis was real and dangerous and action was imperative.

In January 2007, the European Commission rose to the challenge and under a German Presidency released a communiqué calling for limiting global climate change to 2 degrees above pre-industrial times.[19] In the spring of 2007, the European Council committed itself and the EU members to the implementation of what became known as *Europe 2020*. This included a 20 percent reduction of CO2 emissions, a 20 percent share of energy from low-carbon energy sources and a 20 percent reduction in the use of primary energy by improving energy efficiency by 2020, and a pledge to move to even more ambitious targets.[20]

The 2020 strategy proved that these goals were attainable, but also concluded that the targets were still not bold enough to prevent temperature from rising above 2 °C. The EU had committed to re-evaluate its initial plan and as a result produced an even more ambitious strategy to decarbonize its economy. This was the *2030 Climate and Energy Framework*, adopted in October 2014. The EU goal now was to achieve "at least 40 percent cuts in GHG emissions (from 1990 levels); at least 27 percent share for renewable energy; at least 27 percent improvement in energy efficiency."[21] More importantly, this plan was not decided in a vacuum. It did not aim just to respond to emissions controls because of climate action goals, but was in line with wider policy choices looking at 2050. Throughout, EU decisions have reflected a consciousness that climate change is not a distant issue, but that its effects have already begun. This is why the EU decided to increase climate funding, and EU institutions agreed that at least 20 percent of the €960 billion budget for 2014–2020 would now be spent on climate mitigation and adaptation. This represented an increase of three times the previous level of spending. Furthermore, the decision was to earmark €864 million from the Financial Instrument for the Environment (LIFE) for special mitigation and adaptation programming.[22]

The reason behind the prioritization of mitigation and adaptation was based on data which showed that in the last ten years the average land temperature has been 1.3C higher than in pre-industrial times, which meant that Europe was warming faster than other areas of the world. According to EU data, extreme weather conditions had already increased. More frequent heat waves, droughts, forest fires, floods and coastal erosion drove the EU to produce a cost–benefit analysis on a range of areas that were vulnerable to climate change. With regards to flooding, for instance, their calculations showed that every euro spent on flood protection saved €6 in damage costs. Most recently, projections estimated that not adapting to climate change would cost "100 billion a year in 2020 and 250 billion in 2050."[23]

Keeping in line with the understanding that the climate crisis is proof of wider changes that need to take place across the board, the EU made it a priority for climate action goals to intersect with as many policy areas as possible. While Europe's 2050 targets have a strong focus on carbon emission reductions, the plan takes a close look at all the sectors where emissions can be cut more effectively. The EU, much like the US and China, is banking on carbon capture technology and an increase in investment in smart grids, given that the power sector is still considered the predominant area where change can bring solid results. The 2050 plan, however, targets industry more widely, as well as transport, residential and tertiary, which are economic areas ripe for emission reductions.

Examples of how climate action is woven through a wide range of policies include changes in international development funding, linking it to climate action targets for the recipients. Furthermore, support for energy research has become the cornerstone of climate action in the EU with technology and innovation becoming investment priorities. The EU already has an emissions trading scheme in place and has factored in mitigation and adaptation investment into its budget. Additionally, it has incorporated the need for sustainability in its latest agriculture policies[24] that promote the production of safe and healthy food, the conservation of natural resources, and that target a judicial use of pesticides and fertilizers. These policies prioritize animal welfare, the improvement of the quality of life in farming areas and management of the countryside, thus providing a roadmap by which farms can contribute to the preservation of valuable practices and traditions, biodiversity and attractive landscapes. The EU has decoupled its economic support to farmers from production and linked it to sustainable management to comply with EU environmental and other regulations. In this way, farmers become fundamental players in Europe's growing strategy for life in the Anthropocene. Some other practical steps have been to support organic farming, to support biogas on farms, and to introduce precision farming techniques and agro–forestry systems to ensure an income to farmers in order to draw them into a system of best practices for addressing the climate crisis.

Europe's particular attention to the agricultural sector is warranted because growing food demand will represent about a third of the EU's total emissions. The modeling assessment made in the EU low carbon economy roadmap based on the current Common Agricultural Policy (CAP) concluded that the EU agricultural sector could decrease its GHG emissions by between 36 and 37 percent by 2030 and 42 and 49 percent by 2050 depending on different decarbonization scenarios.[25] This makes it imperative to find ways to reduce emissions. Cuts can result from changes in the usage of fertilizer, manure and livestock, but also in the storage of CO_2 from soil and forests. In order for its goals to be reached, the EU does not only look to manage inputs and outputs in the agricultural sector itself, but goes further to highlight the importance of dietary change among citizens to include less meat and more vegetables.[26]

Rural life continues to feature strongly in the EU, though urbanization has been increasing over time. Roughly a quarter of the population in the EU continues to live in rural areas, which means that economic activity in the countryside is critical if the communities are to remain vibrant. Moreover, it is acknowledged that Europeans have been transforming their land for centuries which explains why they view the agricultural landscape as part of their cultural heritage, forming a mosaic of woodlands, wetlands and extensive tracts of open countryside. The centuries long transformation continues to create environmental diversity of fauna and flora from its varied landscapes. Protecting the biodiversity is seen as critical for the countryside's sustainable development. The EU considers farmers stewards of the land, acknowledging their critical role in maintaining the soil, preserving the landscape and protecting biodiversity.[27] Because the EU views these as public goods that the market is not paying for, member–states have opted to provide income support for farmers through the CAP. Moreover, with climate change already impacting agriculture, farmers now need to adjust their methods to cope with its effects. The role of farmers has become increasingly important because they are faced with the double task to produce quality food and to protect nature by safeguarding biodiversity. For these reasons, Europe has sought farmer cooperation through a program of incentives in order for them to work in a sustainable and environmentally friendly matter.[28]

Policy initiatives go further still. Taking the advice of the Stern Review, Europe has been carefully aiming at the expansion of forest areas. According to a 2016 report, forest and wooded land account for more than 40 percent of the EU's land area. Moreover, coverage has increased over the past few decades. Afforestation and natural succession have increased the EU's forest area by around 0.4 percent per year over recent decades. Nearly a quarter of the EU's forest area is protected under Natura 2000, and much of the rest is home to species protected under EU nature legislation. Here too, although the Treaty on the Functioning of the EU makes no reference to specific provisions for an EU forest policy, the EU has a "long history of contributing through its policies to implementing sustainable forest management and to Member States' decisions on forests. Important developments include the Europe 2020 strategy for growth and jobs, the Resource Efficiency Roadmap, Rural Development Policy, Industrial Policy, the EU Climate and Energy Package with its 2020 targets, the Plant Health and Reproductive Materials Strategy and the Biodiversity and Bioeconomy Strategies."[29]

European-wide policies and strategies are additionally and most importantly focused on urban planning. Today, around 75 percent of Europeans live in cities and towns, and that number is set to further increase in the future.[30] Sustainable urban planning and design are among the important foci of the latest 7th Environmental Action Programme launched by the EU. Once again, sustainability is not limited to resource management and energy efficiency, although they remain central issues across many cities in Europe. They are seen alongside other environmental problems and risks, including poor air quality, high levels of noise, GHG emissions, water scarcity, contaminated sites, brownfields and waste.[31] The ultimate goal is to continue improving the quality of life for urban dwellers. Sustainable urban development is a key ingredient to Europe's social cohesion policy. Increasingly, cities across the EU are setting the bar higher through innovative solutions that help further sustainability and for which private–public partnerships are actively sought and encouraged.

In practical terms, and in order to reach these wider objectives in practice, cities have a wide variety of tools at their disposal, such as the Structural Funds and more specifically LIFE+ (a financial instrument supporting environmental and nature conservation projects), URBACT (the European exchange and learning program promoting sustainable urban development that aims to enable cities to work together to develop solutions to major urban challenges), INTERREG IVC (for interregional cooperation), HORIZON 2020 (with an 80 billion budget for research and innovation), Smart Cities and Communities European Innovation Partnership (aiming to pool resources to support the demonstration of energy, transport and information and communication technologies (ICT) in urban areas), and many others.[32] Moreover, the EU Urban Agenda,[33] which is also referred to as the "Pact of Amsterdam," was adopted by the Council on May 30, 2016. This is a policy tool that encourages partnership among European cities with the objective of stimulating growth, livability and innovation. It recognizes the growing challenges such as air quality, housing, integration of migrants and refugees and coping with urban poverty. Working together, cities will help to promote best practices and foster cooperation, improve the EU urban knowledge base and ensure higher access and use of European funding opportunities. Finally, these kinds of partnerships can help set the agenda for new EU legislation.

At the heart of any plan to tackle the climate crisis lies the question of energy security and energy choice. Energy availability and pricing have been at the center of the modern economic miracle. Fossil fuels have reigned supreme as the fuel of choice, and dependency on them has been a major concern for countries around the world. Differences in energy endowments, growing resource competition as a result of the rise of the developing world, and especially the BRICS, have been a source of consternation and anxiety. Although the US, for example, has been experiencing a new energy bonanza after the hydrofracturing revolution, Europe and Japan continue to be resource poor by comparison, aggravating their insecurities.

This pre-occupation has contributed to Europe's decision to deploy renewables to reduce dependence on imported fossil fuels. It simultaneously has sought to create an energy union to ensure that Europe maintains secure, affordable and climate-friendly energy.[34] These concerns have, of course, been aggravated by geopolitical rivalries in the region. Particularly troublesome are the tensions and outright hostility between Russia and the Ukraine and the impact of this rivalry on oil and gas imports from one of its main providers. More than half (53.5 percent) of the EU–28's gross inland energy consumption in 2014 came from imported sources.[35] According to a recent Eurostat report, the

> production of primary energy in the EU–28 was 17.3% lower in 2014 than it had been a decade earlier. The general downward development of EU-28 primary energy production may, at least in part, be attributed to supplies of raw materials becoming exhausted and/or producers considering the exploitation of limited resources uneconomical.[36]

Developing renewables as an alternative to fossil fuels dates back to the 1970s as a result of the oil shocks during that period. The 1980s saw the beginning of the promotion of renewables which increased significantly thereafter as the adverse impacts of emissions became clearer. The strategic push to develop renewable technology and design a program of incentives to help support research and development as well as actual deployment became Europe's signature policy instrument. These technologies were initially expensive, but Europe's strategic decision to support their development increased their competitiveness and demonstrated EU leadership in the climate crisis.

This is why, in 2008, the EU adopted the European Strategic Energy Technology Plan (SET-Plan) to "accelerate the development and deployment of low-carbon technologies ... to improve new technologies and bring down costs by coordinating research and helping to finance projects."[37] With an estimated budget of up to €71.5 billion,[38] the SET-Plan connected to the 2020 Energy and Climate Change goals and marked an EU contribution to the worldwide transition to a low carbon economy by 2050.[39] The Renewable Directive of 2009[40] followed the launch of the SET-Plan. It became the pivotal policy instrument for the deployment of renewables. The scope of this EU-wide project was reminiscent of national industry development schemes that provided generous incentives beyond what the market could offer to rapidly push technological breakthroughs.

With this overarching plan, investment in high tech and especially the renewable energy sector has remained consistently high. By the same token, politicians have heralded it as a win–win proposition for Europe that will help grow the economy and allow for social cohesion. At the keynote speech at the Metropolitan Solutions Conference 2012 in Hannover, former EU Commissioner Connie Hedegaard observed:

Solar, wind and biomass technologies have progressed most rapidly … Europe's renewable energy sector added 320,000 jobs between 2005 and 2009, and it is estimated that meeting our 20% renewables target by 2020 will bring just over 400,000 more. In all, the employment potential from developing the renewable energy sector is estimated at three million jobs by 2020.[41]

EU statistics placed the primary production of renewable energy within the EU–28 at 196 million tons of oil equivalent (TOE), in 2014. That represented an increase of 73.1 percent between 2004 and 2014. Moreover, the most important sources among the renewables were solid biofuels and renewable waste, with hydropower the second contributor to the renewable mix at 16.5 percent and wind at 11.1 percent of the total. Solar accounted for 6.1 percent of the share for 2014. The largest producer of renewable energy was Germany, holding 18.4 percent of the EU–28 share, followed by Italy (12.1 percent) and France (10.7 percent). The mix of renewable technologies deployed among the member–states differed, reflecting the particular climatic conditions and their natural endowments.[42]

The most recent Global Renewables Report (REN21) shows that in 2015, out of the world total of renewable power capacities (not including hydropower), the EU–28 leads the BRICS with 276 gigawatts. In fact, for the eighth consecutive year, renewables accounted for 77 percent of new EU generating capacity. Furthermore, the EU continued to decommission more capacity from conventional sources than it installed.[43] By 2015 renewables had become the largest source of electricity in the EU. Since 2000 and until 2015 the increase has been impressive, going from 24 percent to 44 percent of Europe's total power capacity. Currently, even though there has been somewhat of a slowdown, the focus in Europe has turned to the integration of variable renewable generation.

To achieve these ambitious goals, leadership was instrumental in the early attempts to deploy renewables with such focus and deliberation. This leadership was provided by Germany. In fact, longstanding Chancellor Angela Merkel has been nicknamed "The Climate Chancellor." She has demonstrated leadership both at an international level and domestically. Her perseverance was bold and her decisiveness in particular instances has even proved surprising. After Fukushima, for example, it was Merkel who passed a bill to shut all nuclear power plants in Germany by 2022. Germany's leadership, in creating a robust renewable industry within the EU, was galvanized by the launching of a domestic comprehensive plan for the transition to low carbon energy use named *Energiewende*. The plan's objective from the outset was to produce clean energy and to promote energy efficiency. Public opinion provided the plan the necessary support to move forward because Germans have consistently found climate change to be a serious issue. Polls in 2015 indicated that 55 percent of those questioned found climate change to be the most serious problem (while only 27 percent thought the economic crisis a more important issue). Seventy-nine percent found that both energy efficiency and policies that help to address climate change are also good for the economy. The message that green growth would be a source of economic growth had registered.[44] Furthermore, the reasoning behind what Germans consider good about the *Energiewende* plan is that it helps fight climate change, reduces energy imports, stimulates green growth and technological innovation, reduces risks of nuclear accident, helps build up energy security, strengthens the local economy and provides social justice.[45] So far the plan has been effective, and by the end of 2015, Germany had reduced its emissions by 27.2 percent, while continuing to push for further emission cuts. Germany had also hoped that *Energiewende* would serve as proof that leading industrial nations could continue to perform and remain competitive while moving away from fossil fuels.

With the financial crisis of 2008, there were fears that these efforts would become derailed. Yet the crisis did not dampen Europe's resolve. In fact, the EU turned even more deliberately toward the promotion of renewables and the green economy in response to the crisis. The then President of the EC Manuel Barroso described the economic crisis as a "wake-up call, the moment where we recognize that "business as usual" would consign us to a gradual decline, to the second rank of the new global order. This is Europe's moment of truth. It is the time to be bold and ambitious."[46] Green growth was consistently and intentionally portrayed as an antidote to shrinking growth rates, rising unemployment and a general sense of vulnerability and stagnation. Europe was not willing to give up its vision to create a more socially cohesive continent and a competitive knowledge economy that would be resilient and sustainable in an era of so many unknowns. The EC President in 2010 stated,

> The crisis wiped out years of economic and social progress and exposed structural weaknesses in Europe's economy … We need a strategy to help us come out stronger from the crisis and turn the EU into a smart, sustainable and inclusive economy delivering high levels of employment, productivity and social cohesion.[47]

The persistent question that arises consists of the following: what were the reasons for which Europe, an economic and industrial powerhouse, demonstrated such consistency and resolve *vis-à-vis* the climate crisis when other major economies wavered or even shunned any kind of binding agreement both international and domestic, foregoing their responsibility as global leaders in the process? It is important, therefore, to examine how institutions, interests, society and the media came together to enable Europe to show the kind of resolve that the US, for instance, has not demonstrated.

EU leadership in climate change is the product of multi-level reinforcement among the EU's different political poles. Comprised of 28[48] member–states, the EU has often shown an astonishing flexibility to act as a Union, all the while reinforcing its position through the actions of its states. It is exactly this kind of institutional structure of decentralized governance and unity that has allowed a group of forward thinking states to push the climate action agenda forward.[49]

According to the PEW Research Center of June 2016, Europeans view ISIS and climate change among the top threats facing their nations. Over half the countries that were surveyed for this report answered that they view global climate change as a major threat.[50] According to the 2015 Eurobarometer poll 91 percent of citizens in European member–states consider climate change a serious problem. The breakdown is as follows: 69 percent responded that it is "very serious" and 22 percent characterized it a "fairly serious" problem. There is no doubt that Europeans (polling at 93 percent) are convinced that climate change is a challenge that will only be fought effectively if all countries of the world act together. Similarly 92 percent of those polled support national action on improving energy efficiency and also 91 percent agreed on the increase of renewable energy use by 2030.[51] The countries in Northern Europe are particularly sensitive to the issue of climate and consider it the single most serious challenge facing the world, whereas other parts of Europe, Eastern Europe, for instance, see armed conflict as the most serious issue.[52] According to the findings of the Eurobarometer, Europeans have a positive view of the economic benefits of tackling climate change with

> eight out of ten Europeans (81%) believing that fighting climate change and using energy more efficiently can boost the economy and create jobs in the EU; Roughly two-thirds of Europeans (65%) also think that reducing fossil fuel imports can benefit the EU economy, with around one in four (26%) saying they totally agree.[53]

For any meaningful paradigm shift to take place, business needs to be onboard for climate action to have breadth and durability. Business interests (though not necessarily homogeneous) impact policy choices. They may, for example, express policy preferences in dealing with the climate crisis and prefer market instruments such as the EU ETS versus stringent regulations or a straight carbon tax. Businesses are concerned about how climate change may impact their expansion in the developing world, or how it might impact continuous economic growth. In the case of Europe, although business was initially skeptical and concerned about the impacts of climate action on its own interests, it did not display the same kind of active and vehement opposition as that exhibited in the US. Schreurs and Tiberghien have argued that even though certain industries attempted to thwart the Kyoto Protocol early on, a number of industries later took a more constructive approach, including fossil fuel companies such as BP, OMV and Royal Dutch Shell that have publicly acknowledged that precautionary action was warranted.[54]

Many reasons can account for the difference in behavior. For example, energy efficiency measures can serve a company's bottom line. Other considerations are more intangible and include the fear of reputational damage, especially for a public attune to the problem of climate change and more generally pollution and environmental degradation. Moreover, by engaging and showing leadership, business can partake in the shaping of policy to avoid the most onerous of possible regulations that could threaten profitability and operations. This way they can ensure that decisions are not made without their input and recommendations. By the same token, there are certainly business opportunities that come out of the transition to a low-carbon economy, especially for renewable energy and technology companies, because innovation will be a key element in the fight against climate change. The real impacts of the climate crisis are also being addressed by businesses because they need to now factor in new risks that include resource competition, possible supply disruption, flooding, droughts, declining energy security and insurance planning. Overall uncertainty is a challenge for business entities that prefer more stable environments in which to operate and plan. In order to engage in the wider conversation, business has evolved specialist organizations to rally for its interests. The World Business Council for Sustainable Development (WBCSD) founded on the eve of the 1992 Rio Summit, later merging with the World Industry Council, for instance, has had a prominent voice. The World Economic Forum has repeatedly dealt with climate change and its repercussions on the global economy. Other organizations such as Business Europe, the European Round Table and others have also stayed active in the ongoing dialogue.[55]

The media in Europe has played a supporting role in Europe's climate action plans. Olausson argues, for instance, that in European media "scientific certainty regarding anthropogenic climate change and its already present consequences characterizes the reporting."[56] Moreover, visual prompts of smog spewing factory stacks, floods and drought, and coverage of EU action in dealing with the impacts of climate serve to bolster Europe's policies while also forging a sense of common European mission and identity. European media were highly critical of the Bush decision not to seek Congressional Ratification for the Kyoto Protocol. Though this may not have been surprising for left leaning publications, more conservative papers lashed out against the US administration. Schreurs and Tiberghien cited the Irish Independent (a conservative/populist publication) as commenting: "[Mr. Bush's] stance will be attributed to breathtaking arrogance or his connections with the energy industry, or a combination of the two."[57] More research is needed to assess climate coverage in European media across member–states to better discern the role of the press in this global challenge.[58] Nonetheless, coverage has largely reinforced the action undertaken by both the EU and nation states with respect to climate action, echoing as well as helping to shape public sentiment.

A major change, however, is taking place in the media world. Newspapers are no longer the sole gatekeepers of the news. Initially challenged by TV, today social media in a variety of forms has altered the way information and disinformation reaches the public. There are, for instance, new "digital natives" such as *Buzzfeed*, *Vice* and the *Huffington Post* that dedicate much space to the climate because they have identified it as an area of interest for millennials. Niche sites are also on the rise, ushering in influential bloggers.[59] There are also new sites such as *Upworthy* that features video–stories and whose declared mission is to "change what the world pays attention to."[60] Moreover, a number of apps have become popular that aggregate news sources or curate the news for users, depending on their interests. Coverage tends to be cyclical, and the frameworks alternate between the disaster/catastrophe framework, the coverage of major events and policy announcements, frameworks of growing uncertainty and opportunity for action. Finally, sites like *Avaaz*, which is a global web movement that brings people-powered politics to bear on decision-making, are mobilizing the younger generation with respect to the climate. Undoubtedly, the news landscape is much more fragmented than in the past. These new outlets, moreover, have a global reach, thereby shaping a global audience.

By the same token, NGOs have grown into formidable actors influencing and helping to guide policy agendas and planning. Climate change has become important for European NGOs (ENGOs), and some of them have become the most well-known and active in climate change issues and environmental policies. The list includes Greenpeace, World Wildlife Fund (WWF), Clean Air Now (CAN) Europe and others. Along with a strong public support for climate action, ENGOs have learned to navigate the complex multi-level governance structure of the EU. In this way, they help to forge what the EU ultimately prefers, i.e. a consensus-seeking decision making style of conducting business in Brussels and across its member–states.

Furthermore, the main centers of European power have all played a constructive role in transforming the EU into a leading voice for climate action. The Council and the European Council[61] have overall proven to be critical assets in developing international EU leadership on climate change. The Council of Ministers (Ministers of the Environment), moreover, also took the lead in developing climate policy within the EU. Together with the European Commission and the European Parliament, European Institutions have used their capacities to launch a wave of climate policies within the EU itself and to maintain the pressure for global agreement in an increasingly coherent and effective manner.

Europe's resolve has not wavered, even after a series of external shocks distracted the international community and shook the foundations of the EU itself. The global financial crisis that began in the US and spread through the world took a heavy toll on Europe's weakest members in the Eurozone. Moreover, the aftermath of the Arab Spring has left the Middle East in shambles and Syria at war. This has led to an unprecedented wave of mass population movement to the EU, calling for emergency responses to a humanitarian catastrophe, but also fueling xenophobia and extreme right wing parties. Tensions with Russia over Ukraine and the annexation of Crimea have come to stir unwelcome memories from the time of the Cold War, enlargement fatigue has settled in, threatening the balance in the Balkans, and the recent vote for Brexit are all part of the shifting landscape and unchartered waters that the EU has to now navigate.

Yet, though some may argue that EU appetite for addressing the climate crisis may be declining, it was COP 21 under the leadership of France that produced what has been hailed as an historic global agreement to finally address the crisis. Over the years, the EU has been building a broad coalition of developed and developing countries that favor the kind of "high ambition" that contributed to the successful outcome of the Paris conference.[62] The EU was the first major economy to submit its intended contribution to the new agreement in March 2015 and has taken steps to reduce its emissions by at least 40 percent by 2030.

The EU's position on the way to Paris remained ambitious and unambiguous. It sought a "global, fair, ambitious and legally binding international treaty"[63] to keep average global temperature to well below 2 °C above pre-industrial levels and stressed the importance of finding a clear way forward to achieve this goal. The EU was from the outset a strong advocate for an ambition mechanism, the establishment of a robust system of tracking performance. Furthermore, it recognized the importance of climate financing and adaptation to the growing challenges that climate change is already posing.[64]

Europe's outlook on this unprecedented global challenge was explained in brief by Connie Hedegaard, former EU Commissioner for Climate Action, ahead of the climate summit in New York, in September 2014: "Some voices doubt if this is the right time to focus on climate. With crises raging from Syria to Ukraine and from Sudan to Afghanistan to name just a few, shouldn't we first deal with these more imminent threats?"[65] Her answer was simple and disarming: "Well, the World Meteorological Organization's report last week said that global emissions are still rising and that climate change is already here, adding further instability in an already unstable world. This is why we need a global framework to tackle climate change!"[66] In her estimation, climate change posed the most serious global threat to political stability.

In his speech in Paris, Europe's current Climate Action and Energy Commissioner Miguel Arias Cañete gave a brief but poignant historical account of how Europe's efforts after Copenhagen kept the conversation growing. Perhaps Copenhagen had come too soon and nations were far from ready to make a meaningful commitment to tackling the climate crisis. Moreover, the countries that proved unwilling to commit did not stay by the wayside allowing those willing to move forward. Instead they actively sought to solidify a sharp divide between the developed and developing nations. It took the world some time to understand that today 35 percent of total emissions are coming from the developed world, and these are consistently falling. For an agreement to work, all countries needed to be on board because now developing countries accounted for 65 percent of global emissions. On a practical level, therefore, no real progress can be expected without China, India, Brazil, South Africa or Indonesia accepting responsibility. In the years that followed Kyoto and Copenhagen, the EU did not cease to push for an international agreement, though it frequently found itself left out when compromises were sought between a select few. Still, the Commissioner insisted that the EU did not shy from what it considered its mission and together with a number of other nations in 2011 in Durban, it became more strategic in seeking what could lead to a roadmap for Paris.[67]

It began by building closer ties with countries from the least developed regions and the island nations. They were joined in this endeavor by other developing and developed nations, and they discreetly began meeting to discuss the best way forward. Those few initial countries were, according to Cañete, named "the progressives" and included Angola, the Marshall Islands (Marshall Islands' Foreign Minister, Tony de Brum has been acknowledged as having played a pivotal role in the process), Germany, Grenada, Peru, Santa Lucia, the UK, Gambia, Colombia, Chili, Mexico and Switzerland. They agreed that the goal was to promote five-year reviews of Intended Nationally Determined Contributions (INDC). They decided to push for a common and robust set of transparency and accountability rules. Finally, they wanted a fair agreement on the issues of climate finance and support. In each subsequent meeting, they remained steadfast on these important principles and invited other countries to join their group. They agreed on a meeting before Paris to review the INDCs that were found less ambitious than the situation warranted.[68]

The meeting held in Rabat gave the EU and "the progressives" the opportunity to connect with African nations and begin recruiting by example. The emphasis was on outreach, and gradually 80 ministers found themselves aligning their position and reinforcing their commitment to an ambitious outcome along with Europe and "the progressives". These informal ministerial meetings proved vital for the process. The EU announced that it had "teamed up with 79 African, Caribbean and Pacific countries in calling for an ambitious deal. They had all agreed on the core elements of the Paris deal."[69] This was exciting news and added momentum to the process. The US then joined the "High Ambition Coalition Group," as they became known. As we saw in Chapter 1, the US position on climate change had shifted under President Obama, and it now seemed that the Americans were on board,[70] although, according to the EU, the Chinese were still holding out. Other nations followed: the Philippines, Canada, Seychelles, Switzerland, Fiji, Japan, Uruguay, Australia, Iceland and Micronesia. But it was Brazil that tilted the balance. It had been part of the Brazil, South Africa, India and China (BASIC) group in the climate talks, and as a Brazil, Russia, India, China and South Africa (BRICS) country, its decision to join the High Ambition Coalition Group of Nations meant that progress was now highly likely in Paris. The four keys issues that the group had agreed upon were: a legally binding agreement coming out of Paris; a specific long-term goal on global warming that is in line with scientific findings; the introduction of a mechanism for reviewing countries' emissions commitments every five years; and the creation of a unified system for tracking countries' progress on meeting their carbon goals.

In the end, Paris was deemed a global success. The world had finally decided to come together and act. The EU's role in the negotiations was certainly critical, but the readiness of others to join forces allowed them to succeed. The EU made its presence felt once again at COP 22 in Marrakesh, as it sought to reaffirm its commitment to climate action. According to the announcement by the Adaption Fund, the resource mobilization target of $80 million for 2016 was surpassed in COP 22 mainly because of EU contributions. The following list of countries that made significant contributions include: Germany (€50 million), Sweden (SEK 100 million), Italy (€5 million) and the Flanders region (€6.25 million).[71] EU pledges amounted to 90 percent of the funds currently available. In Marrakesh, the EU proceeded to also announce a €40 million contribution from Germany and another 20 million from the European Commission to the InsuResilience initiative, providing insurance coverage by 2020 to approximately €400 million of the most vulnerable people in the developing world affected by climate change.[72]

With respect to Africa, the EU once again reaffirmed its continued support both to help fight climate change and to promote renewables. The goal that the EU aims to achieve by 2020 is to facilitate investments that will help increase renewable electricity capacity of at least 5GW. That represents half of Africa's Renewable Energy Initiative commitment by 2020. Beyond this Morocco, Germany, France, Spain and Portugal signed a roadmap for sustainable electricity trade. The EU and its members also provided €17.6 billion to developing countries so that they could tackle climate change. Finally, the European External Investment Plan that was revealed in the fall of 2016 has the potential to produce public and private investments of up to €44 billion in African countries and the EU neighborhood area.[73]

A number of scholars have sought to measure in detail Europe's effectiveness in climate negotiations, even with these notable achievements and to assess the extent of its conviction, efficacy and leadership. They ask: does Europe speak with one voice or do member-states disrupt a unified position? Does an EU caught up in its internal battles have the stamina for what will prove an increasingly more difficult road ahead?[74] Can Europe continue to be a leading voice for nations to tackle the climate crisis? Many of these questions raise valid issues. There is no denying the fact that the EU has had to face some very fundamental internal challenges in recent years and that glossing over these difficulties would not be constructive or accurately depict the challenges ahead. Throughout the years of climate negotiations, sometimes the EU has been successful and at other times less so. Yet it has consistently kept the process going, the dialogue relevant and the outreach across the globe robust, especially when the US had turned its back. What might have happened if the EU had emulated the US response to climate negotiations and had never taken action to reduce emissions and introduce sustainability practices? Notwithstanding the difficulties that the EU has faced over the years, it has remained a champion of climate action. Moreover, effective responses to many of the issues that have beset the EU have found solutions through the formulation of a policy framework appropriate for the wider challenges of the Anthropocene. That does not mean, of course, that Europe can fight this battle alone. It most certainly needs other strong players onboard, especially at this time of global transformation. Without the formation of a meaningful, determined and thoughtful international alliance to provide the impetus for continued transformation, piecemeal measures will serve to temporarily lull the nervous public into complacency and allow the crisis to only deepen until it is irreversible.

Notes

1   European Commission, "Press Release – Energy Union and Climate Action: Driving Europe's Transition to a Low-Carbon Economy," accessed March 15, 2017, http://europa.eu/rapid/press-release_IP-16-2545_en.htm.

2   "The Treaty of Rome," accessed March 15, 2017, http://ec.europa.eu/archives/emu_history/documents/treaties/rometreaty2.pdf.
3   Christoph Knill and Duncan Liefferink, *Environmental Politics in the European Union: Policy-Making, Implementation and Patterns of Multi-Level Governance* (Manchester: Manchester University Press, 2007).
4   Knill and Liefferink, *Environmental Politics in the European Union: Policy-Making, Implementation and Patterns of Multi-Level Governance*.
5   Christian Hey, "EU Environmental Policies: A Short History of the Policy Strategies," *Chapter 3* (2005), in *EU Environmental Policy Handbook*, ed. by Stefan Scheuer, 18–30. http://www.eeb.org/publication/policy_handbook.html.
6   Christopher Rootes, "Conclusion: Environmental Protest Transformed?" in *Environmental Protest in Western Europe* (Oxford: Oxford University Press, 2003), 236–40.
7   "Chapter III Reactions of National Authorities – Chernobyl: Assessment of Radiological and Health Impact," accessed November 20, 2016, https://www.oecd-nea.org/rp/chernobyl/c03.html.
8   European Parliament, "Environment Policy: General Principles and Basic Framework" accessed March 15, 2017, http://www.europarl.europa.eu/atyourservice/en/displayFtu.html?ftuId=FTU_5.4.1.html.
9   European Environmental Bureau, "EU Environmental Policy Handbook," accessed December 12, 2016, http://www.eeb.org/publication/policy_handbook.html.
10 The 6th EAP covers the period from 2002–2012."EU Environmental Policy Handbook."
11 "Consolidated Version of the Treaty on the Functioning of the European Union," *Official Journal of the European Union*, no. 326 (October 26, 2012), http://eur-lex.europa.eu/resource.html?uri=cellar:2bf140bf-a3f8-4ab2-b506-fd71826e6da6.0023.02/DOC_2&format=PDF.
12 Neill Nugent, *The Government and Politics of the European Union* (Basingstoke [England] New York: Palgrave Macmillan, 2010), 346.
13 European Commission, "EUROPA - The Economy," July 5, 2016, https://europa.eu/european-union/about-eu/figures/economy_en.
14 Louise van Schaik, *EU Effectiveness and Unity in Multilateral Negotiations* (London: Palgrave Macmillan UK, 2013), 115.
15 Rüdiger Wurzel and James Connelly, eds., *The European Union as a Leader in International Climate Change Politics*, 1st edition (London ; New York: Routledge, 2010).
16 European Commission, "The EU Emissions Trading System (EUETS)," (November 23, 2016), http://ec.europa.eu/clima/policies/ets_en.
17 Nicholas Stern, "The Stern Review: UK Government Web Archive – The National Archives" (UK Government), accessed December 12, 2016, http://webarchive.nationalarchives.gov.uk/20060213210707/http://www.hm-treasury.gov.uk/independent_reviews/stern_review_economics_climate_change/sternreview_index.cfm.
18 For examples of the scholarly critique of the Stern Review see: William D. Nordhaus, "A Review of the Stern Review on the Economics of Climate Change," *Journal of Economic Literature* 45, no. 3 (2007): 686–702. Martin L. Weitzman, "A Review of the Stern Review on the Economics of Climate Change," *Journal of Economic Literature* 45, no. 3 (2007): 703–724.
19 European Commission, "Press Release – Limiting Global Climate Change to 2 Degrees Celsius," accessed December 12, 2016, http://europa.eu/rapid/press-release_MEMO-07-16_en.htm.
20 "Europe 2020: A European Strategy for Smart, Sustainable and Inclusive Growth," accessed December 9, 2016, http://ec.europa.eu/eu2020/pdf/COMPLET%20EN%20BARROSO%20%20%20007%20-%20Europe%202020%20-%20EN%20version.pdf.
21 European Commission, "2030 Climate & Energy Framework," accessed September 30, 2016, http://ec.europa.eu/clima/policies/strategies/2030/index_en.htm.

22 European Commission, "Supporting Climate Action through the EU Budget," *Climate Action - European Commission*, accessed November 23, 2016, http://ec.europa.eu/clima/policies/budget_en; "What Is the EU Doing?" accessed November 23, 2016, https://ec.europa.eu/clima/policies/adaptation/what_en; "Adaptation to Climate Change," accessed November 23, 2016, http://ec.europa.eu/clima/policies/adaptation_en.

23 "Adaptation to Climate Change."

24 "Sustainable Agriculture for the Future We Want," accessed December 17, 2016, http://ec.europa.eu/agriculture/sites/agriculture/files/events/2012/rio-side-event/brochure_en.pdf.

25 CAP Reform, "EU Agriculture: Impacts of Climate Change" accessed November 19, 2016, http://capreform.eu/eu-agriculture-impacts-of-climate-change/.

26 European Commission, "2050 Low-Carbon Economy," accessed November 19, 2016, https://ec.europa.eu/clima/policies/strategies/2050/index_en.htm.

27 European Commission – Agriculture and Rural Development "Agriculture and Landscape," accessed November 21, 2016, http://ec.europa.eu/agriculture/envir/landscape/index_en.htm.

28 European Commission and Directorate-General Communication, *Agriculture: A Partnership between Europe and Farmers* updated in April 2014, http://dx.publications.europa.eu/10.2775/45239.

29 "A New EU Forest Strategy: For Forests and the Forest-Based Sector," 2013, http://www.forestplatform.org/files/EU_Forest_Strategy.pdf.

30 European Environment Agency "Urban Environment," accessed December 17, 2016, http://www.eea.europa.eu/themes/urban.

31 "European Green Capital," accessed December 9, 2016, http://ec.europa.eu/environment/europeangreencapital/about-the-award/policy-guidance/index.html#Urban%20Agenda%20for%20the%20EU.

32 "European Green Capital."

33 "Urban Agenda for the EU Home," *Urbanagenda*, accessed December 9, 2016, http://urbanagendaforthe.eu/.

34 European Commission, "Energy Union and Climate," accessed December 8, 2015, http://ec.europa.eu/priorities/energy-union-and-climate_en.

35 European Commission, "Strategic Energy Technology Plan – Energy," *Energy*, accessed December 9, 2016, https://ec.europa.eu/energy/en/topics/technology-and-innovation/strategic-energy-technology-plan."Energy Production and Imports – Statistics Explained," accessed December 9, 2016, http://ec.europa.eu/eurostat/statistics-explained/index.php/Energy_production_and_imports.

36 "Energy Production and Imports – Statistics Explained."

37 European Commission, "Strategic Energy Technology Plan," https://ec.europa.eu/energy/en/topics/technology-and-innovation/strategic-energy-technology-plan.

38 SETIS – European Commission, "EUROPA – What Is the SET-Plan?," accessed December 9, 2016, https://setis.ec.europa.eu/about-setis/set-plan-governance.

39 If the objectives of the SET Plan are met, then the cost of low carbon energy will continue to decrease and that will help keep Europe at the forefront of this growing technology sector. The hope is that these commitments for a transition to a low carbon economy will help limit the global temperature rise to no more than 2 °C.

40 European Commission, "Renewable Energy Directive – Energy," *Energy*, accessed December 9, 2016, /energy/en/topics/renewable-energy/renewable-energy-directive.

41 Connie Hedegaard, "Keynote Speech at the Opening of the 'Metropolitan Solutions Conference 2012' – European Commission," accessed September 29, 2016, http://ec.europa.eu/archives/commission_2010-2014/hedegaard/headlines/news/2012-04-23_01_en.htm.

42 "Renewable Energy Statistics – Statistics Explained," accessed November 20, 2016, http://ec.europa.eu/eurostat/statistics-explained/index.php/Renewable_energy_statistics.

43 "Renewables 2016: Global Status Report" (REN21), accessed October 1, 2016, http://www.ren21.net/wp-content/uploads/2016/06/GSR_2016_Full_Report.pdf.
44 Crain Morris and Martin Pehnt, "Energy Transition: The German Energiewende," July 2016, http://energytransition.de/wp-content/themes/boell/pdf/en/German-Energy-Transition_en.pdf.
45 Morris and Pehnt, "Energy Transition: The German Energiewende."
46 "Europe 2020: A European Strategy for Smart, Sustainable and Inclusive Growth."
47 "Europe 2020: A European Strategy for Smart, Sustainable and Inclusive Growth."
48 The number of member–states will decline to 27 after the 2016 BREXIT vote.
49 Miranda A. Schreurs and Yves Tiberghien, "Multi-Level Reinforcement: Explaining European Union Leadership in Climate Change Mitigation," *Global Environmental Politics* 7, no. 4 (November 1, 2007).
50 Bruce Stokes, Richard Wike, and Jacob Poushter, "Europeans See ISIS, Climate Change as Most Serious Threats," *Pew Research Center's Global Attitudes Project*, June 13, 2016, http://www.pewglobal.org/2016/06/13/europeans-see-isis-climate-change-as-most-serious-threats/.
51 European Commisssion, "Citizen Support for Climate Action," accessed November 18, 2016, https://ec.europa.eu/clima/citizens/support/index_en.htm; "Special Euro-barometer 435: Climate Change," June 2015, https://ec.europa.eu/clima/citizens/support/docs/report_2015_en.pdf.
52 "Special Eurobarometer 435: Climate Change."
53 "Special Eurobarometer 435: Climate Change."
54 Schreurs and Tiberghien, "Multi-Level Reinforcement."
55 Wyn Grant, "Business : The Elephant in the Room?" in *The European Union as a Leader in International Climate Change Politics*, ed. Rüdiger K. W. Wurzel and James Connelly (New York: Routledge, 2011), 197–213.
56 Ulrika Olausson, "Towards a European Identity? The News Media and the Case of Climate Change," *European Journal of Communication* 25, no. 2 (June 1, 2010): 138–52.
57 Schreurs and Tiberghien, "Multi-Level Reinforcement."
58 Astrid Dirikx and Dave Gelders, "Newspaper Communication on Global Warming: Different Approaches in the US and the EU?" *Communicating Climate Change: Discourses, Mediations and Perceptions*, 2009, 98–109.
59 Karen D. Burke, "Climate Change and Digital and Data Journalism," *GEN*, accessed November 21, 2016, http://www.globaleditorsnetwork.org/press-room/news/2015/10/data-journalism-is-disrupting-climate-change-coverage/.
60 "Upworthy: Because We're All Part of the Same Story," *Upworthy*, accessed December 17, 2016, http://www.upworthy.com/.
61 "The European Council - Consilium," accessed November 21, 2016, http://www.consilium.europa.eu/en/european-council/: "The European Council is the EU institution that defines the general political direction and priorities of the European Union. It consists of the heads of state or government of the member–states, together with its President and the President of the Commission."; "The Council of the European Union – Consilium," accessed November 21, 2016, http://www.consilium.europa.eu/en/council-eu/: "The Council of the EU is the institution representing the member states' governments. Also known informally as the EU Council, it is where national ministers from each EU country meet to adopt laws and coordinate policies."
62 European Commission, "Towards the Paris Protocol," accessed November 23, 2016, http://ec.europa.eu/clima/policies/international/paris_protocol_en.
63 CAN International, "Home Page," accessed November 21, 2016, http://www.climatenetwork.org/.
64 European Commission, "EU Agrees Position for Paris Climate Change Conference," accessed November 23, 2016, http://ec.europa.eu/clima/news/articles/news_2015091801_en.

65 Connie Hedegaard, "'Shaping up for a Global Climate Alliance' – European Commission," accessed December 9, 2016, http://ec.europa.eu/archives/commission_2010-2014/hedegaard/headlines/articles/2014-09-22_01_en.htm.
66 Connie Hedegaard, "'Shaping up for a Global Climate Alliance' – European Commission."
67 Miguel Arias Cañete, "Paris Is Much More Than the Deal," *Vital Speeches of the Day* 82, no. 2 (February 2016): 40–42.
68 "How the EU Helped Build the Ambition Coalition (with Images, Tweets)· EUClimateAction," *Storify*, accessed November 20, 2016, https://storify.com/ EUClimateAction/how-the-eu-helped-build-the-coalition-ambition.
69 Cañete, "Paris Is Much More Than the Deal."
70 Karl Mathiesen and Fiona Harvey, "Climate Coalition Breaks Cover in Paris to Push for Binding and Ambitious Deal," *The Guardian*, December 8, 2015, sec. Environment, https://www.theguardian.com/environment/2015/dec/08/coalition-paris-push-for-binding-ambitious-climate-change-deal.
71 "Adaptation Fund," *Adaptation Fund*, accessed November 20, 2016, https://www.adaptation-fund.org/.
72 "G7 Climate Risk Insurance Initiative Stepping Up Protection for the Most Vulnerable," *UNFCCC*, accessed November 20, 2016, http://newsroom.unfccc.int/ lpaa/resilience/g7-climate-risk-insurance-initiative-stepping-up-protection-for-the-most-vulnerable/.
73 European Commission, "Marrakech Climate Conference: World Forging Ahead on Climate Action," accessed November 19, 2016, http://ec.europa.eu/clima/news/articles/news_2016111801_en.htm.
74 For different perspectives on Europe's role see: Sebastian Oberthür and Claire Roche Kelly, "EU Leadership in International Climate Policy: Achievements and Challenges," *The International Spectator* 43, no. 3 (September 1, 2008): 35–50; Anthony R. Zito, "The European Union as an Environmental Leader in a Global Environment," *Globalizations* 2, no. 3 (December 1, 2005): 363–75. Lisanne Groen and Arne Niemann, "The European Union at the Copenhagen Climate Negotiations: A Case of Contested EU Actorness and Effectiveness," *International Relations* 27, no. 3 (September 1, 2013): 308–24. R. Daniel Kelemen, "Globalizing European Union Environmental Policy," *Journal of European Public Policy* 17, no. 3 (April 1, 2010): 335–49.

Bibliography

Adaptation Fund. "Adaptation Fund." Accessed November 20, 2016. https://www.adaptation-fund.org/.
Burke, Karen D. "Climate Change and Digital and Data Journalism." *GEN*. Accessed November 21, 2016. http://www.globaleditorsnetwork.org/press-room/news/2015/10/data-journalism-is-disrupting-climate-change-coverage/.
Cañete, Miguel Arias. "Paris Is Much More Than the Deal." *Vital Speeches of the Day* 82, no. 2 (February 2016): 40–42.
CAP Reform. "EU Agriculture: Impacts of Climate Change." Accessed November 19, 2016. http://capreform.eu/eu-agriculture-impacts-of-climate-change/.
Chernobyl: Assessment of Radiological and Health Impact. "Chapter III Reactions of National Authorities." Accessed November 20, 2016. https://www.oecd-nea.org/rp/chernobyl/c03.html.
Climate Action Network (CAN) International. "Home Page." Accessed November 21, 2016. http://www.climatenetwork.org/.

Dirikx, Astrid, and Dave Gelders. "Newspaper Communication on Global Warming: Different Approaches in the US and the EU?" *Communicating Climate Change: Discourses, Mediations and Perceptions*, 2009, 98–109.

Eurobarometer. "Special Eurobarometer 435: Climate Change," June 2015. https://ec.europa.eu/clima/citizens/support/docs/report_2015_en.pdf.

European Commission "2030 Climate & Energy Framework." Accessed September 30, 2016. http://ec.europa.eu/clima/policies/strategies/2030/index_en.htm.

European Commission. "2050 Low-Carbon Economy." Accessed November 19, 2016. https://ec.europa.eu/clima/policies/strategies/2050/index_en.htm.

European Commission. "A New EU Forest Strategy: For Forests and the Forest-Based Sector," 2013. http://www.forestplatform.org/files/EU_Forest_Strategy.pdf.

European Commission. "Adaptation to Climate Change." Accessed November 23, 2016. http://ec.europa.eu/clima/policies/adaptation_en.

European Commission. "Citizen Support for Climate Action." Accessed November 18, 2016. https://ec.europa.eu/clima/citizens/support/index_en.htm.

European Commission. "Energy Union and Climate." *European Commission*, December 8, 2015. http://ec.europa.eu/priorities/energy-union-and-climate_en.

European Commission. "EU Agrees Position for Paris Climate Change Conference." Accessed November 23, 2016. http://ec.europa.eu/clima/news/articles/news_2015091801_en.

European Commission. "The EU Emissions Trading System (EU ETS)." Accessed November 23, 2016. http://ec.europa.eu/clima/policies/ets_en.

European Commission. "EUROPA – The Economy." *European Union Website, the Official EU Website*, July 5, 2016. https://europa.eu/european-union/about-eu/figures/economy_en.

European Commission. "Europe 2020: A European Strategy for Smart, Sustainable and Inclusive Growth." Accessed December 9, 2016. http://ec.europa.eu/eu2020/pdf/COMPLET%20EN%20BARROSO%20%20%20007%20-%20Europe%202020%20-%20EN%20version.pdf.

European Commission. "European Green Capital." Accessed December 9, 2016. http://ec.europa.eu/environment/europeangreencapital/about-the-award/policy-guidance/index.html#Urban%20Agenda%20for%20the%20EU.

European Commission. "Marrakech Climate Conference: World Forging Ahead on Climate Action." Accessed November 19, 2016. http://ec.europa.eu/clima/news/articles/news_2016111801_en.htm.

European Commission. "Press Release – Limiting Global Climate Change to 2 Degrees Celsius." Accessed December 12, 2016. http://europa.eu/rapid/press-release_MEMO-07-16_en.htm.

European Commission. "Renewable Energy Directive – Energy." *Energy*. Accessed December 9, 2016. /energy/en/topics/renewable-energy/renewable-energy-directive.

European Commission. "Strategic Energy Technology Plan – Energy." *Energy*. Accessed December 9, 2016. /energy/en/topics/technology-and-innovation/strategic-energy-technology-plan.

European Commission. "Supporting Climate Action through the EU Budget." Accessed November 23, 2016. http://ec.europa.eu/clima/policies/budget_en.

European Commission. "Sustainable Agriculture for the Future We Want." 2012. http://ec.europa.eu/agriculture/sites/agriculture/files/events/2012/rio-side-event/brochure_en.pdf.

European Commission. "Towards the Paris Protocol." Accessed November 23, 2016. http://ec.europa.eu/clima/policies/international/paris_protocol_en.

European Commission. "What Is the EU Doing?" Accessed November 23, 2016. https:// ec.europa.eu/clima/policies/adaptation/what_en.

European Commission – Agriculture and Rural Development. "Agriculture and Landscape." Accessed November 21, 2016. http://ec.europa.eu/agriculture/envir/landscape/index_en.htm.

European Commission, and Directorate-General Communication. *Agriculture: A Partnership between Europe and Farmers*. Updated in April 2014. http://dx.publications. europa.eu/10.2775/45239.

European Council: "The Council of the European Union – Consilium." Accessed November 21, 2016. http://www.consilium.europa.eu/en/council-eu/.

European Environment Agency. "Urban Environment." Accessed December 17, 2016. http://www.eea.europa.eu/themes/urban.

European Environmental Bureau. EU Environmental Policy Handbook." Accessed December 12, 2016. http://www.eeb.org/publication/policy_handbook.html.

Eurostat. "Energy Production and Imports – Statistics Explained." Accessed December 9, 2016. http://ec.europa.eu/eurostat/statistics-explained/index.php/ Energy_production_and_imports.

European Union. "Consolidated Version of the Treaty on the Functioning of the European Union." *Official Journal of the European Union*, no. 326 (October 26, 2012). http://eur-lex. europa.eu/resource.html?uri=cellar:2bf140bf-a3f8-4ab2-b506-fd71826e6da6.0023.02/ DOC_2&format=PDF

Gore, Al (writer) and Davis Guggenheim (director). *An Inconvenient Truth*. Accessed March 15, 2017, https://www.algore.com/library/an-inconvenient-truth-dvd.

Grant, Wyn. "Business: The Elephant in the Room?" In *The European Union as a Leader in International Climate Change Politics*, edited by Rüdiger K. W. Wurzel and James Connelly, 197–213. New York: Routledge, 2011. http://webcat.warwick.ac.uk/ record=b2339626.

Groen, Lisanne, and Arne Niemann. "The European Union at the Copenhagen Climate Negotiations: A Case of Contested EU Actorness and Effectiveness." *International Relations* 27, no. 3 (September 1, 2013): 308–24.

Hedegaard, Connie. 'Shaping up for a Global Climate Alliance' – European Commission." Accessed December 9, 2016. http://ec.europa.eu/archives/commission_2010-2014/ hedegaard/headlines/articles/2014-09-22_01_en.htm.

Hedegaard, Connie. "Keynote Speech at the Opening of the 'Metropolitan Solutions Conference 2012' – European Commission." Accessed September 29, 2016. http://ec.europa.eu/archives/commission_2010-2014/hedegaard/headlines/ news/2012-04-23_01_en.htm.

Hey, Christian. "EU Environmental Policies: A Short History of the Policy Strategies." *Chapter* 3 (2005). In *European Environmental Policy Handbook*, edited by Stefan Scheuer, 18-30. http://www.eeb.org/publication/policy_handbook.html.

Kelemen, R. Daniel. "Globalizing European Union Environmental Policy." *Journal of European Public Policy* 17, no. 3 (April 1, 2010): 335–49.

Knill, Christoph, and Duncan Liefferink. *Environmental Politics in the European Union: Policy-Making, Implementation and Patterns of Multi-Level Governance*. Manchester: Manchester University Press, 2007.

Lima–Paris Action Agenda. "G7 Climate Risk Insurance Initiative Stepping Up Protection for the Most Vulnerable." *UNFCCC*. Accessed November 20, 2016. http:// newsroom.unfccc.int/lpaa/resilience/g7-climate-risk-insurance-initiative-stepping- up-protection-for-the-most-vulnerable/.

Mathiesen, Karl, and Fiona Harvey. "Climate Coalition Breaks Cover in Paris to Push for Binding and Ambitious Deal." *The Guardian*, December 8, 2015, sec. Environment.

https://www.theguardian.com/environment/2015/dec/08/coalition-paris-push-for-binding-ambitious-climate-change-deal.

Morris, Crain and Martin Pehnt. "Energy Transition: The German Energiewende," July 2016. http://energytransition.de/wp-content/themes/boell/pdf/en/German-Energy-Transition_en.pdf.

Nordhaus, William D. "A Review of the Stern Review on the Economics of Climate Change." *Journal of Economic Literature* 45, no. 3 (2007): 686–702.

Nugent, Neill. *The Government and Politics of the European Union.* Basingstoke [England] New York: Palgrave Macmillan, n.d.

Oberthür, Sebastian, and Claire Roche Kelly. "EU Leadership in International Climate Policy: Achievements and Challenges." *The International Spectator* 43, no. 3 (September 1, 2008): 35–50.

Olausson, Ulrika. "Towards a European Identity? The News Media and the Case of Climate Change." *European Journal of Communication* 25, no. 2 (June 1, 2010): 138–52.

REN21. "Renewables 2016: Global Status Report." Accessed October 1, 2016. http://www.ren21.net/wp-content/uploads/2016/06/GSR_2016_Full_Report.pdf.

Rootes, Christopher. "Conclusion: Environmental Protest Transformed? – Oxford Scholarship." In *Environmental Protest in Western Europe*, 236-40. Oxford: Oxford University Press, 2003. http://www.oxfordscholarship.com/view/10.1093/0199252068.001.0001/acprof-9780199252060-chapter-10.

Schaik, Louise van. *EU Effectiveness and Unity in Multilateral Negotiations.* London: Palgrave Macmillan UK, 2013. http://link.springer.com/10.1057/9781137012555.

Schreurs, Miranda A., and Yves Tiberghien. "Multi-Level Reinforcement: Explaining European Union Leadership in Climate Change Mitigation." *Global Environmental Politics* 7, no. 4 (November 1, 2007): 19–46.

SETIS – European Commission "EUROPA – What Is the SET-Plan?" Accessed December 9, 2016. https://setis.ec.europa.eu/about-setis/set-plan-governance.

Stern, Nicholas. "The Stern Review: UK Government Web Archive – The National Archives." UK Government. Accessed December 12, 2016. http://webarchive.nationalarchives.gov.uk/20060213210707/http://www.hm-treasury.gov.uk/independent_reviews/stern_review_economics_climate_change/sternreview_index.cfm.

Stokes, Bruce, Richard Wike, and Jacob Poushter. "Europeans See ISIS, Climate Change as Most Serious Threats." *Pew Research Center's Global Attitudes Project*, June 13, 2016. http://www.pewglobal.org/2016/06/13/europeans-see-isis-climate-change-as-most-serious-threats/.

Storify. "How the EU Helped Build the Ambition Coalition (with Images, Tweets) EUClimateAction." *Storify*. Accessed November 20, 2016. https://storify.com/EUClimateAction/how-the-eu-helped-build-the-coalition-ambition.

Upworthy. "Upworthy: Because We're All Part of the Same Story." *Upworthy*. Accessed December 17, 2016. http://www.upworthy.com/.

Urbanagenda. "Urban Agenda for the EU Home." *Urbanagenda*. Accessed December 9, 2016. http://urbanagendaforthe.eu/.

Weitzman, Martin L. "A Review of the Stern Review on the Economics of Climate Change." *Journal of Economic Literature* 45, no. 3 (2007): 703–724.

Wurzel, Rüdiger, and James Connelly, eds. *The European Union as a Leader in International Climate Change Politics.* 1st edition. London; New York: Routledge, 2010.

Zito, Anthony R. "The European Union as an Environmental Leader in a Global Environment." *Globalizations* 2, no. 3 (December 1, 2005): 363–75.

3 China

Lessons from an unsustainable growth model spur change

From its antiquity, China has transformed and attempted to control its environment to meet its needs. Its geographical position and large population made it frequently susceptible to natural disasters such as droughts and floods. Its enduring quest has been to identify ways to live safely and productively in nature, to temper its force and to mold its landscapes to be more hospitable to human settlement. The transformation of nature has remained a central narrative throughout Chinese history, reaching a violent pitch during the Mao years and progressively gaining speed under Deng Xiaoping's drive for economic growth and prosperity. Today, China finds itself in an environmental crisis far beyond just its CO2 emissions. Pollution and environmental degradation have taken such a toll that they threaten the entire edifice upon which the Chinese dream of modernity has been carefully constructed. Moreover, spillover effects extend to other countries which have become appendages to China's insatiable pursuit for growth and expansion.

China is now facing a unique moment of reckoning. While it is clear that without China there can be no successful response to the climate crisis, this nation more than others will need to quickly decarbonize, embrace notions of sustainability all across its Five-Year Plans (FYP) and begin to robustly tackle the ecological destruction that it has caused itself and others. This imperative has not been lost on China's leaders who have been looking for positive frameworks to express a new narrative of coexistence with nature. This is why President Xi in his speech at COP 21 in Paris declared that, "All things live in Harmony and grow with nourishments. Chinese culture values harmony between man and nature and respects nature. Going forward, ecological endeavors will feature prominently in China's 13th Five-Year Plan."[1] President Xi was attempting to tie present transformation to a bygone era when humanity had achieved a meaningful balance with the natural world. As we will see later on, this framework constitutes more of a nostalgic myth than an accurate depiction of reality.

Nevertheless, President Xi's need to frame the new goals that China seeks to reach in such a way indicates the complexity of the task ahead. While the practical difficulties are numerous, the political difficulty is paramount because the only party that governs the PRC is now faced with having to forge a new path forward that will attempt to bridge the divide between expectations of growth and principles of sustainability, all the while hoping to "eradicate" poverty and repair some of the immeasurable ecological damage it has caused.

It is commonly thought that the environmental crisis in which China finds itself today traces its origins to the Maoist era. History, of course, is never linear and clear-cut. In the days of the empire, the Chinese devoted much attention in deciding how humans should behave in nature. This debate was reflected in the three distinct schools of thought, the Daoist which leaned towards accommodation to Nature's way, the Buddhist which revered all living things, and the Confucian that sought to manage, utilize and control nature.[2] These schools of thought may have proposed different understandings of nature, yet they took a more adaptive and respectful view about the coexistence of humans in nature, as illustrated by the following:

> In hunting, the laws of the former kings did not permit the extermination of the whole herd or flock or the trapping of the young. They did not allow the draining of ponds to fish, the burning of woods to hunt, the spreading of nets in the wild prior to the autumn's wild dog sacrifice, the setting of nets in the water prior to the spring's otter sacrifice, the stretching of bird nets in valleys and river gorges before the autumn falconry, the logging of hill forests before the autumn shedding of the leaves, the burning off of fields before the hibernating of the insects. They did not allow the killing of pregnant animals, the collecting of fledglings and bird eggs, the taking of fish less than a foot in length, or the consumption of piglets less than a year old. Thus grasses and trees billowed forth like rising steam, birds and animals rushed to their domains like a flowing spring, and birds of the air warmed to them like clouds of smoke because they had that which brought all this about.
>
> From the Book of the Prince of Huainan[3] circa 150 BCE

The Confucian tradition, which prevailed, professed a "wise use" of natural resources but, behind this balance, there was an insistence on the regulation and ordering of the non-human environment for the greater good of society. In ancient China, major projects were undertaken based on the technological knowledge of the time. For instance, the Grand Canal linking the North and South of China was constructed in the seventh century CE, as well as many waterworks projects such as the Durjiangyan irrigation systems. As China grew in population and land reach, it overused its natural resources and signs of early environmental degradation can already be traced.

Through centuries of human use and exploitation most arable land in China was transformed, vulnerable species faced extinction as their habitats had already been encroached upon by human development, and deforestation had progressed extensively to clear lands for agricultural pursuits and human habitat. According to Bao Maohong prior to 1949, the Yellow River transported 1.4 billion tons of sediments annually to its lower reaches and estuary. Soil erosion resulted in soil impoverishment and even desertification in the middle and upper reaches of the Yellow River, while frequent floods menaced its middle and lower reaches, and soil salinization spread along its banks. Deforestation occurred on a large scale, and even in Manchuria (a region with the richest forest reserves in China) the forest area decreased 18%, and the forest growing stock decreased by 14.3% from 1929 to 1944. The destruction of forests further contributed to water and soil erosion problems.[4]

While these issues show the gravity of the environmental pressures predating the revolution, there was no one environmental agency tasked with handling these issues. It was in this China that Mao came to rule.

Mao's era was characterized by purposeful never-ending revolutionary fervor, mass mobilization, coercion, dislocation, relocation and a militarist outlook of defying nature, conquering it and bending it to human will, all to build a project of socialist utopia that exalted industrialization at a grand scale.[5] Mao's approach to the environment was overtly adversarial and not only disregarded tradition, but science as well. He brooked no opposition to his plans to rebuild China and create the socialist man. Nature was viewed purely through a utilitarian lens that resulted in numerous failed policies. Throughout this experiment, that culminated in the Great Famine and the Cultural Revolution, voices of opposition were purged and thus silenced. The view that prevailed, as expressed by the cult of Mao, was that man must conquer nature. Mao likely had no respect for the non-human world. In fact his drive to control nature is reflected in a quotation attributed to General Yang Shangkun, "no other world leader looks down with such disdain on great mountains and powerful rivers."[6]

A confidential conversation between Judith Shapiro and a Chinese scholar from Yunnan drives the point home. "Mao's attitude toward nature was an oppositional relationship ..." To catch up with the West Mao launched the "Great Leap Forward" but that led to widespread famine, prompting him to then open up the wilderness for people to plant crops to survive.

> The forests were cut without restraint so as to plant grain in mountains. During the Cultural Revolution ... everything was collective and nature belonged to the country, so there was no individual responsibility to protect nature ... . Officials were ordered to cut down fruit trees. If they resisted, it was terrible ... . After Mao's death ... the farmland that had been state-owned was contracted out to families, as were the forests. But people feared they wouldn't have the right to use the land for long, so there was terrible cutting.[7]

The war against nature in Mao's time was driven forward by a series of policies such as political repression, uniformity in the implementation of countrywide policies without room for the use of local expertise and adaptability to regional conditions, and finally mass relocations of populations into wilderness areas and from cities into the country. In the name of modernization and rapid industrialization, society itself was re-imagined and age old traditions ruthlessly eliminated. The few voices of dissent were silenced, while the vast majority of the largely uneducated poor passively complied with these new dictates. The chaos that Mao's policies instilled into daily life, instead of breeding insurgency, bred complacency born out of despair and incredulity. In 1982, an article published in the Beijing Review, admitted that, between 1957 and 1977, China had a net loss of 29 million hectares of farmland.[8]

The story of Mao's war against nature continues to shock the western public who seem to have forgotten the impact that industrialization had on Europe from the eighteenth century until the late twentieth century. There, too, modernization came hand in hand with the "taming" of nature and its submission to human ambition for the creation of a modern civilization where industry, commerce and technological innovation were the yardsticks of progress. The western expansion in the United States (US), for instance, was driven by a rhetoric of conquest to bring modernity, civilization and economic profit, leaving in its wake deforestation, the extinction of animals and their habitats, the damming of rivers and the destruction of indigenous populations. In fact from the very beginning, the discovery of the New World was seen as a new space in which Europe could expand and shape according to its own image. The first colonialists looked to this new land as an opportunity for new trade routes and for the discovery of new mineral wealth. The entire enterprise was a joint take-over of the forces of empire, trade and Christianity.[9] It was not only the taming of the environment in the name of modernity, however, that characterized the industrialization process in the West. The utilitarian approach to the natural world was then followed by its pollution with manmade chemicals that have left an ongoing toxic legacy. Mao's policies simply appear more dramatic, primarily because they so quickly altered the course of a country of 1.3 billion, the largest population in the world.

While Mao's time in power wreaked havoc on the environment, it must also be noted that his government, while seeking to transform the land, the people and the production model through an ongoing revolutionary process, utilized mass mobilization to attempt to address certain urban and health issues plaguing the country. Through the Patriotic Health Campaign, Mao sought to eliminate certain diseases such as schistosomiasis, filariasis, bubonic plague, encephalitis, cattle plague and hog cholera. He declared a war against pests, identifying four in particular: "rats, sparrows (because they fed on seed and reduced agricultural output), flies and mosquitoes." He amended the list to take off sparrows, after successfully eliminating 1.6 billion of them. According to official figures by 1958 the PRC had disposed of "29.5 billion tons of wastes, collected 61.1 billion tons of manure, dredged 1.65 kilometers of ditches and built and rebuilt 85 million toilets."[10] These mass mobilization campaigns could be seen as the first wave of efforts to deal with environmental issues and improve health and the quality of life.

Scholars argue that 1972 marks an important change in the government's environmental outlook. China took a significant first move to return to the international arena by participating in the UN Conference on the Human Environment in Stockholm. At the conference, the delegation's goal was to make use of a prestigious international event to promote two important messages. First, to curb US interventions in the developing world and second to make known China's efforts in socialist construction as well as its desire to partake in international environmental policy making.[11] China's participation allowed its delegates to be introduced to global environmental movements that were growing around the globe. This exposure had a significant impact marking the official beginnings of what developed into China's environmental awakening. As we have already seen, even during Mao's era environmental problems had become manifest. Both government and the people were becoming increasingly aware of pollution and environmental degradation. The important difference was that during the Mao years, and for some time after his death, the severity of these problems was directly linked to capitalism. Chinese authorities placed the blame on capitalist countries for being unable to resolve them. Set in an ideological framework, Chinese leaders attributed the problems of the West to private ownership, anarchy in production and profit seeking.

As Zhou Enlai put it:

> We can definitely solve industrial pollution because our socialist planning economy serves the masses. While we are engaged in economic construction, we should pay closer attention to solving this issue and avoid doing something absolute, which may create problems for our descendants. The reason that the Soviet Union has environmental problems is that it has become a revisionist country.[12]

At the 1972 meeting, however, the Chinese side also produced a list of principles that they felt should be included in the conference's final declaration. The list provides insight as to how the PRC viewed many of the issues at that point in time.[13] The PRC began its list stating that economic development and social progress are indispensable pre-requisites for the protection and improvement of human environment. China defended the right of developing countries to guard their independence, develop their economy and improve their environment. They went against the "pessimistic" view in which population and environmental conservation are pitted against each other. Moreover, China pushed for a resolute ban on biochemical and nuclear weapons, attributed the greatest destruction of human environment to imperialist wars, supported compensation for any country polluted by another and proposed the establishment of an international environment fund. By the same token, the PRC attempted to promote international cooperation in the conservation of the human environment, encouraged government measures to fight pollution, championed national use of resources and railed against the superpowers of the day for pursuing policies of war and aggression. Finally, China took a clear stance on assuring the right of developing countries to develop first and address their environmental challenges one by one.[14]

Zhou Enlai, in 1973, proceeded to set-up the first National Conference on Environmental Protection. Gradually, especially given the political turmoil on the ground, other institutional structures began to be established, such as the inter-ministerial Environmental Protection Leading Group of the State Council which was mandated to study environmental protection issues. All Chinese provinces, municipalities and autonomous regions were also then tasked with setting up organizations for environmental control, monitoring and research.[15]

Mao's death brought an end to the chaos that was tearing the country apart, yet it left behind a legacy for development that now replaced Maoist ideology with rapid economic gain. When Deng Xiaoping took over in 1978, the per capita income in China was less than $100.[16] He helped launch the wave of explosive economic growth in a country that lay in shambles after the Cultural Revolution. Environmental degradation did not, therefore, cease in the 1980s. In fact, the fear and suspicion that the madness of the previous era had caused, made the population more untrusting of government sponsored decrees and programs. They were, as a consequence, more prone to exploit every opportunity for economic advancement. Reining in the waters, reshaping nature and the overexploitation of natural resources continued. Pollution grew throughout the nation, and the Chinese found themselves increasingly facing problems with their water supply, their waste disposal and the intensity of energy used to generate industrialization and urbanization.

Chinese authorities decoupled pollution from the ideological battle against capitalism and began to characterize it as a product of industrialization. In 1982, the Constitution was revised accordingly, and Article 26 stipulated that, "the state protects and improves the living environment and the ecological environment. It prevents and controls pollution and other public hazards. The state organizes and encourages afforestation and protection of forests." Nevertheless, China's rapid industrialization continued unabated and aimed to accomplish in 30–40 years what had taken developed nations to achieve in two hundred. Economic development remained the nation's principal goal in order to achieve modernization, so even while environmental protection was included as a component of the PRC development model, it became particularly tricky to achieve both because change was happening at such breakneck speed. Throughout its industrial transformation China has portrayed itself as a developing nation seeking to buy time by opting for a model of "pollution first, treatment later."[17]

While Deng Xiaoping's rule is considered the critical moment when China's economy took off and began to join the modern industrial age, his reform and open door policy brought about a rapid economic transformation without any real provisions for protecting the environment. The PRC's metamorphosis into the world's twenty-first century factory did not happen unintentionally. The Party, knowing full well that they had lost legitimacy with the population because of Mao's excesses, focused its energies in creating strong economic performance, raising millions of citizens out of abject poverty into the middle class. It was imperative in Deng Xiaoping's mind to maintain authority and discipline over the country while allowing economic growth to strengthen both the Communist Party as well as his own authority. He took the long view in planning and throughout the period of rapid reform he actively sought to obtain technical knowledge, management skills and popular acceptance for his policies, in order to provide necessary hope without provoking unrealistic expectations in a population that had suffered from waves of devastating experimentation.

To achieve these aims, Deng Xiaoping invited large international industries to the PRC. They hastened to heed his call because China offered them a profitable alternative of cheap labor and lax environmental policies. For the polluting industries especially, it constituted a heaven sent opportunity because they were under increasing scrutiny and facing a growing regulatory environment both in the US and Europe. As a result industries such as steel, coke, aluminum, cement, chemical and petrochemical, plastics, paper production, synthetic fibers and textile production, and auto battery and electronic recycling migrated to the PRC.[18] World prices for the products of these industries collapsed, which meant that the vast majority would not resume production in the developed world. Low prices also had the effect of driving consumption to unprecedented and unsustainable rates in food, clothing and technology, provoking a staggering increase in resource use. China's impressive growth rates that have ranged from 7.9 percent in 1980, 15 percent in 1984, 8.4 percent in 2000,[19] 10.4 percent in 2010, and 6.9 percent in 2015 were lauded by the government and became expected by the population.[20]

A generation of Chinese began to indulge in the trappings of modernity and plenty as their buying power increased, and they joined the ranks of the middle and upper middle class. To be fair, the government began to acknowledge the unsustainability of its project and responded with policies, laws and regulations. Yet, their primary concern was to keep the economy growing and modernizing. Already in 1994, the PRC adopted "China's Agenda 21– White Paper on China's Population, Environment and Development Plan for the 21st century." A directive was subsequently issued by which government institutions at all levels should take Agenda 21 as the strategic guideline for both economic and social policy formulation.[21] The Rio conference of 1992, moreover, had pushed the point home that the resource and energy intensive growth model that China had ascribed to was both unsustainable in the long run and environmentally destructive. The transition into a more sustainable economic model was labeled a strategic priority for the PRC. Nonetheless, building a strong economy remained the paramount concern and government objective, as well as the official excuse for a new wave of environmental degradation.

Jonathan Watts describes the staggering changes that he witnessed living in China in the period following 2003.

> The year after my arrival, China's GDP overtook those of France and Italy. Another year of growth took it past that of Britain. From 2003 to 2010, China stopped receiving aid from the World Food Program and overtook the World Bank as the biggest investor in Africa … To be in Beijing at this time was to witness the consequences of two hundred years of industrialization and urbanization, in close up, playing at fast-forward on a continent-wide screen. It soon became clear to me that China was the focal point of the world's

environmental crisis. The decisions taken in Beijing, more than anywhere else, would determine whether humanity thrived or perished. After I arrived in Beijing, I was first horrified at the chaos and then excited. No other country was in such a mess. None had the greater incentive to change.[22]

The challenge the government faced was voiced in *Der Spiegel* which ran an interview in 2005 with China's Deputy Minister of the Environment, Pan Yue. He was unusually frank in describing China's environmental challenges.

> Of course I am pleased with the success of China's economy. But at the same time I am worried. We are using too many raw materials to sustain this growth. To produce goods worth $10,000, for example, we need seven times more resources than Japan, nearly six times more than the United States and, perhaps most embarrassing, nearly three times more than India. Things can't, nor should they be allowed to go on like that."[23]

Increasingly, media sources have recounted the daily air pollution in cities like Beijing and Shanghai as well as reports of toxic disposal practices that in Europe and the US would no longer be tolerated. In 2008 for example, the *Washington Post*, ran a story about a village in the central plains of Henan Province near the Yellow River where workers from a high tech company nearby were dumping industrial waste in the fields around the village on a daily basis for a period of nine months.[24] The workers "dumped buckets of bubbling white liquid onto the ground."[25] What was even more shocking is that this company was producing a product that we consider vital for our transition to a post fossil fuel economy to rein in climate change, namely polysilicon, used globally in solar panels. The problem is that silicon tetrachloride, which is a byproduct of polysilicon is highly toxic and needs to be disposed of in a safe way. According to the *Washington Post*, that quoted Ren Bingyan, a professor at the School of Material Sciences at Hebei Industrial University, "The land where you dump or bury it will be infertile. No grass or trees will grow in the place … It is like dynamite – it is poisonous, it is polluting. Human beings can never touch it."[26] At the time, and as demand for solar panels soared worldwide, the price for polysilicon grew from $20 per kilogram to $300, making its production an attractive business opportunity, especially if all environmental rules governing its toxic byproducts were ignored.[27]

The shock articulated in the western media over such practices overlooked the fact that similar practices had taken place in the industrialized world in previous decades. Today this no longer constitutes the norm and, moreover, with strides in pollution control methods, ecosystems that had been compromised are making a come-back. Still, many of the newer pollutants are not readily visible, but are entering nature's systems and causing damage the extent of which is yet to be determined and understood. In searching for ways to minimize the cost of production and to stay competitive, western industries today complain about "over-regulation" especially with regard to the high costs of remediation and pollution reduction. They protest that it impedes their competitiveness while giving the upper hand to the developing countries that are not as stringent in their environmental oversight.

The story published by the *Washington Post* is not unique. There are many such stories coming out of China relating to different industries. For example, rare earth production, mining and refining offer salient instances of environmental pollution. In defending its decision to place stringent quotas on rare earth exports, China exposed the extent of the pollution that their extraction and production caused to the environment. Available data continues to indicate the severity of the environmental challenges facing the PRC. A mere one percent of China's 560 million urban dwellers has access to what is considered safe air by European Union (EU) standards. China's cities are amongst the most polluted in the world. According to an announcement by the Chinese government in 2014, out of the ten worst polluted cities, "seven were located in the heavy industrial province of Hebei, which surrounds the capital, Beijing. The cities of Baoding, Xingtai, Shijiazhuang, Tangshan, Handan and Hengshui, all in Hebei, filled the top six places."[28] Furthermore, the World Bank produced a study showing that out of twenty of the most polluted cities worldwide 16 are Chinese. More strikingly, Stern and Zenghelis argued that "air pollution costs millions of lives every year … A recent study by the World Resources Institute put the health impacts, of exposure to the single particulate pollutant PM 2.5 (including premature deaths) in China at a shocking 10–13% of the country's annual GDP."[29]

The situation pertaining to river water is even direr, with over 50 percent of rivers so polluted that the water is not safe to drink without very expensive treatment. Meanwhile groundwater is being quickly depleted, and deserts are expanding in vast areas of the country, with neighbors in South Korea now complaining that sandstorms from China keep them indoors for days at a time. Deforestation rates remain high. Elizabeth Economy claims that China's forest cover is about 16.6 percent while coverage of the US is at 24.7 percent and the world average stands at around 27 percent.[30] Reforestation attempts tend to reflect a haste to plant the fastest growing trees to show progress, a technique that may in fact be causing more problems in the future. Issues of overuse of fertilizers and pesticides in agriculture affecting the food chain and problems of waste disposal and management are also areas of concern, ranging from improper e-waste disposal to household garbage. Fish production has suffered both from overfishing, applied fishing techniques and marine environment degradation, and there is growing international criticism by environmentalists of the mega hydraulic projects currently underway.

The impacts of choices made in China in its pursuit of creating a "moderately affluent society"[31] by 2020 extend beyond its borders. The PRC's increasing energy needs, for example, are the reason behind such projects as the Tar Sands in Alberta, Canada, which aim to bring this low-grade oil to the shores of the PRC. China has also bought exploratory rights for a controversial oil project in a remote corner of Ecuador's rainforest, home to two isolated indigenous tribes but also one of the last remaining pristine ecosystems. China is also buying vast acres of farmland especially in select African countries like Kenya. Its dam projects are also having repercussions in countries like Myanmar, Vietnam and Thailand. Its emissions are a serious cause of acid rain that has destroyed forests in both Korea and Japan. The projects on the Mekong and the Salween River impact these countries' water supplies not only for agriculture but also for other areas of life. As the Chinese have grown wealthier, their tastes are also changing. Today, they represent a growing market for exotic food and medicines that come from endangered species.[32]

A number of scholars and analysts are increasingly pointing directly to China as a source of global environmental degradation and resource abuse. Craig Simons, for example, in a book that portrays China as a "devouring dragon", underscores the massive amounts of resources that the PRC needs to run the manufacturing powerhouse it has created with the help of consumers of cheap and disposable merchandise worldwide. He argues that China's rise is changing the "physical planet."[33] China consumes over half the world's coal and a third of its oil. China is now the largest consumer of lumber and forest products. It's responsible for 90 percent of Mozambique's log exports and 70 percent of exports from Gabon and Cameroon. Nearly half of all the tropical logs and pulp made from tropical logs, which is traded for use in paper, passes through a Chinese port.[34] These kinds of figures highlight the "devouring of natural resources thesis" that is taking place at record speed. Simons means to forewarn publics in industrial nations that what we see in China today will be the trajectory of a rising India, Brazil and, in the future, Russia, and asks his audience to contemplate the limitations of the environment in a world of growing resource competition. There are a number of other voices, however, scapegoating China for the growing climate crisis without simultaneously engaging in a wider discussion on growth and global consumption as drivers of this overwhelming change.

Throughout China's last three decades of unbridled growth, the Communist Party's response has not by any means remained static. It has continued to evolve. During the Presidency of Hu Jintao (2003–2013) the government began to introduce parameters for environmental policy considerations and action in designing China's path to future growth. The growing understanding and scientific acceptance of the climate crisis, climate negotiations and the early signs of its impacts in China itself also stimulated a re-evaluation of how to proceed, especially given that the initial measures that were announced brought mixed results. Moreover, it has become increasingly apparent that environmental degradation and pollution were both a product of difficult economic choices facing the leadership and a result of widespread corruption, unenforced laws by major industries, and the government's continued hesitation to rein in systemic excesses for fear of provoking unrest or slowing down the pace of economic growth.

China has found itself in the Anthropocene facing a pressing urgency to not only reduce emissions, but also to accept and try to reverse the effect of the human activity that has violently transformed the natural environment, impacting quality of life, health, the food chain and overall economic development. Over time, these considerations have been reflected in the Party discourse, and its rhetoric registered a gradual change. Increasingly, new rhetorical frameworks have been utilized to mark the incorporation of environmental considerations and the climate crisis into the list of the PRC's strategic priorities. Themes that have been used to highlight the shift in discourse over the years include a new path of industrialization (2002); a scientific outlook on development (2003); a circular economy (2004); resource efficiency and an environmentally friendly society (2004); a harmonious society (2005); an innovative country (2006); an ecological civilization (2007); a green economy and low carbon economy (2009); a transformation of economic development patterns (2010) and green and low carbon development (2011).[35]

The tide has begun to turn not only out of necessity but also because it increasingly has become easier to find allies in a population that is now directly affected by the rapid, unbridled industrialization process. This helps to bolster the government's determination to act in the name of the people. Public pressure is mounting in all the major cities across the country from China's growing middle classes who fear for their health.[36] Citizen outrage over Beijing's horrific air quality forced the government to take emergency action in 2012, shuttering coal plants in major cities and reducing the number of new cars allowed to be registered in Beijing and other metropolitan areas.[37] In the summer of 2013, moreover, the Ministry of Environmental Protection released data from air quality studies in 74 cities showing harmful levels of pollution. The city of Harbin, the home of 11 million Chinese citizens experienced a shut down when pollution made it impossible to see beyond a few meters.[38] While China's dependence on its domestic coal supply continues to remain exceptionally high at 66 percent in 2014, the government has taken bold action to close down a number of coal mines,[39] decommission older coal fired plants and cancel construction of new ones across fifteen regions.[40]

China may have begun to turn a corner in its pursuit of growth at any cost. Public outcry has been reported rather openly in the Chinese press, even while Xi appears to be cracking down on public dissent in other areas. There are some hopeful success stories that give grounds for optimism, particularly as urbanization continues at high rates. One such example showcased in China was the impressive transformation of the city of Shenyang, located in the industrial northeast. There, efforts to improve environmental conditions have proven successful. Through the implementation of targeted policies such as "dechimneyfication" on a massive scale, there has been a vast improvement in air quality for eight million people. The rivers Hun and Pu are no longer black, there are trees along the banks. Solar panels are producing electricity on the roofs of buildings in parts of the city, and trees have been replanted along streets.[41]

While there is still much work to be done in cities like Shenyang, much has also changed in the last decade. This transformation was not easy. A good part of the industrial infrastructure of the 1950s Maoist era had outlived its production potential and needed to be scrapped and replaced if the factories were to stay open. Many had already closed in the 1990s, and the city was experiencing a rapid decline similar to that of industrial centers of the past. Demolitions began all over the city. Serendipitously, the interests of the construction and development ministries, regional government and the environmental protection bureau chief aligned with those of Tiexi district manager Li Songlin, and reconstruction efforts turned to tapping China's red-hot residential real-estate market and attracting light manufacturing. Soil decontamination efforts on old industrial sites and a general cleanup effort ensued. Costs were covered by the government. Plugged into the political center, Shenyang policy and decision makers made a sound economic argument for the city's transformation that has paid off. Today, according to an Urban China Initiative report[42] quoted by journalist Christina Larson,[43]

> Shenyang had removed virtually all traces of heavy industry from its core by 2010. In new residential areas, coal heating had been replaced by natural gas. Urban green space had increased 30 percent from 2005 to 2007. Perhaps most significantly … Shenyang's plants emit about one-fifth the level of sulfur oxides as the national average in China.

For a country like China that, according to the McKinsey Global Institute's estimates will continue to urbanize so that "the urban population there will expand from about 600 million in 2008 to 926 million in 2025 and more than one billion in 2030,"[44] the search for best practices in greening existing cities and building "smart" cities has led the PRC to closer collaboration with the EU and more recently with a number of US cities to address common challenges and experiment further. The Urban Sustainability Index created by the Urban China Initiative revealed in 2011 that there was a significant gap between the "best- and worst-performing Chinese cities across a number of indicators,"[45] and that China's urban growth model wasn't meeting the "global benchmarks for sustainable development."[46] This kind of data has motivated leadership to develop its new strategies for the future.

It must be clarified that China shares many commonalities with other nations with respect to such drivers of environmental change. However, the size of the country is one major difference that accentuates their significance and impact. Some of these include population growth, globalization of trade and manufacturing, urbanization and the resulting radical changes in land use, new consumption behavior that goes hand in hand with the growth of the middle class, and the adverse effects of climate change not only on temperature and sea level rise, but on the severity of storms and droughts.

There have been important milestones in China's transition toward a more sustainable and decarbonized economy. According to the China Council for International Cooperation on Environment and Development, for instance,

> 2007 was a historic year for China's environmental protection … China has adopted a series of market-based instruments such as green loans from banks, and ecological compensation schemes for those who protect the ecological integrity of watersheds and ecosystem benefits. As a result of the serious control efforts of the 11th Five Year plan … COD (chemical oxygen demand)

and SO2, have started to decrease. China also set out its first National Climate Change Program.[47]

Moreover, a combination of the economic crisis of 2008 and the Copenhagen Climate Change Summit made it readily apparent that China could no longer remain primarily a manufacturing and exporter economy and would inevitably need to switch to a greener growth model. With growth rates declining, the government has begun to speak about adaptation to the "new normal." Of course, the same realizations that are pushing the government to address and steer the economy to a more sustainable economic model are also being influenced by pressure to maintain growth rates through the increase of domestic consumption. Swapping production for export with growth of domestic consumption is under heated debate, but it underscores the difficulties and constraints the PRC government continues to face domestically.

Beyond the rhetorical changes that we have traced, the shifting tides with respect to the environment and the climate crisis can be identified more succinctly in China's socioeconomic FYPs. These reflect the evolution of the Party's thinking and the prioritization of their policies and development strategy for the future. Furthermore, China's evolving position with respect to international climate negotiations also indicates the wider policy shift. Moreover, the influence of public opinion and China's growing risk assessment plans for adaptation and mitigation in the "new normal" are also indicators of its wider considerations about life in the Anthropocene. There are of course countless other areas where researchers can identify challenges, opportunities and possibilities for the transition to a low carbon future, the pursuit of a green economy and continued but sustainable growth. They all, however, share one common understanding. That is, that China's constructive role in Paris was not merely a demonstration of the government's desire to find an area for acceptable US–China cooperation. It also reflected its belief that the climate crisis called for the construction of a new vision forward—a vision that could be supported by its domestic audience as it constituted part of China's path to "national rejuvenation"[48] and declared ambition for the promotion of international win-win cooperation. President Xi Jinping now proudly speaks of building an "ecological civilization," "for a "beautiful China" through quality, efficient and low-carbon development.

In 2014, Li Keqiang, the Chinese Premier, announced that the country would be waging a "war on pollution."[49] First on the agenda was a faster shift towards a low carbon economy. Li Keqiang compared smog—a constant reminder of environmental degradation—to "nature's red-light warning against inefficient and blind development."[50] For the declared Chinese ambition to be realized, according to a report by the Energy Research Institute, there needs to be a peaking of emissions by 2025 and a 2050 target of having 60 percent of energy consumption through renewables as well as 85 percent of its electricity.[51] The government is, moreover, determined to also tackle agricultural pollution. According to the National Development and Reform Commission (NDRC) report of 2014, plans include addressing "the contamination of farmland by heavy metals, with 3.33 million hectares (8 million acres) believed to be too polluted to grow crops."[52] The government earlier had stated that it would spend "2 trillion yuan ($330 billion) on tackling pollution of scarce water resources."[53] Other statements from the Chinese premier underscored the government's ambition to "convert 333,300 hectares of marginal farmland to forest and grassland," as well as to continue fighting desertification and to recover wetlands. The government would ensure that polluters pay "by establishing a new mechanism to compensate victims of environmental damage and by holding local officials accountable." Additionally, another report of 2014, issued by the Ministry of Finance said that "China would spend 21.1 billion yuan on energy conservation and environmental protection in 2014, up 7.1 percent on 2013. It said 64.9 billion yuan would be allocated to agriculture, forestry and water conservation, up 8.6 percent."[54]

Moreover, and according to Professor Teng Fei of Tsingua University, who is also the author of China's Fifth Assessment Report of the Intergovernmental Panel on Climate Change, energy efficiency improvements will continue to play a great role in the decarbonization of the economy, given that growth rates by his estimations will not be going down to 2.5 – 3 percent until 2050. Teng Fei also believes that new energy pricing mechanisms could help reflect social and environmental costs that currently are not adequately taken into account. "The Natural Resources Defense Council found that coal has external costs of 260 yuan per ton – approximately 50% of what coal costs today. But currently only 50 yuan of external costs are factored into the coal price – one fifth of total externalities."[55] Apart from rampant pollution, unprecedented changes in land-use, development strategies and migration from country to city also require that the government turn its attention to climate risk management and adaptation. This is not only a costly endeavor, but it faces a number of hurdles that range from bureaucratic silos, lack of comprehensive data, funding shortages and an overreliance on easy fixes that spring from a preference for technological solutions. Here too, China is making progress as it better understands these risks and how to go about constructing a web of policies to support adaptation initiatives both locally and regionally.

China's overall determined action appears to already be bearing fruit. China lowered its CO2 emissions per unit of GDP by 6.1 percent in 2014. It has taken measures to reduce effects of climate change through intervention in agriculture, water resources, forestry and ecosystems, coastal areas and relevant waters, human health and other areas. The PRC has actively pursued international exchanges and cooperation with India, Brazil, the UK, the EU, the US, and France and participated actively in climate change negotiations in addition to establishing the South-South Cooperation Fund for climate change.[56]

In June 2015, China submitted its Intended National Determined Contribution (INDC) report ahead of COP21.[57] The document made it abundantly clear that China recognizes the adverse effects of climate change already impacting the country.

> As a developing nation … China is among those countries that are most severely affected by the adverse impacts of climate change … To act on

climate change in terms of mitigating greenhouse gas (GHG) emissions and enhancing climate resilience, is not only driven by China's domestic needs for sustainable development in ensuring its economic security, energy security, ecological security, food security as well as the safety of people's life and property and to achieve sustainable development, but also driven by its sense of responsibility to fully engage in global governance, to forge a community of shared destiny for humankind and to promote common development for all human beings."

Later in the winter, at COP 21 in Paris, President Xi Jinping confirmed China's determination to address the challenges of climate change, emphasizing the PRC's commitment to a low carbon economy:

> China is vigorously making ecological endeavors to promote green, circular and low-carbon growth. We have integrated our climate change efforts into China's medium- and long-term program of economic and social development. We attach equal importance to mitigation and adaption, and try to make progress on all fronts by resorting to legal and administrative means, technologies and market forces. China's installed capacity of renewable energy accounts for 24% of the world's total, with the newly installed capacity accounting for 42% of the global total. China tops the world in terms of energy conservation and utilization of new and renewable energies.[58]

From the outset, the Communist Party of China chose to emulate the centralized Soviet FYP model to organize its economic goals. The first plan in 1953 was based on Soviet thinking and at the center of its economic strategy called for rapid industrialization and large-scale construction. Collectivization was initiated under the same model of economic transformation. The rivalry between the Soviets and Mao grew rapidly and those tensions were registered in the second and third FYPs. The second plan coincided with the Great Leap Forward, which pushed for even more rapid industrialization. It dealt a heavy blow to agriculture and resulted in widespread starvation among the population. The third and fourth FYPs continued to reflect the push for industrialization. Mao's revolutionary fervor was meant to create continuous unrest and to build on the geostrategic fears of the Cold War that finally culminated in the Cultural Revolution.

With Mao's death in 1976, the PRC embarked on a new stage of development that now centered on opening up its economy to the world, which ushered in both comprehensive changes and enviable rates of economic growth. China's economy grew at a feverish pace, and the world looked on transfixed by its miraculous transformation. Nonetheless, voices of caution were being raised, expressing fears that this unchecked model of industrialization and growth at any cost was coming at too high an environmental price. They warned that it would not be sustainable in the long run. This is why in the 10th FYP,[59] the first environmental targets began to haltingly make an appearance. The issue of forest coverage, for instance, was addressed in that plan and a target of increasing it by

18.2 percent was included. Raising the urban green rate to 35 percent while also reducing urban and rural pollutants by 10 percent (in comparison to 2000 levels) were goals as well.[60] Moreover, China appropriated 700 billion yuan to six key forestry programs and invested in environmental protection infrastructure. The plan itself underscored the continued emphasis on sustainable development and underlined the need to

> protect and make proper use of valuable resources such as fresh water, farmland and energy in accordance with the law … gradually establish a system of reserves for strategically important mineral resources and ensure their safe supply … strengthen the comprehensive development, utilization and conservation of marine resource … increase our recycling of resources and … [improve] ecological conservation and strengthening environmental protection.[61]

The 11th FYP[62] continued to address environmental challenges and included measures in order to respond. In this particular plan, for example, the Party was aiming to curb energy and water intensity in the industrial sector. Targets such as a 20 percent reduction in energy consumption per unit of GDP over the five years of the plan, and a 30 percent reduction in water consumption per unit of industrial added value reflected the anxiety that the industrial processes in the PRC were wasteful and that resource use needed to be carried out more efficiently. The concept of efficiency was also aimed at water use in agriculture, where the goal was to increase the coefficient of effective use of water for irrigation from 0.45 percent to 0.5 percent. Reforestation continued to remain a goal, as well as the further reduction of major pollutants. Inefficient coal fired plants were closed during this time in order to quickly make headway in this regard. In the words of the Chinese government,

> The outline [of the 11th FYP] carries out two lines of strategic thinking, namely, the Scientific Concept of Development and building a socialist harmonious society. It spells out national strategic intentions, identifies priorities of the government's agenda and reflects the common will and fundamental interests of the Chinese people.[63]

The objective of this plan was that through its implementation "the 'cake' of the national economy will grow further," while bettering the inhabited environment.[64] Specifically the government underscored that it would "promote development by relying on resource conservation and environmental protection and focus on the fundamental change of the economic growth mode, transforming economic growth from being driven by large amount of resources consumption to being driven by the improvement of resources utilization efficiency."[65]

Of course, targets are easier to set than to achieve. While China has many laws, regulations and plans to achieve specific targets, it has not always been successful in reaching them. Part of the problem has been oversight and the enforcement of laws and regulations for a set of different reasons ranging from bureaucratic inefficiencies to corruption and geographic disparity. The difficulty, however, has also been linked to the country's continued desire to grow and transform. Already in the 11th FYP the government was pushing for the build-up of the service sector as a way of reducing the industrial intensity of growth and allowing for the diversification of the economy. This remains a difficult challenge, although there are indications that the country is moving in this direction.

The 12th FYP[66] (2011–2015) placed a strong emphasis on "higher quality growth." Although millions had been raised out of poverty, it became increasingly clear that it was time to grow more sustainably because of pollution, energy intensity and the growing depletion of resources. In the words of Premier Wen Jiabao in 2011: "We should not only make the cake of social wealth as big as possible, but also distribute the cake in a fair way and let everyone enjoy the fruits of reform and opening up."[67] The 12th FYP (2011–2015) also marked the beginning of a new era in climate action. The country was ready to move from more general pronouncements to a framework of climate change policies that would include concrete instruments leading to emission reductions. From the 12th FYP, the leadership began to view the challenges of the climate crisis as an opportunity to diversify the energy mix to reap energy savings and combat pollution, while also creating new economic opportunities and jobs.

The 13th FYP (2016–2020) which is the current "blueprint" for socioeconomic growth, is the first of the Xi era. It marks China's aspiration to move from an investment and export-led economic model to one that is consumption and service-driven. Beyond that, it also reflects a wider shift demonstrating that China is fully onboard in recognizing the growing threat of the climate crisis and the impacts of long-term environmental degradation. President Xi declared that through the 13th FYP,

> China will work hard to implement the vision of innovative, coordinated, green, open and inclusive development. China will, on the basis of technological and institutional innovation, adopt new policy measures to improve the industrial mix, build a low-carbon energy system, develop green building and low-carbon transportation, and build a nation-wide carbon emission trading market so as to foster a new pattern of modernization featuring harmony between man and nature.[68]

China has come a long way since the days of Mao. Today, the per capita GDP stands at $7,800.[69] Its GDP in 2015 was a remarkable $10.87 trillion—up from $59 billion in 1960, $189.65 billion in 1980 and $1 trillion in 2000 (compared to the US with approximately $17.947 trillion and Europe at $16.229 trillion)[70] according to World Bank data.

An overview of the areas of focus for the 13th FYP include: a nationwide real time online environmental monitoring system and an emission permit system that will cover all companies with stationary pollution sources; a continuation of forest protection, a ban on commercial deforestation and an increase of forested areas; the promotion of new energy vehicles and the improved industrialization of electric cars (expanding the electric vehicle market by constructing dedicated parking lots and charging facilities and removing almost four million high-emission vehicles from roads). In addition it calls for subsidies to automakers, local governments for purchase of green fleets, as well as tax breaks and free registration for consumers. The 13th FYP also encourages: clean production, green and low carbon industry and green finance; an audit system for officials who leave their current posts, taking environmental protection under consideration (officials' efforts to protect natural resources will form part of their performance appraisal); improvements in water management and ground water monitoring and the modernization of agriculture.[71]

The five guiding principles of the 13th FYP are "innovative, coordinated, green, open and shared development." The plan also includes concrete environmental and efficiency targets. For instance, China aims to reduce energy consumption per unit of GDP by 15 percent from 2015 levels by 2020. It will actively seek to move away from coal dependency and further promote renewables. Moreover, China will be increasing the efficiency of coal burning power plants and shutting down coal-fired boilers that fail to meet national standards. In addition, the government has restricted construction of new coal-fired power plants. Furthermore, the 13th FYP sets peak emission and water use targets, increased efficiency and a manufacturing overhaul to tackle overproduction. It also contributes to China's decision to increase the cache of the "Made in China" brand, launching the "Made in China 2025" campaign.[72] It focuses on further increasing green energy production and green infrastructure development.

Perhaps, one of the most important mechanisms for reducing carbon emissions is China's decision to create a national Emission Trading System to be launched in 2017 after a successful carbon market pilot project was set-up and operated with the help of the EU in seven of its regions.[73] For the launch of the national ETS system, China is continuing to cooperate with the EU. After the European Union Emission Trading System (EU ETS), China's carbon market was the second largest of the world (in 2016) when only seven pilot regions had been incorporated. It will be the largest in 2017 once it becomes national. Prices of carbon have fluctuated from 9 yuan per ton in Shanghai to 42 yuan in Beijing.[74] The expected average price for the national ETS scheme will be around 39 yuan. This is a game changer because China is the world's largest carbon emitter. This commitment to the utilization of a market mechanism will help put a price on carbon and therefore can dynamically help scale up climate action through carbon markets. It also incentivizes other countries to implement carbon pricing policies and encourages carbon market cooperation.[75]

With respect to renewables, according to a REN21 report, "wind power was the leading source of *new* power generating capacity in Europe and the United States (US) in 2015, and the second largest in China."[76] Already, China is the global leader in the solar sector.[77] In fact, as of 2015 it boasts the top capacity of power generation from wind as well.[78] In 2015, the total installed wind power capacity in megawatts (MW) for China was 145,362 compared to a total of 147,771 for Europe (of which 141,578 was in the EU–28) and 74,471 for the US.[79] By the same token, its solar capacity at the end of 2015 stood at 43 gigawatts (GW).[80] The new domestic priorities of the PRC's FYPs for the future speak to concerted government intervention in the rare earth industry to build the particular high growth economic sector of renewables and high tech applications.[81] The top markets for renewables in China were Xinjian, Inner Mongolia, and Jiangsu. Eighty-six percent of the capacity came from large-scale power plants and the remainder from distributed rooftop systems and other small-scale installations. The rapid increase in solar PV led to congestion, something that posed a problem in a number of areas because of insufficient grid capacity. As a result, further deployment of renewables became problematic so that the government is now urging top solar-producing provinces to prioritize transmission capacity.[82] Although showing a decline from 2014, China commissioned 16 GW of hydropower projects. By the end of the year its total capacity was 296 GW and it had met the targets set-up in the 12th FYP. The PRC has an additional 23 GW of pumped storage capacity. China continues to pursue large-scale hydro projects and some smaller scale ones in Tibet, although there has been some pushback on certain projects because of ecological considerations.[83]

In conclusion, China came to Paris with a strong desire for an international climate change agreement to be reached. How much of a policy change did China's position in Paris signify? It was a significant departure from its previous stance. Until Paris, China had played a leading role as a member of the 77 group of developing countries that had been reluctant to commit to emission reductions or peak emission dates. China and India, the two most populous countries of the developing world, were worried that capping their emissions early would impede their rapid industrialization process, especially if any commitments were binding. US reluctance to agree to any binding targets in Kyoto and beyond bought both China and India time. However, China came to realize that it could no longer hide behind US obstructionism. It was a rising superpower with a one-party system to protect, an economy to grow, and a large enough middle and upper middle class whose calls for pollution control and a growing appreciation for sustainable development have become a force to contend with.

China has now joined the front ranks in climate action. In fact, as we have seen earlier, Xi recognized China's global leadership role by joining forces with Obama to call on other nations to emulate their commitment. It agreed to share this leadership role with the US in what was considered a masterful stroke of diplomacy. However, Donald Trump's election in November 2016 immediately put into question the US's commitment to the Paris Agreement. The election coincided with COP 22 in Marrakesh where a stunned international community began to wonder about America's next steps. During the campaign, Donald Trump had made a range of statements, even calling climate change a "hoax" perpetrated by the Chinese. Trump, moreover, promised to revitalize the coal industry and to withdraw the US from the Paris Agreement altogether. US financing to United Nations (UN) climate programs and clean energy have already been targeted for budget cuts. Appointments in critical positions such as the Environmental Protection Agency (EPA), the Department of Energy, the UN and the State Department suggested an aggressive denial of climate action.[84]

These developments raised questions about the possibility of global resolve at a particularly critical time. The world looked to China to see if they, at least, were still committed to a process that had produced renewed hope. China did not disappoint. Liu Zhenmin, China's Deputy Minister of Foreign Affairs and lead negotiator at this UN summit meeting in Marrakesh told reporters, "Climate change is not, as rumored, a hoax created by the Chinese." In perhaps an effort to keep the US at the climate table he added that, "If you look at the history of climate change negotiations, it was initiated by the Intergovernmental Panel on Climate Change with the support of Republicans in both the Reagan and Bush administrations in the late '80s and early '90s." Liu expressed the hope that the new Republican administration would continue to support and participate in the climate talks and the process initiated in Paris.[85] He furthermore stated that, "Whatever position the U.S. puts forth, China will continue to support the Paris agreement."[86]

China, therefore, is not prepared to rescind a leadership role in tackling climate change. It does not need to, nor is it alone at the helm. Its natural ally and partner, with which it maintains a strategic partnership, is Europe. Together, they should jointly take the lead, and as we will examine later, by creating a new partnership for the Anthropocene, they have the potential to deliver on the promise of a paradigm shift.

Notes

1 Jinping Xi, "Full Text of President Xi's Speech at Opening Ceremony of Paris Climate Summit – World," Chinadaily, accessed November 1, 2016, http://www.chinadaily.com.cn/world/XiattendsParisclimateconference/2015-12/01/content_22592469.htm.
2 Judith Shapiro, *Mao's War against Nature Politics and the Environment in Revolutionary China* (Cambridge; New York: Cambridge University Press, 2001), 7.
3 Cited in: Roger T. Ames, *The Art of Rulership: A Study in Ancient Chinese Political Thought* (Honolulu: University of Hawaii Press, 1983), 201.
4 Bao Maohong, "Environmentalism and Environmental Movements in China since 1949," in *A Companion to Global Environmental History*, ed. J. R. McNeill and Erin Stewart Uldin (Hoboken, NJ: John Wiley & Sons, Ltd, 2012), 475.
5 John Robert McNeill, *Environmental Histories of the Cold War* (New York: Cambridge University Press, 2010), 21–22.
6 Simon Winchester, *The River at the Center of the World: A Journey Up the Yangtze, and Back in Chinese Time* (London: Viking Press, 1997), 199.
7 Shapiro, *Mao's War against Nature Politics and the Environment in Revolutionary China*, 10.
8 Qu Geping and Li Jinchang, *Population and the Environment in China*, translated by Jiang Baozhong and Gu Ran (Boulder, CO: Lynne Rienner Publishers, 1994), 149.
9 John Wills, *US Environmental History: Inviting Doomsday* (Edinburgh: Edinburgh University Press, 2012), 7.
10 J. R. McNeill and Erin Stewart Mauldin, eds., *A Companion to Global Environmental History*, 1 edition (Chichester, West Sussex; Hoboken, N.J: Wiley-Blackwell, 2012), 476.
11 Bao Maohong, "Environmentalism and Environmental Movements in China since 1949," 480.

12   Bao Maohong, "The Evolution of Environmental Policy and Its Impact in the People's Republic of China," *Conservation and Society* 4, no. 1 (January 1, 2006): 36; McNeill and Mauldin, *A Companion to Global Environmental History*, 480.
13   Elizabeth C. Economy, *The River Runs Black: The Environmental Challenge to China's Future*, 2nd edition (Ithaca, N.Y: Cornell University Press, 2010), 98.
14   "Chinese Delegation Makes Statement on 'Declaration on Human Environment,'" *Peking Review*, no. 25 (June 23, 1972): 8. https://www.marxists.org/subject/china/peking-review/1972/PR1972-25.pdf."China's Ten Cardinal Principles on Amending 'Declaration on Human Environment'," *Peking Review*, no. 25 (June 23, 1972): 9-11. https://www.marxists.org/subject/china/peking-review/1972/PR1972-25.pdf.
15   Economy, *The River Runs Black: The Environmental Challenge to China's Future*, 99.
16   Ezra F. Vogel, "China under Deng Xiaoping's Leadership," *East Asia Forum*, September 27, 2011, http://www.eastasiaforum.org/2011/09/27/china-under-deng-xiaopings-leadership/.
17   Susan Chan Shifflett, "Paradigm Shift in Chinese Environmental Sector Needed, Says Activist Wang Canfa," *New Security Beat*, accessed November 16, 2016, https://www.newsecuritybeat.org/2013/03/paradigm-shift-chinese-environmental-sector-needed-activist-wang-canfa/.
18   Richard Smith, "China's Communist-Capitalist Ecological Apocalypse," *Truthout*, accessed December 18, 2016, http://www.truth-out.org/news/item/31478-china-s-communist-capitalist-ecological-apocalypse?tmpl=component&print=1.
19   "China GDP: How It Has Changed since 1980," *The Guardian*, March 23, 2012, http://www.theguardian.com/news/datablog/2012/mar/23/china-gdp-since-1980.
20   "GDP Growth (Annual %) | Data," accessed December 12, 2016, http://data.worldbank.org/indicator/NY.GDP.MKTP.KD.ZG?locations=CN.
21   "Agenda 21 – China – Institutional Aspects," accessed November 13, 2016, http://www.un.org/esa/agenda21/natlinfo/countr/china/inst.htm.
22   Jonathan S. Watts, *When A Billion Chinese Jump: How China Will Save Mankind – Or Destroy It* (London: Faber and Faber Limited, 2003), 3–4.
23   "Interview with China's Deputy Minister of the Environment: 'The Chinese Miracle Will End Soon,'" *SPIEGEL ONLINE*, accessed December 18, 2016, http://www.spiegel.de/international/spiegel/spiegel-interview-with-china-s-deputy-minister-of-the-environment-the-chinese-miracle-will-end-soon-a-345694.html.
24   Ariana Eunjung Cha, "Solar Energy Firms Leave Waste Behind in China," *The Washington Post*, March 9, 2008, sec. Business, http://www.washingtonpost.com/wp-dyn/content/article/2008/03/08/AR2008030802595.html.
25   Cha, "Solar Energy Firms Leave Waste Behind in China."
26   Cha, "Solar Energy Firms Leave Waste Behind in China."
27   Cha, "Solar Energy Firms Leave Waste Behind in China."
28   "China Names 10 Most Polluted Cities," Chinadaily, accessed December 11, 2016, http://www.chinadaily.com.cn/china/2015-02/02/content_19466412.htm."Cost of Pollution in China: Economic Estimates of Physical Damages" (World Bank, State Environmental Protection, China, 2007), http://siteresources.worldbank.org/INTEAPREGTOPENVIRONMENT/Resources/China_Cost_of_Pollution.pdf; Joseph Kahn and Jim Yardley, "China – Pollution – Environment," *The New York Times*, August 26, 2007, http://www.nytimes.com/2007/08/26/world/asia/26china.html; Katherine Morton, "China and the Global Environment: Learning from the Past, Anticipating the Future – CIAO" (Sydney: Lowy Institute for International Policy, 2009), https://www.ciaonet.org/catalog/31411;"China's Environmental Crisis," *Council on Foreign Relations*, accessed December 11, 2016, http://www.cfr.org/china/chinas-environmental-crisis/p12608; Adam Vaughan, "China Tops WHO List for Deadly Outdoor Air Pollution," *The Guardian*, September 27, 2016, sec. Environment, https://www.theguardian.com/environment/2016/sep/27/more-than-million-died-due-air-pollution-china-one-year.

29 Dimitri Zenghelis and Nicholas Stern, "This Is Humankind's 'Great Urbanisation'. We Must Do It Right, or the Planet Will Pay," *The Guardian*, November 8, 2016, sec. Cities, https://www.theguardian.com/cities/2016/nov/08/mankind-great-urbanisation-era-act-now-planet-pay.

30 Economy, *The River Runs Black: The Environmental Challenge to China's Future*.

31 John Wong, *Zhu Rongji and China's Economic Take-Off*, (Singapore: World Scientific, 2016), 36.

32 Judith Shapiro, *China's Environmental Challenges*, 1st edition (Cambridge, U.K.; Malden, MA: Polity, 2012), 2–10.

33 Craig Simons, *The Devouring Dragon: How China's Rise Threatens Our Natural World* (New York: St. Martin's Press, 2013), 8.

34 Simons, *The Devouring Dragon: How China's Rise Threatens Our Natural World*, 9.

35 Yisheng Zheng, ed., *Chinese Research Perspectives on the Environment, Special Volume: Critical Essays on China's Environment and Development*, trans Liang Fan, Special edition (Leiden; Boston: Brill Academic Pub, 2016), 11. Wang Yi, "China's Sustainable Development in the Shifting Global Context," *Bulletin of the Chinese Academy of Sciences* 26, no. 3 (2012): 183-190, http://english.cas.cn/bcas/2012_3/201411/P020141121531782671178.pdf.

36 Rebecca Nadin, Sarah Opitz-Stapleton, and Xu Yinlong, eds., *Climate Risk and Resilience in China* (London/New York: Routledge, 2015).

37 R. Edward Grumbine, "China at Crossroads: Balancing the Economy and Environment," *Yale Environment 360*, accessed December 10, 2016, http://e360.yale.edu/feature/china_at_crossroads_balancing_the_economy_and_environment/2710/.

38 Grumbine, "China at Crossroads."

39 James West, "China to Shut Down 1,000 Coal Mines This Year," *Grist*, February 23, 2016, http://grist.org/climate-energy/china-to-shut-down-1000-coal-plants-this-year/.

40 Qinhua Xu and William Chung, *China's Energy Policy from National and International Perspectives: The Energy Revolution and One Belt One Road Initiative* (Hong Kong: City University of HK Press, 2016), 94. "China to Halt Construction on Coal-Fired Power Plants in 15 Regions," *Reuters*, March 24, 2016, http://www.reuters.com/article/us-china-power-coal-idUSKCN0WQ0ZD.Angel Hsu Xu Andrew Moffat and Kaiyang, "Making Sense of China's Drop in Coal Use," *Scientific American Blog Network*, accessed December 10, 2016, https://blogs.scientificamerican.com/guest-blog/making-sense-of-china-s-drop-in-coal-use/.While the intention to curb coal usage is there it is not yet clear how effective China has been. See also: Lauri Myllyvirta, "China Keeps Building Coal Plants despite New Overcapacity Policy," *Energydesk*, July 13, 2016, http://energydesk.greenpeace.org/2016/07/13/china-keeps-building-coal-plants-despite-new-overcapacity-policy/.

41 Christina Larson, "A Once-Polluted Chinese City Is Turning from Gray to Green," *Yale Environment 360*, accessed December 10, 2016, http://e360.yale.edu/feature/shenyang_a_once-polluted_china_city_is_turning_from_gray_to_green/2454/.

42 The Urban China Initiative (UCI) is a think tank co-founded by McKinsey & Co., Columbia University, and Beijing's Tsinghua University and has begun to produce an "Urban Sustainability Index" for China.

43 Christina Larson, "A Once-Polluted Chinese City Is Turning from Gray to Green."

44 Jonathan Woetzel, "How Green Are China's Cities?" *McKinsey & Company*, accessed December 10, 2016, http://www.mckinsey.com/business-functions/sustainability-and-resource-productivity/our-insights/how-green-are-chinas-cities.

45 Woetzel, "How Green Are China's Cities?"

46 Woetzel, "How Green Are China's Cities?"

47 China Council for International Cooperation on Environment and Development (CCICED), Annual Policy Report 2007, http://www.cciced.net/cciceden/POLICY/APR/201608/t20160803_74631.html. Shapiro, *Mao's War against Nature Politics and the Environment in Revolutionary China*.

48   English.news.cn, "Xinhua Insight: Xi Leads Nation in Pursuing Chinese Dream in New Year," accessed March 15, 2017, http://news.xinhuanet.com/english/2017-02/06/c_136035945.htm.

49   "China to 'Declare War' on Pollution, Premier Says," *Reuters*, March 5, 2014, http://www.reuters.com/article/us-china-parliament-pollution-idUSBREA2405W 20140305.

50   Climate Action Programme, "Premier of China 'declares War' on Pollution," accessed December 10, 2016, http://climateactionprogramme.org/news/premier_of_china_ declares_war_on_pollution.

51   Energy Research Institute and National Development and Reform Commission, "China-2050-High-Renewable-Energy-Penetration-Scenario-and-Roadmap-Study-Executive-Summary.pdf," April 2015, http://www.efchina.org/Attachments/Report/ report-20150420/China-2050-High-Renewable-Energy-Penetration-Scenario-and-Roadmap-Study-Executive-Summary.pdf.

52   "China to 'Declare War' on Pollution, Premier Says."

53   "China to 'Declare War' on Pollution, Premier Says."

54   Climate Action Programme, "Premier of China 'declares War' on Pollution."

55   Sam Geall and Lulu Ning Hui, "China's Low Carbon Future Offers Global Opportunities," accessed December 10, 2016, http://eciu.net/assets/Reports/china_ low_carbon_opportunities_v5.pdf.

56   The National Development and Reform Commission, "China's Policies and Actions on Climate Change (2015)," November 2015, http://en.ccchina.gov.cn/archiver/ ccchinaen/UpFile/Files/Default/20151120095849657206.pdf.

57   "30 June 2015: COP-21 – China Submits Its 'national contribution' (INDC) to the Future International Climate Agreement – CITEPA," accessed December 10, 2016, http://www.citepa.org/en/news/2060-30-june-2015-cop-21-china-submits-its-national-contribution-indc-to-the-future-international-climate-agreement.

58   "Full Text of President Xi's Speech at Opening Ceremony of Paris Climate Summit – World," Chinadaily, http://www.chinadaily.com.cn/world/XiattendsParis climateconference/2015-12/01/content_22592469.htm.

59   "The 10th Five-Year Plan (2001-2005)," accessed December 10, 2016, http://www. gov.cn/english/2006-04/05/content_245624.htm.

60   "China's Green Revolution: Energy, Environment and the 12th Five-Year Plan (English Edition)," accessed December 10, 2016, http://www.offertelettronica.net/ negozio-di-elettronica/Operation=ItemLookup_ItemId=B004WP3EDE.html.

61   "Report on the Outline of the Tenth Five-Year Plan for National Economic and Social Development (2001)," accessed November 13, 2016, http://www.gov.cn/eng-lish/official/2005-07/29/content_18334.htm.

62   Special Report, The 11th Five Year Plan, http://www.gov.cn/english/special/115y_ index.htm

63   Special Report, The 11th Five Year Plan.

64   Special Report, The 11th Five Year Plan.

65   Special Report, The 11th Five Year Plan.

66   "Interactive Timeline of China's 12–13 Five-Year Plans," accessed December 10, 2016, http://visuals.datadriven.yale.edu/china-five-year-plan/

67   "Premier Wen Targets Causes of Instability, Stresses Fair Treatment of Disadvantaged Groups," accessed November 14, 2016, http://www.gov.cn/english/2011-02/27/con-tent_1812292.htm.

68   "Full Text of President Xi's Speech at Opening Ceremony of Paris Climate Summit – World," Chinadaily, http://www.chinadaily.com.cn/world/XiattendsParis climateconference/2015-12/01/content_22592469.htm.

69   *Xinhua*, "Highlights of Proposals for China's 13th Five-Year Plan," accessed October 1, 2016, http://news.xinhuanet.com/english/photo/2015-11/04/c_134783513.htm.

70 "European Union Data," accessed November 17, 2016, http://data.worldbank.org/region/european-union;"GDP (Current US$) | Data," accessed November 17, 2016, http://data.worldbank.org/indicator/NY.GDP.MKTP.CD?locations=US.
71 *Xinhua.* "Highlights of Proposals for China's 13th Five-Year Plan."
72 "madeinchina2025," accessed November 17, 2016, http://english.gov.cn/2016special/madeinchina2025/.
73 "China and EU Make the Case for Emissions Trading - European Commission," accessed November 17, 2016, http://ec.europa.eu/clima/news/articles/news_2015120501_en.htm.
74 Geall and Hui, "China's Low Carbon Future Offers Global Opportunities."
75 Jeff Swartz, "China's National Emissions Trading System," 2016, http://www.ictsd.org/sites/default/files/research/Chinas_National_ETS_Implications_for_Carbon_Markets_and_Trade_ICTSD_March2016_Jeff_Swartz.pdf.Geall and Hui, "China's Low Carbon Future Offers Global Opportunities."
76 "Renewables 2016, Global Status Report," *Renewable Energy Policy Network for the 21st century (REN21)*, 2016, accessed September 20, 2016, http://www.ren21.net/wp-content/uploads/2016/06/GSR_2016_Full_Report.pdf.
77 "China Announces Green Targets," *UPI*, accessed October 1, 2016, http://www.upi.com/Business_News/Energy-Industry/2011/03/07/China-announces-green-targets/33531299517620/.
78 "Renewables 2016, Global Status Report."
79 "Global-Installed-Wind-Power-Capacity-MW—Regional-Distribution.jpg (2094 × 3175)," accessed October 6, 2016, http://www.gwec.net/wp-content/uploads/2012/06/Global-Installed-Wind-Power-Capacity-MW-%E2%80%93-Regional-Distribution.jpg.
80 Adam Rose, "China's Solar Capacity Overtakes Germany in 2015, Industry Data Show," *Reuters*, January 21, 2016, http://www.reuters.com/article/china-solar-idUSL3N15533U.
81 Jost Wubbeke, "Rare Earth Elements in China: Policies and Narratives of Reinventing an Industry," *Resources Policy* 28 (2013): 384–394.
82 "Renewables 2016: Global Status Report" (REN21), accessed October 1, 2016, http://www.ren21.net/wp-content/uploads/2016/06/GSR_2016_Full_Report.pdf.
83 "Renewables 2016: Global Status Report"; International Hydropower Association "China," accessed November 17, 2016, https://www.hydropower.org/country-pro-files/china;Adam Dean, "China May Shelve Plans to Build Dams on Its Last Wild River," *National Geographic News*, May 12, 2016, http://news.nationalgeographic.com/2016/05/160512-china-nu-river-dams-environment/.
84 John Vidal and Oliver Milman, "Paris Climate Deal Thrown into Uncertainty by US Election Result," *The Guardian*, November 9, 2016, sec. Environment, https://www.theguardian.com/environment/2016/nov/09/us-election-result-throws-paris-climate-deal-into-uncertainty.
85 Maggie Haberman, J. David Goodman, Coral Davenport, and Michael D. Shear, "Ivanka Trump and Jared Kushner Will Not Seek Security Clearances, Sources Say," *The New York Times*, November 16, 2016, http://www.nytimes.com/2016/11/16/us/politics/donald-trump-transition.html.
86 Haberman, "Ivanka Trump and Jared Kushner Will Not Seek Security Clearances, Sources Say."

Bibliography

Ames, Roger T. *The Art of Rulership.* Honolulu: University of Hawaii Press, 1983.
Blanchard, Ben, and David Stanway. "China to 'Declare War' on Pollution, Premier Says." *Reuters*, March 5, 2014. http://www.reuters.com/article/us-china-parliament-pollution-idUSBREA2405W20140305.

Cha, Ariana Eunjung. "Solar Energy Firms Leave Waste Behind in China." *The Washington Post*, March 9, 2008, sec. Business. http://www.washingtonpost.com/wp-dyn/content/article/2008/03/08/AR2008030802595.html.

Chan Shifflett, Susan. "Paradigm Shift in Chinese Environmental Sector Needed, Says Activist Wang Canfa." *New Security Beat*. Accessed November 16, 2016. https://www.newsecuritybeat.org/2013/03/paradigm-shift-chinese-environmental-sector-needed-activist-wang-canfa/.

Chen, Kathy, and David Stanway. "China to Halt Construction on Coal-Fired Power Plants in 15 Regions." *Reuters*, March 24, 2016. http://www.reuters.com/article/us-china-power-coal-idUSKCN0WQ0ZD.

China Council for International Cooperation on Environment and Development (CCICED). Annual Policy Report 2007. http://www.cciced.net/cciceden/POLICY/APR/201608/t20160803_74631.html.

Chinadaily. "China Names 10 Most Polluted Cities." Chinadaily. Accessed December 11, 2016. http://www.chinadaily.com.cn/china/2015-02/02/content_19466412.htm.

"China's Ten Cardinal Principles on Amending 'Declaration on Human Environment.'" Peking Review, no. 25 (June 23, 1972): 9-11. https://www.marxists.org/subject/china/peking-review/1972/PR1972-25.pdf.

"Chinese Delegation Makes Statement on 'Declaration on Human Environment.'" *Peking Review*, no. 25 (June 23, 1972). https://www.marxists.org/subject/china/peking-review/1972/PR1972-25.pdf.

CITEPA "30 June 2015: COP-21 – China Submits Its 'national contribution' (INDC) to the Future International Climate Agreement." Accessed December 10, 2016. http://www.citepa.org/en/news/2060-30-june-2015-cop-21-china-submits-its-national-contribution-indc-to-the-future-international-climate-agreement.

Climate Action. "Premier of China 'Declares War' on Pollution." Accessed December 10, 2016. http://climateactionprogramme.org/news/premier_of_china_declares_war_on_pollution.

Council on Foreign Relations. "China's Environmental Crisis." Accessed December 11, 2016. http://www.cfr.org/china/chinas-environmental-crisis/p12608.

Datablog. "China GDP: How It Has Changed since 1980." *The Guardian*, March 23, 2012. http://www.theguardian.com/news/datablog/2012/mar/23/china-gdp-since-1980.

Dean, Adam. "China May Shelve Plans to Build Dams on Its Last Wild River." *National Geographic News*, May 12, 2016. http://news.nationalgeographic.com/2016/05/160512-china-nu-river-dams-environment/.

Haberman, Maggie, J. David Goodman, Coral Davenport, and Michael D. Shear. "Ivanka Trump and Jared Kushner Will Not Seek Security Clearances, Sources Say." *The New York Times*, November 16, 2016. http://www.nytimes.com/2016/11/16/us/politics/donald-trump-transition.html.

Economy, Elizabeth C. *The River Runs Black: The Environmental Challenge to China's Future*. 2nd edition. Ithaca, N.Y: Cornell University Press, 2010.

Energy Research Institute, and National Development and Reform Commission. "China-2050-High-Renewable-Energy-Penetration-Scenario-and-Roadmap-Study-Executive-Summary.pdf," April 2015. http://www.efchina.org/Attachments/Report/report-20150420/China-2050-High-Renewable-Energy-Penetration-Scenario-and-Roadmap-Study-Executive-Summary.pdf.

European Commission. "China and EU Make the Case for Emissions Trading." Accessed November 17, 2016. http://ec.europa.eu/clima/news/articles/news_2015120501_en.htm.

Geall Sam and Lulu Ning Hui. "China's Low Carbon Future Offers Global Opportunities." Accessed December 10, 2016. http://eciu.net/assets/Reports/china_low_carbon_opportunities_v5.pdf.

Geping, Qu and Lin Jinchange. *Population and the Environment in China*, translated by Jian Baozhong and Gu Ran. Boulder, CO: Lynne Reinner Publishers, 1994.

Grumbine, R. Edward. "China at Crossroads: Balancing The Economy and Environment." *Yale Environment 360*. Accessed December 10, 2016. http://e360.yale.edu/feature/china_at_crossroads_balancing_the_economy_and_environment/2710/.

GWEC. "Global-Installed-Wind-Power-Capacity-MW—Regional-Distribution.jpg (2094 × 3175)." Accessed October 6, 2016. http://www.gwec.net/wp-content/uploads/2012/06/Global-Installed-Wind-Power-Capacity-MW-%E2%80%93-Regional-Distribution.jpg.

Hsu, Angel, Andrew Moffat, and Kaiyang Xu. "Making Sense of China's Drop in Coal Use." *Scientific American Blog Network*. Accessed December 10, 2016. https://blogs.scientificamerican.com/guest-blog/making-sense-of-china-s-drop-in-coal-use/.

Environmental Performance Index. "Interactive Timeline of China's 12-13 Five-Year Plans." Accessed December 10, 2016. http://visuals.datadriven.yale.edu/china-five-year-plan/.

Gov.cn. "Premier Wen Targets Causes of Instability, Stresses Fair Treatment of Disadvantaged Groups." Accessed November 14, 2016. http://www.gov.cn/english/2011-02/27/content_1812292.htm.

Gov.cn. "The 10th Five-Year Plan (2001-2005)." Accessed December 10, 2016. http://www.gov.cn/english/2006-04/05/content_245624.htm.

International Hydropower Association. "China." Accessed November 17, 2016. https://www.hydropower.org/country-profiles/china.

Kahn, Joseph and Jim Yardley. "China – Pollution – Environment." *The New York Times*, August 26, 2007. http://www.nytimes.com/2007/08/26/world/asia/26china.html.

Larson, Christine. "A Once-Polluted Chinese City Is Turning from Gray to Green." *Yale Environment 360*. Accessed December 10, 2016. http://e360.yale.edu/feature/shenyang_a_once-polluted_china_city_is_turning_from_gray_to_green/2454/. Lorenz, Andreas (trans. Patrick Kessler). "Interview with China's Deputy Minister of the Environment: 'The Chinese Miracle Will End Soon.'" *SPIEGEL ONLINE*. Accessed December 18, 2016. http://www.spiegel.de/international/spiegel/spiegel-interview-with-china-s-deputy-minister-of-the-environment-the-chinese-miracle-will-end-soon-a-345694.html.

McNeill, John Robert. *Environmental Histories of the Cold War*. New York: Cambridge University Press, 2010.

McNeill, J. R. and Erin Stewart Mauldin, eds. *A Companion to Global Environmental History*. 1st edition. Chichester, West Sussex/Hoboken, N.J: Wiley-Blackwell, 2012.

Maohong, Bao. "The Evolution of Environmental Policy and Its Impact in the People's Republic of China." *Conservation and Society* 4, no. 1 (January 1, 2006): 36.

Maohong, Bao. "Environmentalism and Environmental Movements in China since 1949." In *A Companion to Global Environmental History*. Edited by J. R. McNeill and Erin Stewart Mauldin. Hoboken, NJ: John Wiley & Sons, Ltd, 2012, pp. 474–92. http://onlinelibrary.wiley.com/doi/10.1002/9781118279519.ch26/summary.

Morton, Katherine. "China and the Global Environment: Learning from the Past, Anticipating the Future – CIAO." Sydney: Lowy Institute for International Policy, 2009. https://www.ciaonet.org/catalog/31411.

Myllyvirta, Lauri. "China Keeps Building Coal Plants despite New Overcapacity Policy." *Energydesk*, July 13, 2016. http://energydesk.greenpeace.org/2016/07/13/china-keeps-building-coal-plants-despite-new-overcapacity-policy/.

Nadin, Rebecca, Sarah Opitz-Stapleton and Xu Yinlong, eds. *Climate Risk and Resilience in China*. London New York: Routledge, 2015.

The National Development and Reform Commission. "China's Policies and Actions on Climate Change (2015)," November 2015. http://en.ccchina.gov.cn/archiver/ccchinaen/UpFile/Files/Default/20151120095849657206.pdf.

Offerte Elettronica. *"China's Green Revolution: Energy, Environment and the 12th Five-Year Plan (English Edition)."* Accessed December 10, 2016. http://www.offertelettronica.net/negozio-di-elettronica/Operation=ItemLookup_ItemId=B004WP3EDE.html.

REN21. "Renewables 2016: Global Status Report." Accessed October 1, 2016. http://www.ren21.net/wp-content/uploads/2016/06/GSR_2016_Full_Report.pdf.

Rongji, Zhu. "Report on the Outline of the Tenth Five-Year Plan for National Economic and Social Development (2001)." Accessed November 13, 2016. http://www.gov.cn/english/official/2005-07/29/content_18334.htm.

Rose, Adam. "China's Solar Capacity Overtakes Germany in 2015, Industry Data Show." *Reuters*, January 21, 2016. http://www.reuters.com/article/china-solar-idUSL3N15533U.

Shapiro, Judith. *Mao's War against Nature Politics and the Environment in Revolutionary China*. Cambridge; New York: Cambridge University Press, 2001.

Shapiro, Judith. *China's Environmental Challenges*. 1st edition. Cambridge, U.K. ; Malden, MA: Polity, 2012.

Simons, Craig. *The Devouring Dragon: How China's Rise Threatens Our Natural World*. New York: St. Martin's Press, 2013.

Smith, Richard. "China's Communist-Capitalist Ecological Apocalypse." *Truthout*. Accessed December 18, 2016. http://www.truth-out.org/news/item/31478-china-s-communist-capitalist-ecological-apocalypse?tmpl=component&print=1.

The State Council, the People's Republic of China. "madeinchina2025." Accessed November 17, 2016. http://english.gov.cn/2016special/madeinchina2025.

Swartz, Jeff. "China's National Emissions Trading System," 2016. http://www.ictsd.org/sites/default/files/research/Chinas_National_ETS_Implications_for_Carbon_Markets_and_Trade_ICTSD_March2016_Jeff_Swartz.pdf.

United Nations. "Agenda 21 – China –Institutional Aspects." Accessed November 13, 2016. http://www.un.org/esa/agenda21/natlinfo/countr/china/inst.htm.

UPI. "China Announces Green Targets." UPI. Accessed October 1, 2016. http://www.upi.com/Business_News/Energy-Industry/2011/03/07/China-announces-green-targets/33531299517620/.

Vaughan, Adam. "China Tops WHO List for Deadly Outdoor Air Pollution." *The Guardian*, September 27, 2016, sec. Environment. https://www.theguardian.com/environment/2016/sep/27/more-than-million-died-due-air-pollution-china-one-year.

Vidal, John, and Oliver Milman. "Paris Climate Deal Thrown into Uncertainty by US Election Result." *The Guardian*, November 9, 2016, sec. Environment. https://www.theguardian.com/environment/2016/nov/09/us-election-result-throws-paris-climate-deal-into-uncertainty.

Vogel, Ezra F. "China under Deng Xiaoping's Leadership." *East Asia Forum*, September 27, 2011. http://www.eastasiaforum.org/2011/09/27/china-under-deng-xiaopings-leadership/.

Wang Yi. "China's Sustainable Development in the Shifting Global Context." *Bulletin of the Chinese Academy of Sciences* 26, no. 3 (2012). http://english.cas.cn/bcas/2012_3/201411/P020141121531782671178.pdf.

Watts, Jonathan S. *When A Billion Chinese Jump: How China Will Save Mankind -- Or Destroy It*. Faber and Faber Limited, 2003.

West, James. "China to Shut Down 1,000 Coal Mines This Year." *Grist*, February 23, 2016. http://grist.org/climate-energy/china-to-shut-down-1000-coal-plants-this-year/.

Wills, John. *US Environmental History: Inviting Doomsday*. Edinburgh: Edinburgh University Press, 2012.

Winchester, Simon. *The River at the Center of the World: A Journey Up the Yangtze, and Back in Chinese Time*. Viking Press, 1997.

Woetzel, Jonathan. "How Green Are China's Cities? | McKinsey & Company." Accessed December 10, 2016. http://www.mckinsey.com/business-functions/sustainability-and-resource-productivity/our-insights/how-green-are-chinas-cities.

Wong, John. *Zhu Rongji and China's Economic Take-Off*. Singapore: World Scientific, 2016.

World Bank. "European Union Data." Accessed November 17, 2016. http://data.worldbank.org/region/european-union.

World Bank. "GDP (Current US$) Data." Accessed November 17, 2016. http://data.worldbank.org/indicator/NY.GDP.MKTP.CD?locations=US.

World Bank. "GDP Growth (Annual %) | Data." Accessed December 12, 2016.http://data.worldbank.org/indicator/NY.GDP.MKTP.KD.ZG?locations=CN.

World Bank, State Environmental Protection, China, 2007. "Cost of Pollution in China: Economic Estimates of Physical Damages." http://siteresources.worldbank.org/INTEAPREGTOPENVIRONMENT/Resources/China_Cost_of_Pollution.pdf.

Wubbeke, Jost. "Rare Earth Elements in China: Policies and Narratives of Reinventing an Industry," *Resources Policy* 28 (2013): 384-394.

Xi, Jinping. "Full Text of President Xi's Speech at Opening Ceremony of Paris Climate Summit – World". Chinadaily. Accessed November 1, 2016. http://www.chinadaily.com.cn/world/XiattendsParisclimateconference/2015-12/01/content_22592469.htm.

Xinhua. "Highlights of Proposals for China's 13th Five-Year Plan." Accessed October 1, 2016. http://news.xinhuanet.com/english/photo/2015-11/04/c_134783513.htm.

Xu, Qinhua, and William Chung. *China's Energy Policy from National and International Perspectives: The Energy Revolution and One Belt One Road Initiative*. Hong Kong: City University of HK Press, 2016.

Zenghelis, Dimitri, and Nicholas Stern. "This Is Humankind's 'Great Urbanisation'. We Must Do It Right, or the Planet Will Pay." *The Guardian*, November 8, 2016, sec. Cities. https://www.theguardian.com/cities/2016/nov/08/mankind-great-urbanisation-era-act-now-planet-pay.

Zheng, Yisheng, ed. *Chinese Research Perspectives on the Environment, Special Volume: Critical Essays on China's Environment and Development*. Translated by Liang Fan. Special edition. Leiden; Boston: Brill Academic Pub, 2016.

4 US–China

Rivalry trumps partnership in the Anthropocene

As China grows in influence and power around the globe, nations that have thus far shaped the way the world works wonder what kind of superpower China will become. How will it use its influence? This is an especially strong pre-occupation for the United States (US). More than other nations in the world, the US has been the driving force behind the formulation of theories of international relations, especially as they crystallized after the Second World War. The stakes, therefore, for the maintenance of super power status are the highest for the US, because it has dominated world affairs, spreading its values and practices of liberal democracy and free trade around the globe.

Because US dominance has contributed to the country's prosperity and influence, it has garnered the necessary bipartisan support in Washington, D.C. At the same time, however, it has saddled the US with the burden of acting in the capacity of "world policeman". Increasingly, other industrial actors are being asked by the US to take on more responsibility and share some of this burden. This would allow the US to more effectively compete and lead in areas which it identifies with its more important core interests. The request for burden sharing does not imply that the US is ready to relinquish its hegemony. It is seeking, however, to recalibrate its strategic focus toward the Asia–Pacific region where it perceives the geopolitical balance rapidly shifting. China is at the center of US strategic thinking and planning[1] because its rise poses economic and political challenges to US hegemony. Viewing its role as vital to regional stability, the US has decided to actively bolster its presence in the Asia–Pacific region, to focus on existing alliances and broaden networks of cooperation in the pursuit of common interests.[2]

In order to assess the realistic possibilities of Sino–US leadership on climate and the Anthropocene, it is necessary to first examine the strategic considerations shaping US foreign and security policies in the Asia–Pacific region, how they impact China's rise and the PRC's response in turn. In 2009, the Obama administration called for a "return to Asia." Building on many of the previous administration's initiatives—such as the US–China Strategic Economic Dialogue (SED)—[3]it combined them with a number of innovative and proactive policies in the region. It signed the ASEAN Treaty of Amity and Cooperation and joined the East Asia Summit, for instance. The Obama administration referred to the twenty-first century as America's Pacific Century and the President himself described the US as "a Pacific power,"[4] intent to play both a larger and a more long-term role in shaping the Asia–Pacific region's future. Undoubtedly, the rapid growth of the Asian economies contributed to their elevation in the list of important US interests. Following the Bush years, which had predominantly focused on the "war on terror," the Obama administration sought to rebalance the US global footprint by focusing on the Asia–Pacific region and extricating itself from the Middle East. This pronounced shift in policy appears to have been influenced by President Obama's own worldview. Bogged down in the Middle East where problems continually flared up, the President sought a new, more hopeful focus, an opportunity to build anew in an Asia that appeared full of potential. He looked for an opportunity to move forward with dynamism and optimism. As the US became less reliant on oil imports and the problems in the Middle East grew more intractable and violent, Obama turned to other nations with both the capabilities and interests in the region, reminding them of their obligation to pitch in, show commitment and decisiveness, share—if not take on—responsibility in that turbulent part of the world. His outlook and policy drew much criticism especially regarding his unwillingness to intervene in Syria and his eagerness to "quickly" normalize relations with Iran—decisions that caused unease among "traditional" regional US allies.[5]

The major policy shift began in 2011, when the US outlined what became known as the "strategic pivot" toward Asia. In November 2011,[6] Hillary Clinton, then Secretary of State, in a speech entitled "America's Pacific Century," highlighted the nature of the administration's renewed embrace of the Asia–Pacific region. The tone of the announcement, although upbeat, clearly indicated what the US considered as its role "shaping the architecture of the Pacific" in the twenty-first century. Clearly, this shift toward Asia was not only a transfer of resources or a mere exercise of US policy being smarter and more systematic. Rather, it was an unequivocal declaration of the US intention to sustain its global leadership position, secure its interests and advance its values.

> It is becoming increasingly clear that in the 21st century, the world's strategic and economic center of gravity will be the Asia Pacific … And one of the most important tasks of American statecraft over the next decades will be to lock in a substantially increased investment – diplomatic, economic, strategic, and otherwise – in this region … And just as the US played a central role in shaping that architecture across the Atlantic – to ensure that it worked, for us and for everyone else – we are now doing the same across the Pacific. The 21st century will be America's Pacific century.

In that same speech, Clinton went on to single out the US relationship with China, characterizing it as "most complex and consequential." It indicated that while the US would promote active engagement with the PRC on numerous fronts, it was not taking China's rise in stride. Rather, it sought to actively frame and direct its ascent in a way that would be "constructive", non-threatening, and even complimentary to the US worldview. She took both the time to extoll the administration's increased efforts in working with China and enumerated the areas in which cooperation was proving fruitful; she also underscored their differences, however, with a biting critique of the PRC's human rights record and asked for both respect of international law and a more open political system.

A few months later in its January 2012 report, the US Department of Defense stressed America's interest in strengthening its bilateral ties with China, but simultaneously underlined that "the growth of China's military power must be accompanied by greater clarity of its strategic intentions in order to avoid causing friction in the region."[7] Furthermore, the report indicated the US intention to

> make the necessary investments to ensure that we [the US] maintain regional access and the ability to operate freely in keeping with our treaty obligations and with international law. Working closely with our network of allies and partners, we [the US] will continue to promote a rules-based international order that ensures underlying stability and encourages the peaceful rise of new powers, economic dynamism, and constructive defense cooperation.[8]

Although the US has framed its efforts as part of its agenda to deepen multilateral cooperation, it is not surprising that in the eyes of Chinese leaders, this might suggest an attempt to continue dominating the global order. A number of Chinese scholars have argued that the US presence in the Asia–Pacific region tempts third parties to feel more comfortable in challenging the regional giant.[9] Furthermore, by setting the stage and drawing China into prescribed notions of power relations, the US may in fact be aiming at locking China into binding commitments that may or may not fit its own perceived national interests. Their view attempts to burden China with additional "costs, risks and commitments" within the framework of "China responsibility theory"[10] as a way of limiting its options or even overextending its involvement beyond what the PRC considers its current limit. Some Chinese scholars, moreover, consider the US and China as having significant differences in the guiding principles on which the international system is currently built. Furthermore, in this line of thought, "Sino-American interaction in the international system features duality, with both cooperation and competition."[11]

Some analysts, scholars and politicians, particularly in the US, seek to downplay the competitive nature of the relationship. They argue that the US aspires to avoid the patterns of the past when the trajectory for a rising power was the inevitable clash with other established powers. They tout the emergence of a new model of cooperation and subscribe to the new model of major power relations, echoing the concept put forth by President Xi Jinping himself. Others claim that the US is gradually exhibiting a preference for multipolarity in response to a changing world. They point to US encouragement of rising powers to become increasingly engaged in international institutions and to adhere to the rule of law, while sharing the overall burden of stability, security and prosperity in pursuit of mutually beneficial cooperation. As Joseph Nye points out, new global challenges pose numerous constraints, transforming the current agenda of world politics into a "three-dimensional chess game in which one can win only by playing vertically as well as horizontally."[12] A turn to multipolarity, therefore, constitutes an attempt to avoid falling into the "Thucydidean Trap." The emerging "Responsibility Doctrine,"[13] as it is often called in the policy literature and as pursued by the Obama administration, supports the view that emerging powers have an "obligatory" duty to become stewards in the new global order, having benefitted from the existing status quo. Today emerging powers contribute to larger global problems to which they too need to respond, using their significant capabilities. There are still others who argue that perhaps even the theories that inform the current system of international relations aggravate the rivalry and subsequent tensions[14] between established and rising powers.

These views all hold partial truths, especially given the rise of new powers in the global system. Yet it is the US that continues to consistently view the world in strategic terms, still heavily involved in its architecture and invested in its operation.[15] While this is true, the US has historically also exhibited ambivalence about its appetite for engagement. As Henry Kissinger points out: "No nation has been more pragmatic in the day-to-day conduct of its diplomacy, or more ideological in the pursuit of its historic moral convictions. No country has been more reluctant to engage itself abroad even while undertaking alliances and commitments of unprecedented reach and scope."[16] Today, this ambivalence seems to be growing in the view of many analysts who describe it as new isolationism or retrenchment. The US presidential election of 2016 brought this ambivalence very much to the fore through the mixed messages candidates sent to nations across the globe about what US "leadership" might look like in the coming decades. In other words, while the US seeks to funnel China's rise through a lens that reflects its own vision of the world, it struggles with increasing volatility in its own perceptions of what US leadership will entail moving into the future.

This internal debate has been interpreted by many both within and outside the US as a sign of US decline. In the widely held view expressed by Yuan Peng of the Chinese Institutes for Contemporary International Relations, the Chinese see the current system as undergoing its "fourth historical transformation."[17] The first three were: the Westphalian system of 1648, the Versailles–Washington system of 1918 (a result the First World War) and the post-Second World War Yalta system of 1945. Today's fourth transformation is a result of the rise of new powers like China and the other BRICs. However, as he points out, it is not just because new powers are rising that the system is changing. It is also because the power players of the twentieth century are in the twenty-first century faced with a new set of political and economic challenges. Non-state actors, which range from NGOs to terrorist networks, are increasingly making an impact in international affairs. New challenges of a global nature are also transforming the discourse and the priorities of the world community, with climate change topping the list, but also demographic changes, energy issues and resource competition.

From the Chinese perspective, a possible US "decline" gives way to new perceived challenges. First there is a danger of a chaotic non-polar system emerging as the alternative. Second, as China rises, there might be inevitable friction between the PRC and the US. Most important, however, is China's own hesitation in light of these changes and its own newfound importance that contributes to the uncertainty.

> China itself has not yet made adequate psychological and strategic preparations for changes in the international system. This is because China's total GDP is the second largest worldwide, but its per capita GDP is 88th in the world; China's economic influence in the world is expanding, while its military, political, and cultural influence is still quite limited … China has become the first poor country with the title of second largest power in the world. It has become a reluctant No. 2.[18]

Perhaps an insistence on showing one's cards, being fully transparent about leadership goals *vis-à-vis* the workings of the international system, and having preconceived notions about the required areas in which an emerging power must be active, leads the US to label China as a "selective stakeholder,"[19] feeding China's suspicions and increasing its discomfort. In the words of Hillary Clinton, speaking at the US Institute of Peace China Conference, in celebration of the 40-year anniversary of President Nixon's trip to China in 1972,

> the U.S.-China project of 2012 is something altogether different; indeed, it is unprecedented in the history of nations. The United States is attempting to work with a rising power to foster its rise … we are trying to do this without entering into unhealthy competition, rivalry, or conflict; … We are, together, building a model in which we strike a stable and mutually acceptable balance between cooperation and competition … And this is where China has its own choices to make. Its power, wealth, and influence have pushed it rapidly to a new echelon in the international order … the world is looking for China to play a role that is commensurate with its new standing. And that means it can no longer be a selective stakeholder.[20]

To the ears of non-US actors, these types of policy speeches sound extremely prescriptive, if not heavy handed. They offer a set menu of scripted choices for what engagement in international affairs should entail, and they insist on a predetermined playbook for actors to follow if their intentions and goals are to be understood by others. It is no wonder that those on the receiving end of these recommendations seek to proactively strengthen themselves and bolster their defenses and outreach in order to ensure their preparedness, respond to challenges or offer another way forward that does not subscribe to the US vision of the world.

Though the rest of the world looks upon China with interest and degrees of apprehension, internally the Chinese government is exploring its options and developing the narrative of its new status. Initially, after Deng Xiaoping assumed leadership, China's main position was one of peaceful relations with other powers because its main focus had been on its own internal development. It sought cooperation and help from the West and other more advanced neighboring powers in Asia to help its modernization efforts. Today, China is seeking to balance different goals and priorities under rapidly changing circumstances at home and abroad. Under the leadership of President Xi Jinping, China is gradually moving out of a more passive role into one that is more active because its national interests are increasingly becoming intertwined with those of the international community.

While the main red lines of foreign policy pertaining to Taiwan, the South China Sea and the Diaoyu Islands (or Senkaku, according to the Japanese) have not changed, China is also seeking to present its credentials to the outside world to showcase its successes and new found strength. The splendor of the 2008 Beijing Olympics was a visible testimony to China's renaissance. Its sixtieth-anniversary in 2009[21] celebrated its nationhood in the modern era with patriotic and military displays, while the Shanghai expo in 2010 underscored its economic might. Yet China is also making its influence felt through the use of soft power diplomacy tools and development aid; its economic strength is being exerted through trade, investment and initiatives such as the new development bank and the revival of the Silk Road. As China considers its path forward, its historical understanding of power relations and its newfound understanding of its growing superpower status are inflecting its efforts to produce a more coherent world view with Chinese characteristics. As it does so, it relies on a strategic culture of prudence and patience, always taking the long view, showing measured assertiveness and tempered reaction.

Because of its geography, China through most of its history hadn't felt pressured to deal with other countries that could compare to it in scale and sophistication. It did not embark on naval expeditions, or a search for conquest and new markets, not because it lacked the sophistication and the technological advancement to do so, but because of its worldview. Its territorial claims stopped at the water's edge.[22] This kind of isolation led to China's developing a view of itself as being unique. China was not just another great world civilization, but the center of civilization itself. That is not to say that China was oblivious to the fact that there were other neighboring nations such as Korea, Vietnam, Thailand, and Burma. But those countries' importance was measured on a scale of how they compared to China. China was the standard by which it assessed others' importance. Henry Kissinger summarizes the Chinese experience as follows,

> China … was never engaged in sustained contact with another country on the basis of equality for the simple reason that it never encountered societies of comparable culture or magnitude. That the Chinese Empire should tower over its geographical sphere was taken virtually as a law of nature, an expression of the Mandate of Heaven. For Chinese Emperors, the mandate did not necessarily imply an adversarial relationship with neighboring peoples; preferably it did not. Like the United States, China thought of itself as playing a special role. But it never espoused the American notion of universalism to spread its values around the world. It confined itself to controlling the barbarians immediately at its doorstep. It strove for tributary states like Korea

to recognize China's special status, and in return, it conferred benefits such as trading rights.[23]

In contrast to China's historical experience, Europe during the sixteenth and seventeenth centuries developed concepts of competitive international relationships. The way the world looked to the European states at the time was very different. The continent was mostly divided into small states and their strength was nearly equal. They needed to find a way to balance the power system. A form of diplomacy emerged hand in hand with sovereignty and with the legal equality of states forming the basis of international law and diplomacy. The "state" construct spread throughout the world through colonization. At the end of this period and with decolonization, the colonial borders previously drawn largely remained the same, and political authority transferred to the new nation's capital. The recognition of sovereign status was conferred by the new state's participation in the United Nations.

To this systemic approach to international relations borne from a different historical experience, China is slowly but surely forming its own counterproposition to world affairs. No longer as passive, it now has shifted its emphasis to offer a diplomacy that is active and, by its own description, intends to provide guidance toward a global "community of shared destiny." Xi's style of diplomacy moves "beyond the constraints of Western international relations theory." This description alone sends a clear signal that perhaps China's intention is to offer an alternative framework to the one state actors use to deal with each other on a global scale. As a counter to these frameworks, China seems to be offering a more nuanced approach which builds on its cultural tradition to pursue "peace and cooperation with neighboring countries."[24]

Xi's diplomacy suggests "Chinese solutions" to global problems by building mutual trust with other countries and winning their respect for the PRC. Its "One Belt One Road" initiatives aim to revitalize the old trade route and establish a twenty-first Century Maritime Silk Road that represents the "concentrated embodiment of China's equality, mutual benefit and win-win diplomatic philosophy."[25] In his 2014 visit to Brazil commemorating 40 years of relations, President Xi publicly hailed the relationship between the two BRICS nations as a manifestation of a "community of shared destiny."[26] In April 2015, Beijing held the first Lancang–Mekong River Dialogue and Cooperation meeting with Thailand, Cambodia, Laos, Burma and Vietnam themed "Six countries, one community of shared destiny: build Lancang–Mekong River Dialogue and Cooperation Mechanism to promote regional sustainable development."[27] President Xi has visited over 50 countries since he came to office.[28] He has repeatedly spoken of a new Chinese dream, which is a call for rejuvenation and a renewal of the Chinese nation. These words resonate with the Chinese because they indicate the end to what China considers the years of National Humiliation that began in the mid-nineteenth century as the empire's strength rapidly declined and was overrun by the great powers of the day.

The shift in policy received its official stamp of approval during a foreign affairs meeting that took place in November 2014. It was the first such meeting after an eight-year hiatus and was attended by high-ranking Party leaders who gathered to introduce and announce significant policy changes regarding China's relations with the world. Signaling a departure from Deng Xiaoping's legacy, Xi focused on making his first priority relations with countries around China, offering more initiatives and a renewed vision for enhancing regional cooperation. According to Yan Xuetong, the Dean of the Institute of Modern International Relations at Tsinghua University, the new Chinese president is determined to gain the international respect that the PRC now feels it deserves as he seeks to rejuvenate the nation. While China sought to deal primarily with the biggest economies, now it is turning its attention to those smaller than itself because it is now the second largest economy in the world[29]. The shift signals an understanding that the time is now ripe for more of an economic give and take so that China can continue to develop its economy, but in a more equitable fashion while addressing its partners' needs as well.

Nonetheless, with the passage of time, China will also find itself faced with new challenges that are part of the price to be paid for its rise. In a 2011 paper published in *East Asia*, Yinhong Shi, outlines some of the most critical challenges the PRC will need to respond to:

> the changing shape of modernity regarded by the universalistic and demanding West (and, it should be added, increasingly by the Chinese ourselves); Persistent calls for "self-determination" by those who are hostile to China's present political system and national unification as well as territorial integration; Leadership's ability to inspire the Chinese society that has become more pluralist; Requirement for a new body of ethics for the contemporary China and the difficulty in developing it; Popular and conservative nationalism and its possible echoes in the political high echelon. However, the most basic challenge will still be China's huge magnitude in size and population: perhaps the greatest constant for China's domestic tasks, her position in the world, and her foreign policy situation.[30]

The transition of power to Xi Jinping, moreover, ushered in a new period of dynamism and action. The new Chairman's agenda focuses on reforms, especially in the economy, as he seeks ways to maintain high growth rates and stimulate internal consumption. He is also targeting rampant corruption and sending a message that he is responding to public discontent on this issue. Thousands of Communist Party officials have been charged. Xi, however, has not extended the same reforms with regards to human rights and greater political freedoms. Internally, he seeks control and has been accused of increasingly stifling conversation and dissent while seeking to consolidate power around him.

On May 15, 2016, the *Wall Street Journal* ran an article comparing some of his tactics to Mao's Cultural Revolution, describing Xi as "borrowing [Mao's] rhetoric and aping his practices."[31] Furthermore, Xi's anticorruption campaign, while popular among citizens, is also seen as an attempt to settle scores within the Party. The Panama papers have fueled internal fires because they showed that many relatives of past and current Party members of the leadership have set up offshore firms. These revelations have led Chinese censors to "scrub" domestic sites and social media of mentions of Chinese involvement in order to contain public outcry.[32] On the surface, the papers do not necessarily point to wrongdoing on the part of those who have created off-shore companies. China does not bar its citizens from forming or investing in off-shore firms if they are not being used to tax evade or to move illicit funds outside the country. The rules for Communist Party members, however, are clear; they are barred from such actions. The Party rules do not, however, specify the same or similar restrictions for family members and relatives, but there is an internal understanding that senior cadres should rein in all "excessive behavior" because it feeds public resentment.

In another telling move, Xi further resurrected Mao's 1949 treatise on work style which was a set of guidelines urging "consultative leadership and unity among cadres."[33] This was a call for coordination among the leaders, pointing also to the need to multitask and avoid divisiveness among the cadres. Mao used the piano playing allegory in 1949 to make this message clear, "In playing the piano all ten fingers are in motion; it won't do to move some fingers only and not others … [to] produce good music, the ten fingers should move rhythmically and in co-ordination."[34]

In this fluid and rapidly changing landscape, both within their nations and on the global scene, the US and China have sought to engage with one another while genuinely looking to avoid unnecessary confrontation, all without giving up their perceived national interests and their place of power in world affairs. The underlying mistrust that exists close to the surface often emerges and reminds both them and the world that tensions can quickly rise and that varying degrees of confrontation remain possible. Whether a full-fledged confrontation is inevitable or even probable remains to be seen, but there is certainly a long and difficult history between the two powers that colors their analysis of each other's actions and explains the deeply rooted suspicion exhibited by both sides.

Tensions with the US have existed since the PRC emerged. In 1912, the last Chinese Emperor abdicated and the post-imperial modern Chinese state was born out of war and revolution. For the first 60-odd years, the PRC experienced hardship and difficulties and played only a small part during the Cold War that was an era of fierce ideological conflict and power politics. During the original ideological battles of communism versus democracy and free markets, China offered limited support for radical groups across the globe.[35] At the time, the PRC's foreign policy was shaped by ideological concerns and the sales of arms to raise hard currency for domestic development.

For these reasons, but also because of its radical reach, size and geography, in the eyes of the US, Maoist China was not to be underestimated or ignored. An isolated China posed a far greater threat to the world than one that was brought into the international fold and interacted with other nations in world organizations. This belief shaped the Nixon administration's goal to open the door to China, especially after its rift with the other super power of the era, the Soviet Union. For the Nixon administration this indicated an opportune moment for engaging the PRC. The presidents who succeeded Nixon shared that same view and sought ways to engage China until the normalization of diplomatic relations took place under the Carter administration.

The first significant bump in the road came after the tragic events on Tiananmen Square that shook Western public opinion in 1989 and put the cultivation of bilateral cooperation on hold. In response, the US and a number of its allies imposed economic and diplomatic sanctions on the PRC. While sanctions differed among participating countries, they included the suspension of high-level official visits, the halting of both technology transfer and development assistance and the cessation of military and police equipment sales. Both the World Bank and the Asian Development Bank were pressured to stop lending money to China. Naturally, this backlash caused much consternation in Beijing, and there were voices asking for a re-orientation of Chinese foreign policy away from the US and toward the developing world. Although the debate was robust, China's reaction was tempered and, soon after, relations began to progressively thaw. The Clinton White House moreover, went on to support China's accession to the World Trade Organization (WTO), a step that caused a lot of angst to other members because of China's size and the uncertainty over whether it would subsequently play a disruptive role in the WTO.[36]

Subsequent US presidents continued to engage with China, although a spirit of competition and underlying suspicion of the PRC's intentions and goals continued unabated. It has been common for the US government to often allude to the brewing rivalry targeting both domestic and international audiences with its message. Already in the democratic primary in 2007 Barack Obama spoke about China in the following way. "China is rising and it's not going away. They're neither our enemy or our friend … But we have to make sure that we have enough military-to-military contact and forge enough of a relationship with them that we can stabilize the region."[37]

Once Barack Obama became president, he sought to strengthen ties and contacts with the Chinese leadership, though this did not preclude some strong language where deemed appropriate or useful. For example, Obama used harsh language when discussing "'alleged" cyberattacks emanating from China: "We have been very clear to the Chinese that there are certain practices that they are engaging in, that we know are emanating from China and are not acceptable."[38] The president suggested that the two nations work together to agree on rules for cyberspace but reiterated US intentions on the matter, stressing that "there comes a point at which we consider this a core national security threat and we will treat it as such," adding that in an online confrontation, "I guarantee you we will win if we have to."[39]

In the State of the Union Address in January 2016, Obama asked Congress to approve the Trans-Pacific Partnership (TPP) agreement, pointing out to elected officials that this agreement allowed the US to set the rules in the region.

> we forged a Trans-Pacific Partnership to open markets, and protect workers and the environment, and advance American leadership in Asia. It cuts

18,000 taxes on products made in America, which will then support more good jobs here in America. With TPP, China does not set the rules in that region; we do. You want to show our strength in this new century? Approve this agreement. Give us the tools to enforce it. It's the right thing to do.[40]

The US has furthermore maintained pressure on China with regard to human rights, political dissidents, religious freedom and the status of Tibet. While human rights activists may say that the issue goes up and down the priority ladder for the US government, depending on what it deems a higher priority of challenges that need to be dealt with in its relationship with the Chinese,[41] US rhetoric on these topics is a source of displeasure for the Chinese government.

US–China competition has manifested itself throughout the years in many distinct ways. After the end of the Cold War that had seen the engagement of both the US and the Soviet Union in proxy wars and a game of building strategic influence, great power focus on the African continent dwindled. This was not the case with China. It established connections during the years of US–Soviet rivalry by selling arms to rebel movements in order to secure hard currency under the Mao regime. The ties and relations that had been cultivated proved important when China began to open up and build its vibrant economy and needed new markets and resources in order to keep growing.

Trade exploded between China and Africa and by 2015 had reached nearly $300 billion.[42] These figures in combination with the generous use of soft diplomacy in the region have raised concerns among other industrial powers that are watching the PRC's influence continue to grow through its effective development aid program. This strategic approach, furthermore, is not confined to the African Continent. China has followed a similar tack in Latin America, where trade reached $255.5 billion in 2012,[43] as well as the rest of the developing world.

China has been criticized extensively for developing these kinds of relationships without taking a moral stance on the politics of the region, that is to say that China's overall policy has been one of non-interference in the domestic affairs of countries it works with, especially in the developing world where domestic conflicts, governance by corrupt, violent and undemocratic regimes often deter Western powers from engaging financially and diplomatically. While this policy of non-interference may have perhaps been true in the first decades of China's engagement, gradually there is growing evidence that the PRC is partaking in crisis situations and is engaging diplomatically (although not heavy-handedly) in places like Liberia during the Ebola crisis, the peacekeeping mission in Haiti following the earthquake in 2010 and in the Sudan–South Sudan crisis of 2012 where it joined other powers to help thwart the outbreak of renewed conflict.[44]

For those who see the US–China rivalry as the center of geopolitical tensions in the decades to come, this kind of nuance is brushed over, and China's overall reluctance to intervene in the domestic affairs of sovereign nations highlighted as being expedient and part of China's decision to defend its economic interests at all costs. Yet, as China's power grows, its own interests need to be protected as well, and that too accounts for its careful but growing participation in international peacekeeping efforts and its use of diplomatic intervention when it deems it necessary.

Many analysts take for granted that in the twenty-first century, a US–China rivalry is inevitable because China's rapid rise makes it the natural challenger to US hegemony. Those who prefer a bipolar model in international relations to that of a multipolar world are underscoring the aspects of what they see as a power competition. In powerful Washington, D.C. circles the rivalry scenario is played out vocally. Statements such as that of Clyde Prestowitz, former US Trade Negotiator during the rare earths crisis that began in 2010, indicate that distrust persists and that economic interdependence is by no means a guarantee for peace:

> The mantra in the U.S. ever since the late 1990s has been that globalization will make everybody rich. By being rich, they will all become democratic. By being democratic, they will all be peaceful. Well, globalization is working in a somewhat different way. China is getting rich and India is getting rich. But China's not getting democratic. We've seen in the recent case of China embargoing the export of rare earths that it's a kind of a mercantilist economy. The economy is being run for strategic purposes in ways that we didn't anticipate.[45]

Although there is a tacit understanding that US politics especially during election years may call for the use of tough language on certain issues, China consistently figures as an easy target. In the 2012 election, Republican nominee Mitt Romney accused the Obama administration of "not standing up to China," stating outright that this behavior leads to the US getting "run over" by its competitor. In fact, he even went so far as to claim that "On day one, I will label China a currency manipulator, which will allow me as president to be able to put in place, if necessary, tariffs where I believe that they are taking unfair advantage of our manufacturers."[46] Romney's belligerence impacted Obama's rhetoric during the campaign. Although the Chinese leadership may have been able to understand the nature of this kind of rhetoric as part of the US political cycle, it did adversely impact public opinion in China. According to a Pew survey, by 2012 faith in Obama had plunged to 38 percent from 62 percent in 2008. It also had an effect on US public opinion. According to a Pew Research Center Poll in 2015, Americans exhibit numerous concerns with regards to China[47] especially the economy, jobs, trade and cyber-attacks but also its growing military power. Eighty-nine percent find the large amount of US debt held by China to be a serious issue. In addition, other issues that stood out as serious concerns for respondents were the loss of US jobs to China (89 percent) and the PRC's impact on the environment (85 percent).

Albeit less openly in Beijing, the spillover of the contest between the two countries impacts both geostrategic and economic realms. In response to the US's declared pivot toward Asia, China under Xi has turned its attention westward with its Silk Road initiative linking the PRC and its neighbors through projects and initiatives. China's decision for a "western lean" can be interpreted in different ways depending on one's point of view. A closer engagement with Central Asia and the Middle East may be China's attempt to avoid a direct confrontation with the US on a strategic level by turning in another direction. Another interpretation, however, could be that China reads the US pivot toward the Asia–Pacific as a direct reaction to the PRC's rise and therefore now chooses to flex its own muscles by expanding its influence westward and offering an alternative to US power encroachment in that region. The regional initiatives that China is promoting have excluded the US, Japan and Australia. In the eyes of the US it is an indication that China is trying to push the US out of the region so that the PRC alone can be the hegemon. The competition is also fueled by the "ideological" differences between the two superpowers, a chasm that cannot be breached.

In a policy brief drafted by the Institute of Defense and Strategic Studies (IDSS), the S. Rajaratnam School of International Studies (RSIS) and Nanyang Technological University, which was based in Singapore and focused on security issues of South East Asia and China's rise, the authors took the opportunity to describe the November 2014 summit between Presidents Obama and Xi, as an opportunity for "robust engagement" at a time when there is an "ongoing need to put Asia's future on a more stable footing." [48] The brief that was released ahead of the summit went on to raise three important items for discussion in Beijing.

1   Express the desire to move away from big conceptual frameworks toward practical cooperation and the management of differences;
2   Engage President Xi in a conversation about how China perceives the "status quo" in Asia; and
3   Clarify that China's assertiveness in East Asia is challenging vital national interests of the US.[49]

This brief sought to reflect a growing anxiety of how a "new model" of relations between the US and China (announced during Xi's US visit in June 2013) would in fact work in practice, with Asian allies of the US voicing concerns that the "new relationship" might be managed by "Washington and Beijing without sufficient care or consultation with other countries."[50] Clearly, this kind of analysis highlights the inherent difficulties of re-dividing the world into two camps where the two greatest powers of the day will have the most direct and lasting influence. Lyle J. Goldstein, in his recent *Meeting China Halfway* (2015), argues that

> For the moment at least, the study of key mandarin language sources seems to reveal that cooler heads still prevail, and that China is not seeking to follow the belligerent and risky Russian model. The overall guidance in Beijing with respect to US-China relations still seems to be 'struggle but do not break'. Nevertheless, it is quite evident that Chinese discourse regarding the United States has become more bellicose, even as a similar trend has developed in the United States, reflecting a clear and dangerous evolution toward intensified rivalry.[51]

To be sure, there are analysts who argue that while China is rising economically, it lacks the depth of relationships and alliances that make the US the most formidable of powers. While China follows a principal of forming cooperative partnerships and has established strategic partnerships with 47 countries and three international organizations, mostly since the early 2000s,[52] the US is a proponent of the alignment principle and has close to sixty such allies around the world.[53] That is not to say, however, that China's national strength is not growing. To the contrary, China is building up its military capabilities, cracking down on corruption, showing political astuteness and growing its economy.

Whether the glass is half empty or half full, there are some undeniable factors that are shaping the US–China relationship as it evolves. The much touted strategic pivot toward Asia fed into China's worries of encirclement and containment and created a sense of abandonment in the eyes of its traditional European allies and nations in the Middle East, while raising expectations and fears in the Asian region. For US allies in Asia, the muscular language of the "pivot" indicated change, not continuity, suggesting that the US would no longer be multitasking and was turning to Asia having abandoned other allies and other commitments. While Asian allies were supposed to be reassured because the US had unwittingly suggested that it could not handle two problems at once, predictably some of them now worry that the US might pivot away again whenever problems arise in other regions.

Furthermore, the word "pivot" was somewhat inaccurate because the US had never left Asia and therefore did not need to pivot back to it. In fact, many of the policies later associated with the so-called "pivot"—such as sending more submarines to Guam, rotating F-22 aircraft through Japan, sending littoral combat ships to Singapore, entering a free-trade pact with South Korea and negotiating the TPP—were in the works before Obama took office. But some new positive elements were added. The Obama administration sent top officials to Asia more frequently than its predecessors; it improved relations with Myanmar; it signed the Treaty of Amity and Cooperation in Southeast Asia, the founding document of the Association of Southeast Asian Nations; it joined the East Asia Summit, and it saw to it that the EAS and the ASEAN Regional Forum, often dismissed as talk shops, actually addressed important security issues. To its credit, the administration recognized the need for clarification of its Asia–Pacific policy and dropped the term "pivot," replacing it with the more benign "rebalance," although much of the damage had already been done.

Against this background of simmering rivalry in the Asian Pacific, events took an unexpected turn. In November 2014, Presidents Obama and Xi jointly addressed the problem of climate change during their Summit in Beijing.[54] The world was surprised that these two leaders whose countries had previously shown reluctance to limit national emissions were now taking a vocal stand to address the climate crisis together. In truth, this did not constitute a sudden change of heart. Their respective teams had been working on a joint statement for some time reflecting the concern of both presidents about the effects of the climate crisis. The Climate Change Working Group (CCWG), established during Secretary of State Kerry's visit to Beijing on April 14, 2013, aimed to bring about cooperative action in order for the two powers to address the climate crisis. Topics on the CCWG's agenda included: "reducing emissions from heavy-duty and other vehicles; increasing carbon capture, utilization and storage (CCUS); increasing energy efficiency in buildings, industry and transport; improving greenhouse gas (GHG) data collection and management; and promoting smart grids."[55] Moreover, the two sides began a larger discussion for cooperation ahead of Paris 2015 and renewed efforts to phase down hydrofluorocarbons (HFCs).

Cooperation between the US and China on the environment more broadly had already enjoyed a 30-year history,[56] although relations on climate change had been rather low key.[57] The US Environmental Protection Agency (EPA) worked with ministries and commissions, provincial and special administrative regions, as well as other key stakeholders in China to share expertise and advance environmental protection. Together the EPA and the Ministry of Environmental Protection of the PRC addressed:

> air and water pollution; pollution from persistent organic pollutants and other toxics; hazardous and solid waste; prevention and restoration of contaminated sites; emergency preparedness and response; environmental institutions; and environmental law development, implementation, compliance and enforcement.[58]

The EPA also collaborated with China's National Development and Reform Commission (NDRC) as well as China's Ministry of Science and Technology. The EPA, moreover, also participated in the US–China Ten Year Framework for Cooperation on Energy and Environment (TYF), SED and the CCWG.

Given that the US and China are the world's two largest emitters that remain heavily dependent on coal to power their large economies, they represent important actors that need to take an active part in the transition to a low carbon future to ensure a drastic reduction of global emissions. Unlike the US, which took considerable measures to protect the environment especially in the 70s and 80s, China's environmental degradation, a result of rapid industrialization, has taken a heavy toll. Because the PRC's environmental challenges at the moment far surpass those of the US, this necessitates a whole range of measures that the Chinese government is undertaking to help rectify decades-long problems emanating from policies that now need to be urgently reversed.

Dependence on coal is one of the main culprits. Coal not only has a higher carbon-to-hydrogen ratio than oil and natural gas, releasing more carbon into the environment, but its prevalence in the energy mix of both nations continues to remain alarmingly high. According to Merritt T. Cooke, "Coal currently supplies almost half the electric power generated in the US. In China, coal supplies more than 70 percent of electric power generation. These "facts on the ground" are unlikely to change."[59] The issue, of course, does not only impact the environmental situation at a local level, but it goes well beyond the borders of each nation by causing acid rain and ocean acidification as well as respiratory problems since environmental repercussions do not limit themselves to man-made boundaries.

After the Xi–Obama joint declaration of 2014, the world continued to hope that in Paris the two superpowers would once again demonstrate their commitment to international climate negotiations that constituted an effective departure from both their previous national positions in the talks. They did not disappoint. In September 2015 and prior to the Paris Conference, Xi visited Washington, D.C. and both leaders again spelled out their commitment to a positive outcome at COP 21. In their joint communiqué they articulated their shared understanding of what such an agreement might entail, supporting a system of enhanced transparency which should include both reporting and review, as well as support for action.[60] They furthermore made progress on the issue of differentiation and agreed that the outcome of Paris needed to adhere to the principle of common but differentiated responsibilities and respective capabilities. They also expressed the desire to see that adaptation is addressed more thoroughly in international climate negotiations.[61]

In Paris itself, in December 2015, both presidents once again re-affirmed their commitment and support for the historic Treaty on Climate. In the end and after many setbacks since the international climate talks first began, Paris was hailed as a major breakthrough for climate action, providing the world with a much needed boost of optimism for the future. In September 2016, moreover, Obama and Xi added another "milestone" to their "legacy of climate leadership."[62] Together they formally joined the Paris Agreement, an important step for it to enter into force. They also stated their intention to prepare and publish their respective "mid-century, long-term low greenhouse gas emission development strategies" required under the Paris Agreement. In their joint statement, the two sides declared their commitment to bilateral climate cooperation that has been instrumental in their arriving to joint leadership positions in the international climate arena. Frameworks under which their collaboration was meant to continue and deepen included: the U.S.-China Climate Change Working Group, and the U.S.-China Clean Energy Research Center (CERC). The plan was to also participate in U.S.-China Climate-Smart/Low-Carbon Cities Summit, to be held in Boston in 2017, and the Clean Energy Ministerial, to be held in China in 2017.[63] Furthermore, they also reaffirmed their commitment to work together in order to reach a successful outcome in adopting "an ambitious amendment to the Montreal Protocol to phasedown HFCs and on a market-based measure to reduce carbon emissions from international aviation, and announced continued bilateral climate cooperation and domestic action."[64] The two presidents additionally agreed to continue to demonstrate robust domestic action in order to encourage and accelerate the "transition towards green, low-carbon and climate-resilient economies both domestically and internationally."[65]

At first glance, and after drawing such global attention, the challenges of climate change and the environment may seem to be an important and attractive area for US–China cooperation. However, their efforts remain tainted by the overall geopolitical rivalry that has increasingly become the framework in which cooperation and engagement take place. In the view of some Chinese experts, for instance, in pushing for cooperation on climate change, the US is in fact looking for another way to contain China's rise before its economy far surpasses its own. This pervasive suspicion,[66] held by experts such as Yu Hongyuan, of the Shanghai Institute for International Studies,[67] is not uncommon in China, especially given the US record in climate change negotiations and its own rhetoric on how a binding agreement would negatively impact its growth and its economy.

While skepticism in certain circles abounds, growing discontent within China itself about the extent of environmental degradation and its impacts on daily life and public health make climate action an important domestic policy priority. The Chinese government is facing growing internal pressure to act immediately to reverse the damage, improve on air quality and diversify the energy mix. Over the last few years, there have been many incidents that have shaken that nation to the core, like the 2003 SARS epidemic which highlighted the problematic nature of agricultural practices as well as issues of hygiene in the growing megacities all over the country. Then there was the 2005 inadvertent release of poisons in the Songhua River that was reported only after Russia brought it to the world's attention. Air pollution in cities like Beijing and Shanghai is out of control, and protests by the citizenry are increasing, while the health issues that are caused by this are impacting the Chinese economy.

As the two superpowers seek to cooperate on climate, other regional challenges continually threaten to derail their efforts. Geopolitical tensions both in the East and South China Sea have given Japan the opportunity to vocalize its opposition to Chinese practices in the area, calling for the improvement of maritime security and the implementation of the "rule of law." China's actions in the South China Sea, meanwhile, may stop short of military conflict, but the ongoing reclamation project that has thus far brought the PRC 3,200 acres of land continues and is decried by other interested nations in the disputed waters. The Pentagon,[68] furthermore, released to Congress its annual review of China's military power in May 2016. This report estimates China's military spending at a total of $180 billion which is $40 billion more than its official 2015 defense budget. According to the Pentagon, China can continue to increase its defense spending by 9.8 percent annually for the foreseeable future even though its economic growth rates are lower than years past.[69] In a very interesting shift in tone from the same report in 2015, the Pentagon's executive summary is more focused on China's increasing assertiveness in its periphery.

> The long-term, comprehensive modernization of the armed forces of the People's Republic of China (PRC) entered a new phase in 2015 … to strengthen the Chinese Communist Party's (CCP) control over the military, enhance the PLA's ability to conduct joint operations, and improve its ability to fight short-duration, high-intensity regional conflicts at greater distances from the Chinese mainland. China's leaders seek ways to leverage China's growing military, diplomatic, and economic clout to advance its ambitions to establish regional preeminence and expand its international influence. Chinese leaders have characterized modernization of the People's Liberation

Army (PLA) as essential to achieving great power status and what Chinese President Xi Jinping calls the "China Dream" of national rejuvenation.[70]

Additionally, in the same report, the Pentagon estimated that China's military modernization will produce capabilities that "have the potential to reduce core U.S. military technological advantages."[71] As security concerns escalate in the region, they have a sobering effect on wider US–China collaboration efforts.

The Obama administration most likely had every intention to make the climate an area of cooperation that might help ease the underlying suspicion and competition that feeds into the US–China relationship and rivalry. Engagement and collaborative partnerships help keep distrust at bay and bring actors closer together to learn about each other, form bonds, exchange information and build an agenda of mutually beneficial areas in which to cooperate. Cooperation in areas that seem less controversial and where core national interests are not at stake *prima facie* may help avert clashes. As such, the environment and the climate crisis did offer themselves as common areas of interest in which collaboration might take place. Senator Cardin voiced this view during a hearing about the future of US–China Relations in the US Senate,

> We have a common interest on the environment. And it seems to me we can work together on that. We have common interests in trade. The United States market is very important to China, and commerce between China and the United States is very important to America's economy. So, we have a lot of common interests. And, as you point out, we have some significant challenges.[72]

Such claims subscribe to the theory that a good solution is to work on smaller problems to deepen engagement and avoid tensions and conflict. While this approach has delivered important benefits in many cases, the climate crisis in the Anthropocene does not lend itself to such a narrow and selective view of cooperation. This kind of thinking represents the old. Environmental challenges cannot be on equal footing with trade disputes. The climate crisis is not one small peripheral problem that needs to be addressed on the sidelines so that the two parties have something to keep talking about in order to build trust. Moreover, the best political plans may fall to the wayside after an electoral upset such as the one that took place in the US in November 2016 that made Donald Trump the 45th president of the US. Before even assuming office, the president-elect reached out to the president of Taiwan in a move that provoked the Chinese side, threatening to derail not only cooperation on the climate but relations that have been delicately constructed and developed since Nixon's visit to China.[73] A Trump presidency will certainly need more time to manifest its true intentions toward China, but there is growing concern that as president, Trump will perhaps seek to disrupt lasting conventions in international affairs. China may perceive itself to be cornered and will need to sacrifice any meaningful cooperation in order to stand its ground on what it perceives as being in its core interests.

Therein lies the problem of a US–China leadership model regarding climate change and the Anthropocene. What the climate crisis demands is new thinking, one that acknowledges the interconnectivity of the challenges and offers holistic solutions if there is to be an effective response to this unprecedented global challenge. In this crisis there are no stand-alone issues. Even if US–China cooperation were to continue, their solutions for the climate crisis and life in the Anthropocene would be chosen on an ad hoc basis because of the closed parameters defining their relationship. Already the Xi–Obama agreements showed a strong emphasis for bilateral energy cooperation. Although this represents an important sector, it remains limited in scope. Furthermore, the belief that the world has time to innovate out of the problem is erroneous and short sighted. And yet, both the US and China capitalize on this approach by focusing heavily on solutions such as carbon capture, a technology which is still in a nascent state. More specifically, while carbon capture and storage (CCS) technology is projected to account for 13 percent of global emission reductions by 2050, the reality is that deployment since the 2008 financial crisis has been slower than anticipated. By the end of 2017, the global total of CCS projects will number 22 and increase the carbon captured annually to around 40 million tons.[74] These numbers, while significant, are nowhere near what the International Energy Agency has projected as necessary to have by mid-century; namely 2 billion tons stored per year in 2030 and up to 7 billion tons in 2050. CCS projects featured prominently in the US–China Joint Announcement on climate change in 2014. This created optimism but simultaneously obscured the difficulties that the rapid deployment of CCS would entail. Such difficulties include the high initial capital costs compared to other clean energy technologies, as well as the high probability of a project failure that would discourage public and private investment. In addition, there is a widely held impression that the use of CCS applies almost exclusively to power generation and because of that it merely serves as an excuse for the continued use of coal.

In their joint statement, the US and China spoke about cooperation in mitigation, adaptation, transparency, the importance of technological advancement for the transition to green and low-carbon, and climate-resilient and sustainable development. They emphasized the need for an increase in research and development funding both at a national and global level and agreed that emission reductions should reflect the principle of common but differentiated responsibilities and respective capabilities, in light of different national circumstances.[75]

In climate collaboration, those who did not see the US–China relationship as a zero-sum game advocated that the two superpowers could lead the world through a great transformation to a low-carbon economic future. The reasoning was that although the European Union (EU) had already made great strides in this area, it still lacked the clout to achieve this transition without the joint leadership of the US and China.[76] The logic behind this analysis was that these two powers would become the largest markets for renewable energy and thereby the most effective leaders ushering in the era of sustainable energy.[77] China in particular has in recent years made a staggering investment in the deployment of renewables (wind, solar, hydro) and also nuclear. The US as well boasts considerable investment in renewable applications and green technology. However, market size alone offers a limited lens through which to define climate leadership. Those who have been staunch proponents of US–China collaboration on climate have inexplicably failed to extend an invitation to the EU to join them at the helm at such a critical juncture, especially given its size and proven record on energy transformation and climate action.

The US–China joint announcements on climate action may have captured headlines and raised hopes around the globe that perhaps the two largest emitters could now take the lead in the Anthropocene. Yet more breadth in the framing of their partnership and the forming of their agenda would be needed to reflect an acknowledgement of the complexities facing the planet in the Anthropocene. To deal with the new realities in the Anthropocene, US–China cooperation would need to extend, for instance, into other crucial areas such as agriculture, which is a large contributor to climate change. According to some estimates, "the overall food system could contribute 25–50 percent of global GHG emissions. Therefore, reducing agriculture's GHG emission should be central to limiting climate change."[78]

Selective recipes for partial change wherever most politically expedient or financially profitable render a skewed picture of the kind of global mobilization and coordination needed to thwart the impending disaster. The climate crisis and the age of the Anthropocene cannot fit into the existing parameters of international relations. In Paris, President Hollande put the issue into a compelling context.

> It is in the name of climate justice that I speak to you today. It is in the name of climate justice that we must take action. We need to take note of the seriousness of the threat to the world's equilibrium. Global warming heralds conflicts just as clouds herald a storm. It causes migration which throws more refugees out onto the roads than warfare itself. Governments may no longer be able to satisfy the vital needs of their citizens with the risks of famine, rural exodus and conflicts to access a good that is increasingly scarce: water … Our greatest challenge is to move on from a globalization based on competition to a model based on cooperation, where protection will be more viable than destruction. We need to think of our planet as a single space, establishing a pact of fairness between the North and South and a partnership between mankind and nature.[79]

Leadership in the age of the Anthropocene should reflect these wide-ranging concerns that need to be dealt with simultaneously. As Naomi Kline emphasizes, "we are left with a stark choice: allow climate disruption to change everything about our world, or change pretty much everything about our economy to avoid that fate. But we need to be very clear: because of our decades of collective denial, no gradual, incremental options are now available to us."[80] In the next chapter, I will argue that Europe has shown it can provide such a vision for the future. It is for this reason that Europe and China should pursue joint and proactive leadership to address the challenges of the future.

Notes

1 Cf: Stephen S. Roach, *Unbalanced: The Codependency of America and China* (New Haven: Yale University Press, 2014).The overt shift of US focus toward Asia has EU policy makers worrying about the future of transatlantic cooperation. Javier Solana, former Secretary-General of NATO and former EU High Representative for the Common Foreign and Security Policy wrote that a transatlantic free trade agreement would be crucial for the EU. He underscored that "if current trends continue, Asia could soon surpass North America and Europe in global power. It will have a higher GDP, larger population, higher military spending, and more technological investment. In this geopolitical context, Europe and the US need each other more than ever, making greater transatlantic co-operation crucial." Furthermore, Solana added that Secretary Clinton had extended an invitation to the EU to join the US in its re-orientation toward Asia so that "Asia is seen not only as a market, but also as a focus of common strategic action." From "Transatlantic Free Trade?" *POLITICO*, January 4, 2013, accessed February 14, 2013 http://www.politico.eu/article/transatlantic-free-trade/.
2 U.S. Department of Defense, "Sustaining U.S. Global Leadership: Priorities for 21st Century Defense," January 5, 2012, accessed May 10,2013,http://www.defense.gov/news/Defense_Strategic_Guidance.pdf.
3 Bureau of Public Affairs Department Of State, "U.S.-China Strategic and Economic Dialogue," July 29, 2009, accessed August 30, 2016, http://www.state.gov/e/eb/tpp/bta/sed/.
4 "Remarks By President Obama to the Australian Parliament," *Whitehouse.gov*, November 17, 2011, accessed August 1, 2016, https://www.whitehouse.gov/the-press-office/2011/11/17/remarks-president-obama-australian-parliament.
5 Jeffrey Goldberg, "The Obama Doctrine," *The Atlantic*, April 2016, http://www.theatlantic.com/magazine/archive/2016/04/the-obama-doctrine/471525/.
6 U.S. Department of State, "America's Pacific Century," accessed December 7, 2016, http://www.state.gov/secretary/20092013clinton/rm/2011/11/176999.htm.
7 U.S. Department of Defense, "Sustaining U.S. Global Leadership: Priorities for 21st Century Defense," January 5, 2012, http://archive.defense.gov/news/Defense_Strategic_Guidance.pdf.
8 "Sustaining U.S. Global Leadership."
9 Chi Wang, *Obama's Challenge to China: The Pivot to Asia* (Farnham, Surrey, UK: Ashgate, 2015).
10 Junxian Gan. "The Analysis of 'China's Responsibility' and Its Diplomatic Countermeasures," *Global Review*, April 2014," accessed December 7, 2016, http://en.cnki.com.cn/Article_en/CJFDTOTAL-GJZW201004016.htm.
11 "China's Responsibility and 'China Responsibility Theory," *International Studies*, March 2007, accessed December 7, 2016, http://en.cnki.com.cn/Article_en/CJFDTOTAL-GJWY200703000.htm.
12 Joseph S. Nye Jr, *Soft Power: The Means To Success In World Politics* (New York: Public Affairs, 2004), 4.
13 Nina Hachigian and David Shorr, "The Responsibility Doctrine," *The Washington Quarterly* 36, no. 1 (February 2013): 73–91.
14 Chi Wang, *Obama's Challenge to China: The Pivot to Asia* (Farnham, Surrey, UK: Ashgate, 2015).
15 Michèle Flournoy and Janine Davidson, "Obama's New Global Posture: The Logic of U.S. Foreign Deployments," *Foreign Affairs* 91, no. 4 (2012): 54–63.

16 Henry Kissinger, *Diplomacy* (New York: Simon and Schuster, 1994), 12.
17 Nina Hachigian, ed., *Debating China: The U.S.-China Relationship in Ten Conversations*, 1st edition (Oxford; New York: Oxford University Press, 2014), 89.
18 Hachigian, *Debating China: The U.S.-China Relationship in Ten Conversations*, 90.
19 U.S. Department of State, "Remarks at the U.S. Institute of Peace China Conference," accessed December 11, 2016, http://www.state.gov/secretary/20092013clinton/rm/2012/03/185402.htm.
20 "Remarks at the U.S. Institute of Peace China Conference."
21 "China Celebrates 60 Years," *Boston.com*, accessed December 11, 2016, http://www.boston.com/bigpicture/2009/10/china_celebrates_60_years.html.
22 Henry Kissinger, *On China*, Reprint edition (New York: Penguin Books, 2011), 8.
23 Kissinger, *On China*, 16–17.
24 Gao Yanjun, "On Route toward a Shared Destiny – Asia Weekly – China Daily," accessed December 11, 2016, http://epaper.chinadailyasia.com/asia-weekly/article-7960.html.
25 Gao Yanjun, "On route toward a shared destiny."
26 "Xi Hails China-Brazil As 'community of Shared Destiny,'"*Xinhuanet*, July 18, 2014, http://news.xinhuanet.com/english/china/2014-07/18/c_126766944.htm.
27 "To Promote a Closer China-ASEAN Community of Shared Destiny – Asia News – China-ASEAN Expo," August 14, 2015, http://eng.caexpo.org/index.php?m=content&c=index&a=show&catid=10021&id=200376.
28 Jonathan Kaiman and Yingzhi Yang, "China's President Is the Country's Most-Travelled Leader since Communism," *The Sydney Morning Herald*, December 26, 2015, http://www.smh.com.au/world/chinas-president-is-the-countrys-mosttravelled-leader-since-communism-20151226-glv49i.html.
29 Ken Moriyasu, "Yan Xuetong Interview: China Needs to 'Purchase' Friendships, Scholar Says," *Nikkei Asian Review*, March 2, 2015, http://asia.nikkei.com/Viewpoints-archive/Perspectives/China-needs-to-purchase-friendships-scholar-says.
30 Yinhong Shi, "China's Contemporary Political Leadership, Foreign Policy, and Their Chineseness," *East Asia* 28, no. 3 (2011): 247–57.
31 Andrew Browne, "Xi Embraces Mao's Radical Legacy," *Wall Street Journal*, May 13, 2016, sec. Life, http://www.wsj.com/articles/in-china-xi-embraces-maos-radical-legacy-1463153126.
32 Chun Han Wong and Josh Chin, "Chinese Link to 'Panama Papers' Widens," *Wall Street Journal*, April 7, 2016, sec. World, http://www.wsj.com/articles/chinese-link-to-panama-papers-widens-1459965602.
33 Chun Han Wong, "Advice From Mao Recycled in the Era of Xi Jinping: 'Play the Piano?,'" *Wall Street Journal*, March 2, 2016, http://blogs.wsj.com/chinarealtime/2016/03/02/advice-from-mao-recycled-in-the-era-of-xi-jinping-play-the-piano/.
34 Wong, "Advice From Mao Recycled in the Era of Xi Jinping."
35 Joshua Eisenman, Eric Heginbotham, and Derek Mitchell, eds., *China and the Developing World: Beijing's Strategy for the Twenty-First Century* (Armonk, N.Y: M.E. Sharpe, 2007), ix.
36 David L. Shambaugh, "The New Strategic Triangle: U.S. and European Reactions to China's Rise," *The Washington Quarterly* 28, no. 3 (June 15, 2005): 7–25.
37 J. Stapleton Roy, "The Obama Administration Approach to U.S. Relations with China," *The Asia Foundation*, February 4, 2009, http://asiafoundation.org/2009/02/04/the-obama-administration-approach-to-us-relations-with-china/.
38 Gao Yanjun, "Obama: China Cyber Attacks 'Unacceptable,'" *BBC News*, September 12, 2015, sec. US & Canada, http://www.bbc.com/news/world-us-canada-34229439.
39 Yanjun, "Obama: China Cyber Attacks 'Unacceptable.'"
40 President Donald Trump is abandoning the TPP.
41 "Clinton: Chinese Human Rights Can't Interfere with Other Crises," *CNN.com*," accessed December 11, 2016, http://edition.cnn.com/2009/POLITICS/02/21/clinton.china.asia/.

42 "China-Africa Trade Approaches $300 Billion in 2015," Chinadaily, sec. Business, accessed December 3, 2016, http://www.chinadaily.com.cn/business/2015-11/10/content_22417707.htm.

43 "China/Latam Trade Expanded 8% in 2012 and Region's Deficit Jumped to 6.6bn," *MercoPress*, accessed December 11, 2016, http://en.mercopress.com/2013/05/22/china-latam-trade-expanded-8-in-2012-and-region-s-deficit-jumped-to-6.6bn.

44 Lyle J. Goldstein, *Meeting China Halfway: How to Defuse the Emerging US-China Rivalry* (Washington, DC: Georgetown University Press, 2015), 140.

45 Robert Looney, "Recent Developments on the Rare Earth Front," *World Economics* 12, no. 1 (January 2011): 47–78.

46 Danny Vinik, "The Trump Platform That Mitt Romney Just Attacked Looks a Lot like Mitt Romney's," *The Agenda*, accessed December 11, 2016, http://politi.co/1oThM8K.

47 Richard Wike, "Americans' Concerns about China: Economics, Cyberattacks, Human Rights Top the List," *Pew Research Center's Global Attitudes Project*, September 9, 2015, http://www.pewglobal.org/2015/09/09/americans-concerns-about-china-economics-cyberattacks-human-rights-top-the-list/.

48 Ely Ratner, "The Obama-Xi Summit: Three Essential Messages from Washington" (RSIS, November 2014), https://www.rsis.edu.sg/wp-content/uploads/2014/11/PB141106_the_obama_xi_summit.pdf.

49 Ratner, "The Obama-Xi Summit."

50 Ratner, "The Obama-Xi Summit."

51 Goldstein, *Meeting China Halfway*, 11.

52 Feng Zhongping and Huang Jing, "China's Strategic Partnership Diplomacy," 2014, http://papers.ssrn.com/sol3/papers.cfm?abstract_id=2459948.

53 Yan Xuetong, "A Bipolar World Is More Likely Than a Unipolar or Multipolar One," *Carnegie-Tsinghua Center*, accessed December 11, 2016, http://carnegietsinghua.org/2015/04/20/bipolar-world-is-more-likely-than-unipolar-or-multipolar-one-pub-59915.

54 "U.S.-China Joint Presidential Statement on Climate Change," *Whitehouse.gov*, September 25, 2015, https://www.whitehouse.gov/the-press-office/2015/09/25/us-china-joint-presidential-statement-climate-change.

55 "U.S.-China Climate Change Working Group and Ten-Year Framework for Energy and Environment Cooperation Meetings," *U.S. Department of State*, accessed November 26, 2016, http://www.state.gov/r/pa/prs/ps/2014/03/223631.htm.

56 "EPA Collaboration with China," Overviews and Factsheets, accessed November 26, 2016, https://www.epa.gov/international-cooperation/epa-collaboration-china.

57 David Belis et al., "China, the United States and the European Union: Multiple Bilateralism and Prospects for a New Climate Change Diplomacy," *Carbon & Climate Law Review* 9, no. 3 (2015): 203–18.

58 US EPA, "EPA Collaboration with China."

59 Merritt T. Cooke, *Sustaining US-China Cooperation in Clean Energy* (Washington DC: Woodrow Wilson International Center for Scholars, 2012), 50–51.

60 "FACT SHEET: The United States and China Issue Joint Presidential Statement on Climate Change with New Domestic Policy Commitments and a Common Vision for an Ambitious Global Climate Agreement in Paris," *Whitehouse.gov*, September 25, 2015, https://www.whitehouse.gov/the-press-office/2015/09/25/fact-sheet-united-states-and-china-issue-joint-presidential-statement.

61 Feng Zhongping and Huang Jing, "China's Strategic Partnership Diplomacy," 2014, http://papers.ssrn.com/sol3/papers.cfm?abstract_id=2459948.

62 "FACT SHEET: U.S.-China Cooperation on Climate Change," *Whitehouse.gov*, September 3, 2016, https://www.whitehouse.gov/the-press-office/2016/09/03/fact-sheet-us-china-cooperation-climate-change-0.

63 "FACT SHEET: U.S.-China Cooperation on Climate Change."

64 "FACT SHEET: U.S.-China Cooperation on Climate Change."

65 "U.S.-China Climate Change Cooperation Outcomes," *Whitehouse.gov*, September 3, 2016, https://www.whitehouse.gov/the-press-office/2016/09/03/fact-sheet-us-china-cooperation-climate-change.

66 Kenneth Lieberthal and Wang Jisi, *Addressing US-China Strategic Distrust* (Washington, D.C.: Brookings, 2012), http://yahuwshua.org/en/Resource-584/0330_china_lieberthal.pdf.

67 Rosemary Foot and Andrew Walter, *China, the United States, and Global Order* (Cambridge University Press, 2010), 223. Yu Hogyuan, The Process of the Copenhagen Negotiations and the Development of US-China Carbon Diplomacy, Asia Pacific Studies, no3 (2010): 98.

68 Office of the Secretary of Defense, Annual Report to Congress: Military and Security Developments Involving the People's Republic of China 2016, 26 April 2016, http://www.defense.gov/Portals/1/Documents/pubs/2016%20China%20Military%20Power%20Report.pdf.

69 Paul Sonne, "U.S. Report Decries Beijing's Sea Tactics," *Wall Street Journal*, May 15, 2016, sec. World, http://www.wsj.com/articles/u-s-report-decries-beijings-sea-tactics-1463182533.

70 "Annual Report to Congress: Military and Security Developments Involving the People's Republic of China 2016," April 26, 2016, http://www.defense.gov/Portals/1/Documents/pubs/2016%20China%20Military%20Power%20Report.pdf.

71 "Annual Report to Congress: Military and Security Developments Involving the People's Republic of China 2016."

72 "The Future of U.S.-China Relations," accessed March 15, 2017, https://www.gpo.gov/fdsys/pkg/CHRG-113shrg91140/html/CHRG-113shrg91140.htm.

73 Roberta Rampton and Ben Blanchard, "U.S. Seeks to Reassure Beijing after Trump Call with Taiwan Leader," *Reuters*, December 6, 2016, http://www.reuters.com/article/us-usa-trump-china-idUSKBN13T0SQ.David Smith, "Donald Trump Rails against China as Team Runs Damage Control over Taiwan," *The Guardian*, December 5, 2016, sec. US news, https://www.theguardian.com/us-news/2016/dec/04/trump-foreign-policy-faces-scrutiny-as-team-defends-taiwan-phone-call.

74 "Carbon Capture and Storage: Prospects after Paris | ChinaFAQs," accessed December 11, 2016, http://www.chinafaqs.org/blog-posts/carbon-capture-and-storage-prospects-after-paris.

75 "U.S.-China Joint Presidential Statement on Climate Change."

76 "Common Challenge, Collaborative Response: A Roadmap for U.S.-China Cooperation on Energy and Climate Change," *Asia Society*, accessed November 13, 2016, http://asiasociety.org/center-us-china-relations/common-challenge-collaborative-response-roadmap-us-china-cooperation-energ.

77 National Academy of Engineering and National Research Council, *The Power of Renewables: Opportunities and Challenges for China and the United States*, 2010, https://www.nap.edu/catalog/12987/the-power-of-renewables-opportunities-and-challenges-for-china-and.

78 Zhang Hongzhou, "China-US Climate Change Cooperation: Beyond Energy," *The Diplomat*, accessed December 11, 2016, http://thediplomat.com/2015/10/china-us-climate-change-cooperation-beyond-energy/.

79 French Embassy in South Africa/*Ambassade de France En Afrique Du Sud*, "COP21 Opening Speech: President François Hollande," accessed March 15, 2017, http://www.ambafrance-rsa.org/COP21-opening-speech-President-Francois-Hollande; Président de la République M. Francois Hollande, "Ouverture Du « Leaders' Event » COP21," accessed November 30, 2015, http://unfccc.int/files/meetings/paris_nov_2015/application/pdf/cop21cmp11_statement_hollande.pdf.

80 Naomi Klein, "How Will Everything Change under Climate Change?," *The Guardian*, March 8, 2015, http://www.theguardian.com/environment/2015/mar/08/how-will-everything-change-under-climate-change.

Bibliography

Asia News. "To Promote a Closer China-ASEAN Community of Shared Destiny." August 14, 2015. http://eng.caexpo.org/index.php?m=content&c=index&a=show&catid=10 021&id=200376.

Belis, David, Paul Joffe, Bart Kerremans and Ye Qi. "China, the United States and the European Union: Multiple Bilateralism and Prospects for a New Climate Change Diplomacy." *Carbon & Climate Law Review* 9, no. 3 (2015): 203–18.

The Big Picture: News Stories in Photographs. "China Celebrates 60 Years." *Boston.com*. Accessed December 11, 2016.

Browne, Andrew. "Xi Embraces Mao's Radical Legacy." *Wall Street Journal*, May 13, 2016, sec. Life. http://www.wsj.com/articles/in-china-xi-embraces-maos-radical-legacy-1463153126. http://www.boston.com/bigpicture/2009/10/china_celebrates_60_years.html.

Chinadaily. "China-Africa Trade Approaches $300 Billion in 2015." Chinadaily, sec. Business. Accessed December 3, 2016. http://www.chinadaily.com.cn/business/2015-11/10/content_22417707.htm.

CNN. "Clinton: Chinese Human Rights Can't Interfere with Other Crises." Accessed December 11, 2016. http://edition.cnn.com/2009/POLITICS/02/21/clinton.china.asia/.

Department Of State. The Office of Website Management, Bureau of Public Affairs. "U.S.-China Strategic and Economic Dialogue," July 29, 2009. http://www.state.gov/e/eb/tpp/bta/sed/.

Eisenman, Joshua, Eric Heginbotham, and Derek Mitchell, eds. *China and the Developing World: Beijing's Strategy for the Twenty-First Century*. Armonk, N.Y: Routledge, 2015.

Flournoy, Michèle, and Janine Davidson. "Obama's New Global Posture: The Logic of U.S. Foreign Deployments." *Foreign Affairs* 91, no. 4 (2012): 54–63.

Foot, Rosemary and Andrew Walter. *China, the United States, and Global Order*. Cambridge: Cambridge University Press, 2010.

Gan, Junxian. "The Analysis of 'China's Responsibility'and Its Diplomatic Countermeasures – 《Global Review》2010年04期." Accessed December 7, 2016. http://en.cnki.com.cn/Article_en/CJFDTOTAL-GJZW201004016.htm.

Goldberg, Jeffrey. "The Obama Doctrine." *The Atlantic*, April 2016. http://www.theatlantic.com/magazine/archive/2016/04/the-obama-doctrine/471525/.

Goldstein, Lyle J. *Meeting China Halfway: How to Defuse the Emerging US-China Rivalry*. Washington, DC: Georgetown University Press, 2015.

Hachigian, Nina, ed. *Debating China: The U.S.-China Relationship in Ten Conversations*. 1st edition. Oxford; New York: Oxford University Press, 2014.

Hachigian, Nina and David Shorr. "The Responsibility Doctrine." *The Washington Quarterly* 36, no. 1 (February 2013): 73–91. doi:10.1080/0163660X.2013.751652.

The Initiative for U.S.-China Cooperation on Energy and Climate. "Common Challenge, Collaborative Response: A Roadmap for U.S.-China Cooperation on Energy and Climate Change." *Asia Society*. Accessed November 13, 2016. http://asiasociety.org/center-us-china-relations/common-challenge-collaborative-response-roadmap-us-china-cooperation-energ.

Jonathan Kaiman and Yingzhi Yang. "China's President Is the Country's Most-Travelled Leader since Communism." *The Sydney Morning Herald*, December 26, 2015. http://www.smh.com.au/world/chinas-president-is-the-countrys-mosttravelled-leader-since-communism-20151226-glv49i.html.

Kissinger, Henry. *Diplomacy*. New York: Simon and Schuster, 1994.

Kissinger, Henry. *On China*. Reprint edition. New York: Penguin Books, 2011.

Klein, Naomi. "How Will Everything Change under Climate Change?" *The Guardian*, March 8, 2015. http://www.theguardian.com/environment/2015/mar/08/how-will-everything-change-under-climate-change.

Lebling, Katie, and Xiaoliang Yang. "Carbon Capture and Storage: Prospects after Paris." *ChinaFAQs*. Accessed December 11, 2016. http://www.chinafaqs.org/blog-posts/carbon-capture-and-storage-prospects-after-paris.

Lieberthal, Kenneth, and Wang Jisi. *Addressing US-China Strategic Distrust*. Washington, D.C.: Brookings, 2012. http://yahuwshua.org/en/Resource-584/0330_china_lieberthal.pdf.

Looney, Robert. "Recent Developments on the Rare Earth Front." *World Economics* 12, no. 1 (January 2011): 47–78.

MercoPress. "China/Latam Trade Expanded 8% in 2012 and Region's Deficit Jumped to 6.6bn." *MercoPress. Accessed December 11*, 2016. http://en.mercopress.com/2013/05/22/china-latam-trade-expanded-8-in-2012-and-region-s-deficit-jumped-to-6.6bn.

Moriyasu, Ken. "Yan Xuetong Interview: China Needs to 'Purchase' Friendships, Scholar Says." *Nikkei Asian Review*, March 2, 2015. http://asia.nikkei.com/Viewpoints-archive/Perspectives/China-needs-to-purchase-friendships-scholar-says.

National Academy of Engineering and National Research Council. *The Power of Renewables: Opportunities and Challenges for China and the United States*, 2010. https://www.nap.edu/catalog/12987/the-power-of-renewables-opportunities-and-challenges-for-china-and.

Nye Jr, Joseph S. *Soft Power: The Means To Success In World Politics*. New York: PublicAffairs, 2004.

Office of the Press Secretary. "FACT SHEET: The United States and China Issue Joint Presidential Statement on Climate Change with New Domestic Policy Commitments and a Common Vision for an Ambitious Global Climate Agreement in Paris." *Whitehouse.gov*, September 25, 2015. https://www.whitehouse.gov/the-press-office/2015/09/25/fact-sheet-united-states-and-china-issue-joint-presidential-statement.

Office of the Press Secretary. "Remarks By President Obama to the Australian Parliament." *Whitehouse.gov*, November 17, 2011. https://www.whitehouse.gov/the-press-office/2011/11/17/remarks-president-obama-australian-parliament.

Office of the Press Secretary. "U.S.-China Joint Presidential Statement on Climate Change." *Whitehouse.gov*, September 25, 2015. https://www.whitehouse.gov/the-press-office/2015/09/25/us-china-joint-presidential-statement-climate-change.

Office of the Press Secretary. "FACT SHEET: U.S.-China Cooperation on Climate Change." *Whitehouse.gov*, September 3, 2016. https://www.whitehouse.gov/the-press-office/2016/09/03/fact-sheet-us-china-cooperation-climate-change-0.

Office of the Press Secretary. "U.S.-China Climate Change Cooperation Outcomes." *Whitehouse.gov*, September 3, 2016. https://www.whitehouse.gov/the-press-office/2016/09/03/fact-sheet-us-china-cooperation-climate-change.

Rampton, Roberta, and Ben Blanchard. "U.S. Seeks to Reassure Beijing after Trump Call with Taiwan Leader." *Reuters*, December 6, 2016. http://www.reuters.com/article/us-usa-trump-china-idUSKBN13T0SQ.

Ratner, Ely. "The Obama-Xi Summit: Three Essential Messages from Washington." RSIS, November 2014. https://www.rsis.edu.sg/wp-content/uploads/2014/11/PB141106_the_obama_xi_summit.pdf.

Roach, Stephen S. (Stephen Samuel). *Unbalanced: The Codependency of America and China*. Princeton, NJ: Yale University Press, 2014.

Shambaugh, David L. "The New Strategic Triangle: U.S. and European Reactions to China's Rise." *The Washington Quarterly* 28, no. 3 (June 15, 2005): 7–25.

Shi, Yinhong. "China's Contemporary Political Leadership, Foreign Policy, and Their Chineseness." *East Asia* 28, no. 3 (2011): 247–57.

Smith, David. "Donald Trump Rails against China as Team Runs Damage Control over Taiwan." *The Guardian*, December 5, 2016, sec. US news. https://www.theguardian.com/us-news/2016/dec/04/trump-foreign-policy-faces-scrutiny-as-team-defends-taiwan-phone-call.

Solana, Javier. "Transatlantic Free Trade?" *POLITICO*, January 4, 2013. http://www.politico.eu/article/transatlantic-free-trade/.

Sonne, Paul. "U.S. Report Decries Beijing's Sea Tactics." *Wall Street Journal*, May 15, 2016, sec. World. http://www.wsj.com/articles/u-s-report-decries-beijings-sea-tactics-1463182533.

Stapleton Roy, J. "The Obama Administration Approach to U.S. Relations with China." *The Asia Foundation*, February 4, 2009. http://asiafoundation.org/2009/02/04/the-obama-administration-approach-to-us-relations-with-china/.

U.S. Department of State. "America's Pacific Century." Accessed December 7, 2016. http://www.state.gov/secretary/20092013clinton/rm/2011/11/176999.htm.

U.S. Department of Defence. "Annual Report to Congress: Military and Security Developments Involving the People's Republic of China 2016," April 26, 2016. http://www.defense.gov/Portals/1/Documents/pubs/2016%20China%20Military%20Power%20Report.pdf.

U.S. Department of State. "Remarks at the U.S. Institute of Peace China Conference." *U.S. Department of State*. Accessed December 11, 2016. http://www.state.gov/secretary/20092013clinton/rm/2012/03/185402.htm.

U.S. Department of Defense. "Sustaining U.S. Global Leadership: Priorities for 21st Century Defense," January 5, 2012. http://archive.defense.gov/news/Defense_Strategic_Guidance.pdf.

U.S. Department of State. "U.S.-China Climate Change Working Group and Ten-Year Framework for Energy and Environment Cooperation Meetings." Accessed November 26, 2016. http://www.state.gov/r/pa/prs/ps/2014/03/223631.htm.

US EPA, OITA. "EPA Collaboration with China." Overviews and Factsheets. Accessed November 26, 2016. https://www.epa.gov/international-cooperation/epa-collaboration-china.

Vinik, Danny. "The Trump Platform That Mitt Romney Just Attacked Looks a Lot like Mitt Romney's." *The Agenda*. Accessed December 11, 2016. http://politi.co/1oThM8K.

Wike, Richard. "Americans' Concerns about China: Economics, Cyberattacks, Human Rights Top the List." *Pew Research Center's Global Attitudes Project*, September 9, 2015. http://www.pewglobal.org/2015/09/09/americans-concerns-about-china-economics-cyberattacks-human-rights-top-the-list/.

Wang, Chi. *Obama's Challenge to China: The Pivot to Asia*. Farnham, Surrey, UK: Ashgate, 2015.

Wong, Chun Han. "Advice From Mao Recycled in the Era of Xi Jinping: 'Play the Piano?'" *Wall Street Journal*, March 2, 2016. http://blogs.wsj.com/chinarealtime/2016/03/02/advice-from-mao-recycled-in-the-era-of-xi-jinping-play-the-piano/.

Wong, Chun Han and Josh Chin. "Chinese Link to 'Panama Papers' Widens." *Wall Street Journal*, April 7, 2016, sec. World. http://www.wsj.com/articles/chinese-link-to-panama-papers-widens-1459965602.

Xinhua. "Xi Hails China-Brazil As 'community of Shared Destiny'". Xinhua, July 18, 2014. http://news.xinhuanet.com/english/china/2014-07/18/c_126766944.htm.

Xuetong, Yan. "A Bipolar World Is More Likely Than a Unipolar or Multipolar One." *Carnegie-Tsinghua Center*. Accessed December 11, 2016. http://carnegietsinghua.org/2015/04/20/bipolar-world-is-more-likely-than-unipolar-or-multipolar-one-pub-59915.

Yanjun, Guo. "Obama: China Cyber Attacks 'Unacceptable.'" *BBC News*, September 12, 2015, sec. US & Canada. http://www.bbc.com/news/world-us-canada-34229439.

Yanjun, Guo. "On Route toward a Shared Destiny - Asia Weekly - China Daily." Accessed December 11, 2016. http://epaper.chinadailyasia.com/asia-weekly/article-7960.html.

Zhang, Hongzhou, "China-US Climate Change Cooperation: Beyond Energy." *The Diplomat*. Accessed December 11, 2016. http://thediplomat.com/2015/10/china-us-climate-change-cooperation-beyond-energy/.

Zhengang, Ma. "China's Responsibility and 'China Responsibility Theory.'" *International Studies* 2007. Accessed December 7, 2016. http://en.cnki.com.cn/Article_en/CJFDTOTAL-GJWY200703000.htm.

Zhongping, Feng and Huang Jing. "China's Strategic Partnership Diplomacy," 2014. http://papers.ssrn.com/sol3/papers.cfm?abstract_id=2459948.

5 What makes EU–China collaboration a better fit for the Anthropocene

A truly wise man is apt at seizing opportunities rather than simply working out plans.

Old Chinese saying quoted by PM Jiabao in 2004[1]

Though China and the European Union (EU) do not share close geographic proximity, they are not strangers to one another. They have shared a long and mixed history of interaction through trade and empire. Europe's involvement in the construction of the post-Second World War order and the rapid impacts of globalization make engagement with China a top priority for the EU. While trade and economic exchanges have been an important focal point for the burgeoning relationship, they are not the sole reason the Sino–European partnership presents great potential. China and Europe are not in direct confrontation with each other, neither rhetorically nor literally. In contrast to the United States (US), Europe does not see itself as a Pacific power. Moreover, both the EU and China present themselves as "emerging" powers that do not have underlying conflicts of national interest. The European view of a rising China, in contrast to that of the US, has not been shaped by the same intense anxiety over a looming political rivalry.[2] By the same token, China and the EU exhibit a preference for multilateral diplomacy and actively partake in the workings of international institutions. With the exception of isolated incidents which have occasionally dampened their enthusiasm for robust rapprochement, their relations are more stable, more mature and more productive than Sino–US relations and have not been subject to the same ups and downs.

China's official relationship with the European Commission (EC, preceding the EU) began in 1975 and laid the legal foundations for the building of its ties with European Community member states. This was followed by a series of important steps in a process aimed at bringing the two actors closer for the purpose of solidifying cooperation. In 1978, they agreed to offer each other "most-favored nation status." They signed an economic and trade agreement in 1985 and exchanged diplomatic missions in 1988. Sino–European relations, however, were set back in 1989 because the EU imposed sanctions and an arms embargo on China after the bloody crackdown against demonstrators in Tiananmen Square. In 1994, the EU launched its Strategic Framework for Enhanced Partnerships with Asian countries[3] along with its long-term policy plans for its relations with China.[4] A dialogue on human rights was initiated in 1996 and in 1998 a Leaders' Summit was established. In 2001, China gained entrance into the World Trade Organization (WTO) with the strong support of the EU which had insisted that the organization would not be a truly global one without China's participation. That same year, the cooperative partnership was renamed a "comprehensive partnership."[5] In 2003, moreover, the partnership's status was further upgraded to "comprehensive strategic partnership."[6] This constituted a turning point in EU–China relations and both sides held high expectations.

This relationship of "strategic closeness" went through a number of phases during its first ten years: the honeymoon phase, the restoration period and the progressive evolution of the partnership. At the outset both the EU and China issued policy papers outlining their respective understanding of what kind of relationship they sought to build, stating their objectives and contextualizing their partnership within the wider global picture.[7] Both sides underscored particular facets of the relationship that enabled them to be truly cooperative, less adversarial and accorded recognition to the fact that both had a significant role to play in regional and global affairs.

Although disagreements on some issues continued to exist, it was clear to both sides that there were no lurking threats or fundamental conflicts of interest that could hamper a successful progression of their partnership. The Chinese in particular made these points abundantly clear by specifically underscoring that,

> given their differences in historical background, cultural heritage, political system and economic development level, it is natural that the two sides have different views or even disagree on some issues. Nevertheless China-EU relations of mutual trust and mutual benefit cannot and will not be affected if the two sides address their disagreements in a spirit of equality and mutual respect.[8]

In that first honeymoon period, high-level visits between the EU and China became noticeably more frequent. Premier Wen Jiabao visited Brussels to attend the China–EU Investment and Trade Forum on May 6, 2004 and discussed the meaning and importance of the strategic partnership that the two powers sought to build.[9] In Prime Minister Jiabao's own words,

> By 'comprehensive,' it means that the cooperation should be all-dimensional, wide-ranging and multi-layered. It covers economic, scientific, technological, political and cultural fields, contains both bilateral and multilateral levels, and is conducted by both governments and non-governmental groups. By 'strategic,' it means that the cooperation should be long-term and stable, bearing on the larger picture of China-EU relations. It transcends the differences in ideology and social system and is not subjected to the impacts of individual events that occur from time to time. By 'partnership,' it means that the cooperation should be equal-footed, mutually beneficial and win-win.[10]

The relationship appeared to be on track and to be moving forward by a momentum that found support on both sides.

Despite Premier Wen Jiabao's earnest advocacy for EU–China cooperation and hopes that the two powers would be able to create a strategic axis,[11] things would quickly change. David Shambaugh argues that, "… like all marriages, the more the two interacted, the more differences and frictions inevitably surfaced. After a decade of rosy rhetoric and expanding ties, relations turned sour between 2006 and 2010."[12] One problem was that the Chinese may have been looking for a partner to help end US unilateralism and interventionism of the sort that had led to the second Iraq war.

The US's looming shadow significantly impacted the relationship between the two powers. The bonds that Europe and the US share have been among the strongest in the international arena, having become particularly important after the Second World War. The closeness of this relationship has been based on shared values such as democracy and human rights, cultural connections, a strong economic and trade relationship, joint participation in institution building, and particularly during the Cold War years, shared foes. There has been a trust and maturity in their relationship that has endured through more recent divergences of opinion and agendas. As European states came closer together by launching a single currency and strengthening their political bonds, the EU began to perhaps come out of the US's shadow to champion a belief of a multipolar world system that does not rely on superpower politics and agendas. Still, Europe's commitments in the North Atlantic Treaty Organizaiton (NATO) have limited some of its flexibility, for example, in resuming weapon sales to China after the initial boycott following events at Tiananmen. This attachment to the US could perhaps be construed as Europe's Achilles' heel, especially from the perspective of the Chinese who had hoped that it would provide an alternative leadership paradigm to the more interventionist model of US power projection.

It seemed that China's expectations on this front were being dashed, even though over the last two decades US commitment toward Europe has begun to waver. The disagreement over the second Iraq war and the growing political isolationist mood in Washington, D.C. have been responsible for cracks in the deep-rooted conviction that Europe and the US were bound to each other above and beyond the economic and strategic. In fact, at times it seemed that the two chief allies were quasi-estranged. Although the Obama administration tried to repair the growing chasm, his vociferous pivot toward Asia and the push for the establishment of the Trans-Pacific Partnership (TPP)[13] constituted clear indications that the US was shifting priorities and resources toward Asia while trying to disentangle itself from the Middle East and loosening its bonds to Europe. Even though this decision speaks more to the fact that the US seems incapable or unwilling to multitask, however much globalization demands that it do so, the power and military shifts toward Asia have left European policymakers with a bitter aftertaste.

The US was not the only factor that impacted the EU–China relationship. The closer relations became, the more the EU began to wonder about the breakneck speed of China's rise both economically and politically. Friction ensued over trade issues, such as the granting of market status to China ahead of 2016. On the EU side as well, there were concerns over intellectual property and technology transfer, as well as other issues pertaining to market access into China. Furthermore, the Iranian nuclear program became a point of contention. Human-rights issues were pushed to prominence by some critics of China's record, and heads of state in the UK, France and Germany met with the Dalai Lama, provoking China to postpone the 11th China–EU summit scheduled to take place in Lyon France in 2008.[14]

Global events also took away from the luster of this partnership, particularly the global financial crisis from which the world has yet to fully recover. While the world economy scrambled to find its footing, China found itself heavily impacted by the contagion which provoked a host of domestic reactions. For some policy makers in China, this was the moment that showed that the reign of the West (and particularly the US) was coming to an end and that China should use this opportunity to take a more assertive stance. China, after all, held vast amounts of US debt (over a $1 trillion). Chinese statements at the highest level reflected both apprehension over the contagion, but also a growing desire to influence US policy through financial statecraft. This produced mixed results.[15] The crisis, however, signaled a new normal, pointing to the extent of economic/financial interdependence of all the major economies.

European economies were hard-hit as a result, and while they took brave measures to boost the real economy, protect jobs and contain the damage,[16] the crisis was taking place in real time, and it was difficult for them to act as a union, given the range of interests of different member–states. In the height of the financial meltdown, China proved its commitment to Europe and to global financial stability by buying Eurozone government bonds[17] and also bonds by the European Financial Stability Facility. Still, the crisis was the first serious challenge to the euro and raised questions about its durability and design. The repercussions in the Eurozone amongst some of its members have been such that they have brought into question the level of solidarity among member-states. As a result of these outcomes, Europe's status as an important global actor was put into question and raised concerns about whether the EU could continue to speak in one voice. Moreover, the shock of the Brexit vote in 2016, the wave of migrants and refugees arriving starting in the summer of 2015, and terrorist attacks have all put European unity to the test.

While the partnership was meant to be multidimensional, the emphasis was overwhelmingly in the economic sector, followed by the political-diplomatic sector, then security, rule of law and finally the environment.[18] According to research conducted by Jonathan Holslag, data from joint statements made after each annual Sino–European summit from 2001–2007 indicated that identified interests (needs or necessities) were low compared to dialogues and exchanges that were viewed as necessary.[19] Although the prioritization of the economy was to be expected, during the period for which the aforementioned data provides some insight, the environment at least was already on the table for discussion, although it still ranked low in the declared priorities of defined common interests.

The partnership that Europe and China had claimed to be building was from the outset heavily focused on trade. They had seen each other as providing lucrative markets in which their goods could find an outlet. In 2014, they had become leading trading partners, trading well over €1 billion per day.[20] In 2015, trade had risen to €520,812 billion.[21] According to EU data, the EU imports industrial and consumer goods from China such as machinery and equipment, footwear and clothing, furniture and lamps, and toys. European exports to China are concentrated on machinery and equipment, motor vehicles, aircraft and chemicals. Service trade accounts for only one-tenth of the total trade of goods. Investment flows were rising but still accounted for 2 to 3 percent of overall European investments abroad. Chinese investment in Europe started from a lower base but continues to rise.[22] The EU is now China's top trading partner, and China is Europe's second largest trading partner.

Chinese investment has been a source of both relief and angst because the trade deficit between them remains high, giving rise to protests and opposition by European industries such as textiles and steel that have met with overwhelming competition. The trade deficit in 2015, for instance, stood at approximately €180,060 billion.[23] China too has its own grievances such as the continued arms embargo[24] (not lifted at the time of writing) and the denial of market economy status[25] (not yet granted at the time of writing). These issues continue to weigh negatively on China's assessment of what their relationship with Europe truly means. While both sides acknowledge the importance and breadth of their association, much of the literature tends to see the glass as half empty rather than half full, pointing out obstacles and arguing that the "comprehensive strategic partnership" lacks the "comprehensive and strategic" character that is implied in its name. Scholars and analysts are not alone in their assessments. It appears that the actors themselves, while trying hard to achieve such a partnership, are hampered by constraints. They have largely missed the core opportunity that presents itself in the form of needed global leadership for the Anthropocene. The real but limited priorities which both put forth as pre-requisites for a meaningful "comprehensive strategic partnership" may possibly never be met. The EU can neither ignore its domestic populations nor will it be able to completely overlook issues of human rights and democracy. They are the values that the Continent safeguards as a result of its long historical procession through revolution and the Enlightenment. Europe, moreover, cannot and does not want to break its relationship with the US, which it does not view as a global rival but as an ally it traditionally can count on. Although the Cold War is over, there are new threats facing the Europeans both internal and external that are a result of an aging population, mass migration, terrorism, economic stagnation and an unpredictable and increasingly aggressive Russia. For these reasons, they continue to value their relationship with their partner across the Atlantic.

For China, the problem, perhaps, lies in the fact that the economy has been the primary goal for the Chinese government outside its declared and evolving core interests,[26] which include national re-unification with Taiwan, continued territorial integrity, maintaining national security, the preservation of its political system and claims in the South and East China Seas.[27] China's pre-occupation with internal stability and growth often conflates domestic and international priorities, merging them under the rubric of economic opportunity, investment and trade.[28] Such an outlook dates back to the years of Deng Xiaoping who saw "economics" as the strategic path by which China would develop swiftly and would gain both military and international leverage and influence. In 1975, Deng Xiaoping had declared that,

> The whole Party must now give serious thought to our country's overall interest … The first stage is to build an independent and relatively comprehensive industrial and economic system by 1980. The second will be to turn China into a powerful socialist country with modern agriculture, industry, national defense and science and technology by the end of this century, that is, within the next 25 years … This constitutes the overall national interest.[29]

Deng Xiaoping understood full well that in order to achieve his goal, China needed to emerge from isolation and work with other powers, especially those that could help with economic transformation. In a speech before the Central Committee in 1983, he expressed the urgency of building ties with Western Europe to achieve the strategic goal of economic rebirth,

> We should open our country wider to the outside world. Now that the West European countries are beset with economic difficulties, we should lose no time in seeking their cooperation, so as to speed up our technological transformation … China provides a huge market, so many countries wish to develop cooperation or do business with us. We should seize this opportunity. It is a matter of strategic importance.[30]

At present, the single-mindedness governing Chinese transformation both internally and externally may have reached its limit. The overwhelming emphasis of international cooperation through trade and development may also have reached its limit. Although global trade continues to grow, so does the backlash against it. New trade deals are facing more public scrutiny and opposition.[31] The Transatlantic Trade and Investment Partnership (TTIP) and the TPP both seem to have been derailed by opposition. The EU–Canadian Agreement was initially vetoed by the French-speaking Wallonia region of Belgium with just 3.6 million people, shocking both the EU and Canada. In the end, the agreement was signed, but such is the climate surrounding new free trade agreements.[32] Trade deals are now being vilified and branded as being responsible for the growing economic malaise of many Organization for Economic Cooperation and Development (OECD) countries. They are seen as prompting unfair competition that threatens a lifestyle that has come to be expected. China has predominantly built its image of ascendancy on its growing economic strength. This often works against its interests over time, because populations feel that there is an unclear agenda behind the PRC's generosity and that its heavy-handed promotion of its exports threatens their livelihoods.

According to the Pew Report of 2014, confidence in President Xi to do the right thing in world affairs was a resounding no in Spain at 72 percent, in Germany at 62 percent, in Italy at 64 percent, in Greece at 60 percent and in Poland at 63 percent.[33] In answering a question about whether the growing Chinese economy is good for their country 53 percent of those polled in France responded that it wasn't, and in Italy the number was a staggering 75 percent.[34] In a 2015 PEW poll, when asked whether China will/has replaced the US as a superpower, 66 percent of the French say it had, along with 59 percent of Germans, 60 percent of the Spanish and 57 percent of the Italians. Ratings of favorability toward China are also informative, with 60 percent of Germans giving China unfavorable ratings, along with 57 percent of Italians, 44 percent of Poles, 49 percent of the French and 37 percent of the British.[35] These numbers reflect the apprehension that China will overtake Europe economically, altering the standard of living on the continent. Basing so much of its prestige as a rising nation on its dramatic economic achievements may be more of a vulnerability than the PRC had banked on. Moreover, the slow-down in growth rates within China, the dramatic stock market collapse in 2016[36] and recent moves in the South China Sea have tainted their image of invulnerability and given rise to a discourse of paper tigers.

These constraints notwithstanding, the EU and China continue to work on enriching their contacts and deepening their cooperation. President Xi Jinping's trip to Europe in 2014 was meant to revitalize the relationship.

> We need to build four bridges for peace, growth, reform and the progress of civilization, so that the China-EU comprehensive strategic partnership will take on even greater global significance … We must uphold the open market, speed up negotiations on the investment agreement, actively explore the possibility of a free trade area, and strive to achieve the ambitious goal of bringing two-way trade to $1 trillion by 2020,

President Xi told dignitaries in Belgium.[37] The message that he sought to convey was that through the Silk Road economic belt, Asia and Europe could be integrated to transform themselves into the "twin engines" of economic growth. However upbeat Xi's message strove to be, continued constraints often result in frustration, disappointment and distrust and run the danger of stifling meaningful cooperation.

Yet, I submit that there is one key area of global importance that provides China and Europe a tangible goal for a transformative strategic partnership. A full-blown partnership for the Anthropocene with climate action at its core gives the world its best chance for confronting the coming crisis. While such a partnership enables China and Europe to achieve their economic and investment objectives and build their technological cooperation, it more importantly fashions a common vision that allows them to bypass the pitfalls of US–style realpolitik.

Fortunately, many crucial structures for such a partnership are already in place. In 2005, the EU–China Partnership on Climate Change was launched and a climate change action plan drafted. By 2007, green growth and clean energy had become a new frontier for collaboration. As a result, the climate crisis became a vehicle for more meaningful and robust cooperation. The reasons for the convergence of interests in this area are manifold. For the EU, public awareness and activism with respect to the climate crisis pushed political elites to make the climate crisis a mainstream concern for all political parties. Furthermore, the Stern Review in 2005[38] opened the door to the realization of the heavy economic burden that rising temperatures would entail, transforming climate change into a priority for action. Moreover, renewables offered an attractive new possibility for growth in a continent whose economy was stagnating and did not have adequate fossil fuel resources. By the same token, the sheer urgency of transitioning to a low carbon economy called for investment in research and development and technology development.

China, too, embraced the idea of collaborating with Europe on climate action for a series of reasons. Its environmental challenges, as we have seen in chapter four, had become enormous, and public pressure for action was mounting. In the 10th Five-Year Plan (FYP) (2001–2005), the government offered some acknowledgement of the crisis, pointing to the need to diversify its energy mix and promote a less intensive model of industrialization. It addressed environmental protection and public health and set out to reverse some of the damage done by extensive deforestation and the lax handling of pollutants.[39] Moreover, renewable energy production was a win–win for China, allowing it more energy independence from coal and mostly imported oil. Renewables could boost its energy capacity in response to its ever-growing needs. Renewables, furthermore, helped create a new market for the production and export of renewable energy source (RES) applications and provided the possibility for reducing the atmospheric pollution that was chocking its cities. Europe had much to offer China in this domain both through technology transfer and extensive expertise in energy efficiency and more sustainable urban planning.

There was initial enthusiasm about building up this industrial exchange in renewable applications. For Europeans the exchange would lower costs of production, making RES more affordable and widespread. This would make it possible to help fulfill its ambitious goals to decarbonize the economy. China too recognized the opportunity to build up a new industry, acquire technological knowledge that it lacked and boost its energy security. Producing energy locally had the added bonus of not having its energy supplies vulnerable to disruption given that the US "controlled" the seas by which the majority of China's fossil fuels were being transported. Clean energy, furthermore, could help reduce China's dependence on coal that was responsible for the staggering pollution of large cities.[40] As these exchanges deepened, they produced tangible results. China's turn to renewables, for example, produced a significant decline in coal use in 2015. Li Junfeng, Director General at the National Climate Change Research and International Cooperation Center, noted that,

This trend may continue for 3–5 years or even longer … Today's figures are sending the strong signal of the clear acceleration of China's energy transition. I think thermal [coal] power generation will continue to drop with an annual speed of 2–4% and the non-fossil power generation will stay in a high growth rate of 20%.[41]

The early stage of optimism was tempered by the disappointment that followed Copenhagen in 2009. There was a worry that in the end the technological exchanges and the close working relations on tackling the climate crisis failed to alter China's position on the multilateral climate change talks. In Copenhagen, China "firmly upheld the principle of "common but differentiated responsibilities", steadfastly defended the development rights and interests of the vast number of developing countries and unswervingly safeguarded their unity and coordination."[42] Wen Jiabao himself defended China's position on climate change in his address at the Climate Summit:

The principle of 'common but differentiated responsibilities' represents the core and bedrock of international cooperation on climate change and it must never be compromised … It is totally unjustified to ask them [developing countries] to undertake emission reduction targets beyond their due obligations and capabilities in disregard of historical responsibilities, per capita emissions and different levels of development … emissions from developing countries are primarily survival emissions and international transfer emissions …
    Developed countries must take the lead.[43]

In searching for a party to blame, both the US but especially China were accused of dragging their feet.[44] "It was obvious that the US and China didn't want more than we achieved at Copenhagen," commented Andreas Carlgren the Environment Minister of Sweden, the country that had been holding the rotating EU presidency at the time.[45]

    Europeans began to grow more apprehensive, as well, of China's low cost production of renewables. In 2012, following complaints lodged by the renewables industry, the EC conducted two parallel investigations concerning imports of solar panels from China, an anti-dumping investigation and an anti-subsidy investigation. The duties that were subsequently imposed were on average 47.7 percent, for those exporters who cooperated with the investigation and for the others who accounted for less than 20 percent of imports, they were set at 64.9 percent.[46] The rationale behind the Commission's decision to impose duties was that the renewable energy industry was vital for Europe to be able to achieve its climate goals. Unfair trade practices did not contribute to the health of the global solar industry. The debate over whether or not to scrap duties on Chinese solar imports continues, although there is a divergence of opinions within European industry itself. There are those who believe that the barriers set up to protect Europe's solar industry are impacting the deployment of solar technology because they maintain costs artificially high, resulting in the loss of jobs and a decrease in solar installation across the EU area.[47] Others believe that if they are scrapped, then Chinese overcapacity will send the market crashing.[48]

Bilateral cooperation continued, nonetheless, in a number of policy areas such as domestic emissions reduction policies, low-carbon cities, carbon capture and storage (CCS), greenhouse gas (GHG) emissions from the aviation and maritime industries, and hydrofluorocarbons (HFC). There has also been extensive collaboration over carbon markets. More recently, and following a successful pilot launch of China's first carbon market, with the collaboration of the EU, the two actors are working toward the launching of a national carbon market in China in 2017. According to the EU announcement, more than

> 1500 Chinese carbon market experts have received training on emissions trading under an EU funded project, which started in 2014. The successful results of the roll-out of the seven regional pilot system led the Commission to double its funding for cooperation on carbon markets and is making 10 million euros – more than 70 million yuan - available under the EU's Foreign Partnership Instrument for a new three year co-operation project starting in 2017.[49]

Europe's experience in launching the European Union Emission Trading System (EU ETS) has proven a significant asset. Bringing China on board with a national carbon ETS mechanism will contribute to finally putting a price on carbon, proving that the two powers can achieve concrete and measureable outcomes in the fight against climate change when they collaborate.[50] Miguel Arias Cañete, Commissioner for Climate Action and Energy said:

> This is an exciting time as China prepares to launch the biggest emissions trading system in the world. The Chinese ETS will play an important role in China's development towards a low-carbon economy. I look forward to continuing our excellent cooperation and to supporting China as it takes this ambitious step. Cooperation between the world's two largest emission trading systems represents a strong and promising signal for the development of future carbon markets worldwide.[51]

The disappointment of Copenhagen lingered for quite some time. It may have been too early for the world to accept the full impact of the climate crisis and the role of nations in stopping its accelerating speed, especially given the fact that it impacted both developed and developing countries indiscriminately. Without the deep disappointment of Copenhagen,[52] and the unwavering leadership of the EU that kept up the momentum even when worldwide pessimism had taken over, the outcome of COP 21 in Paris may not have been possible. The question that begs for an answer is whether today it is merely enough to pursue joint cooperation for emission reductions, deployment of renewable energy applications and adaptation and mitigation. Does the response to the climate crisis necessitate only a logistical framework of dos and don'ts encompassed in a plan, or does it necessitate something more to mobilize global society quickly and effectively? I contend that it needs a narrative that transcends mere planning and a functional logic of engagement. Climate change action and leadership in the Anthropocene should become important components of a grand strategy. There are contending views on what might constitute "grand strategy." In this context, a plausible analogy is provided by Paul Kennedy who claims that the

> crux of grand strategy lies … in policy, that is in the capacity for the nation's leaders to bring together all of the elements [of national power], both military and non-military, for the preservation and enhancement of the nation's long-term (i.e. in wartime and peacetime) best interests."[53]

Such a grand strategy informs Xi Jinping's attempt to define China's vision with notions of national rejuvenation, the launch of a Chinese Dream and by the Asia–Pacific Dream. Included in his vision was the creation of a global network of partners, the use of soft power and a new type of great power relations[54] that would promote win–win cooperation.[55] Of course, the fact that President Xi has broken from the low profile that Deng Xiaoping had advocated is drawing attention to China's possible underlying "true" intentions. While these words sound noble to Chinese ears, they often have the opposite effect on their audience. National rejuvenation in itself raises warning flags for neighboring South East Asian countries that are fearful of China's rise. Japan is increasingly feeling vulnerable and nationalistic,[56] while incidents in the South China Sea have led the parties in the dispute to worry about a China that is increasingly intransigent over what it perceives as its interests.[57] Soft power may not be enough to alleviate these fears, even though China has been employing it abundantly across its region and throughout the globe. As a result, the US, Japan and South Korea have responded by strengthening their alliance.

Sensing that climate change is an area where political legacies will be made in the future, President Obama in the last half of his second term, made a final push to bring the US back into the climate conversation. Indeed, by jointly making statements about the climate with Xi, first in 2014 and then again in announcing the ratification of the Paris Agreement in 2016, the US was hailed in the media for its leadership. Experts and activists alike expressed optimism that with the two largest emitters on board, now there would be greater global effort to respond to the climate crisis. Obama announced to the world that

> Where there is a will and there is a vision and where countries like China and the United States are prepared to show leadership and to lead by example, it is possible for us to create a world that is more secure, more prosperous and more free than the one that was left for us.

President Xi, in turn, declared: "Our response to climate change bears on the future of our people and the well-being of mankind."[58] Indeed, the two presidents may have even sounded visionary. Even so, Obama framed US–China cooperation as a decision to put aside rivalries and work together on this particular issue. Unfortunately, while his political instincts were correct about the importance of such a leadership paradigm, he did not have the domestic political support to commit the US in following through.

The immediate reaction of the US Congress expressed by Senate Environment and Public Works Chairman Jim Inhofe (R-Okla.) was that "History already shows that this Paris Agreement will fail." He added that, "This latest announcement is the president attempting to once again give the international community the appearance that he can go around Congress in order to achieve his unpopular and widely rejected climate agenda for his legacy."[59] His sentiments were echoed by Sen. John Barrasso (R-Wyo.) who added that, "This questionable unilateral action by the president can and should be struck down as soon as possible."[60] Obama was sharply criticized by his opponents for abusing his executive authority to promote an agenda that will be too costly on the US economy. What these "historic" declarations did prove, however, was that much of the rest of the world desired ambitious leadership for climate action. Obama himself lamented that his rallying cry has not galvanized the US public.[61]

Strikingly absent from the Obama publicity bonanza was any mention of Europe's key contribution to international climate action. For a time, it seemed that Europe had been sidelined. Nonetheless, the EU ratified the Paris Agreement, quietly showing consistency and resolve in its pursuit of concrete action *vis-à-vis* the climate crisis. In contrast to its own previous declarations, however, the EU sounded more subdued and seemed left out of the loop by the world's hegemon and the rising superpower. There was a sense that although Europe continued to actively pursue its climate agenda, internal divisions between members on a number of other issues were distracting it from its commitment and its potential for leadership. Miguel Arias Cañete, the EU Commissioner for Climate Action and Energy sought to rectify this impression:

> They said Europe is too complicated to agree quickly. They said we had too many hoops to jump through. They said we were all talk. Today's decision shows what Europe is all about: unity and solidarity as Member States take a European approach, just as we did in Paris. We are reaching a critical period for decisive climate action. And when the going gets tough, Europe gets going.[62]

Moreover, Jean-Claude Juncker, EC President, who is a fervent believer in European integration, sounded more upbeat when he declared that this

> decision shows that the European Union delivers on promises made. It demonstrates that the Member States can find common ground when it is clear that acting together, as part of the European Union, their impact is bigger than the mere sum of its parts. I am happy to see that today the Member States decided to make history together and bring closer the entry into force

of the first ever universally binding climate change agreement. We must and we can hand over to future generations a world that is more stable, a healthier planet, fairer societies and more prosperous economies. This is not a dream. This is a reality and it is within our reach. Today we are closer to it.[63]

Juncker's statement highlighted what the US president could not bring to the table, public consensus supporting climate action. The Commissioner's tone, furthermore, served to contextualize the importance of the Paris agreement's ratification and underscored that international collaboration was no longer a dream but a growing reality.

Given the outcome of the US presidential election of November 2016, Obama's cameo appearance with China on the climate stage no longer seems pertinent. This leaves Europe and China to fulfill the kind of global hopes expressed by Juncker. Even those who are skeptical about the achievement of the Paris agreement must acknowledge that it sparked new life into the push toward a low carbon future. How much progress nations make will be assessed in the near future, but there is a growing global acceptance that the climate crisis is both real and worsening. Technological innovation and the considerable decrease of prices for the deployment of renewables have already made the case for energy mix diversification. Even while fossil fuel prices have remained low, data shows a steady worldwide increase in the use of renewables.[64] Global extreme weather events have not passed unnoticed and are increasingly worrying states across the globe. Warnings about the acceleration of melting glaciers and the rise of sea levels are also raising alarms. Global mass migration is increasing as a result of the climate crisis. As governments in the developed world are getting a taste of the future, those in the developing world are feeling the brunt of increased population displacements. Although developing nations continue to feel that the developed countries need to do more, they too now are coming to the realization that this is a global problem which impacts every country apart from their particular past contribution in generating the crisis.

While it is too early to discuss in concrete terms future changes in US policy *vis-à-vis* international climate negotiations, it is abundantly clear that the kind of leadership that Obama sought in dealing with the climate crisis will not be in the offing from Donald Trump. With the US becoming once again more of a problem than a solution, China need not find itself alone at the helm nor shy away from its global responsibility. Moreover, it already has a strategic partner that is engaged and has an admirable track record of commitment to both the process of international climate talks and to its objectives.

Paris and later Marrakesh (COP 22) demonstrated that the world is ready to embrace change that the climate crisis necessitates. It does, however, need a more concerted push. Here is where the EU and China have a pivotal role to play. Through their vast network of friends and allies in the developing world, and with their soft power and network diplomacy, they can reach out to offer support, cajole nations to follow up with their pledges and encourage them to become more ambitious. As Xi Jinping said at the opening ceremony of COP 21 in Paris in 2015,

China ... takes an active part in international cooperation on climate change ... China announced in September the establishment of an RMB 20 billion South-South Climate Cooperation Fund. Next year, China will launch cooperation projects to set up 10 pilot low-carbon industrial parks and start 100 mitigation and adaptation programs in other developing countries and provide them with 1,000 training opportunities on climate change ... China will also help other developing countries to increase their financing capacity.[65]

Europe, too, has taken action on this front and is the largest contributor of climate finance to developing countries and the world's biggest aid donor, collectively providing more than half of global official development assistance (ODA). Moreover, the broader EU development strategy has increasingly been integrating climate change.[66] The EU has committed to spend at least 20 percent of its budget by 2020 on climate action. At least €14 billion will support activities in developing countries between 2014 and 2020.[67]

Opting to partner more closely on this issue with the EU, moreover, would demonstrate China's commitment to multilateral diplomacy that has won it many friends in the developing world. It shows consistency with the ideals of the revolution and China's newly evolving grand strategy of win–win cooperation. Furthermore, because the EU has not overtly sought to express its own strength in terms of superpower status, it can partner with China without the baggage of an imbedded competition for supremacy.[68] Such a partnership provides China a way to move beyond relationships driven solely by commercial interests. It would, moreover, enable China to translate economic power into an assertion of ideas and norms in a way that is closer to its own designs instead of preconceived US recipes of how a "responsible stakeholder" is expected to engage internationally.

The climate crisis and the overarching challenges of the Anthropocene are multi-tiered, multi-layered and increasingly complex. As a consequence, they give rise to problems of resource competition, food security, water scarcity, changes in agricultural production, production management, environmental protection, mass population movements, global health, and the design of smart cities. The wide range of challenges and areas ripe for action offer China more flexibility in setting an international agenda that it might prefer to foster in the coming decades. For Europe, a leadership role in the Anthropocene will provide a new narrative for European unity in the face of a global crisis. It will certainly maximize the win–win cooperation with a giant like China and empower the relationship with much more than just an appreciation for each other's long civilization and the benefits of their economic give- and-take. Ultimately, both Europe and China need to decide if they want to be a leaders or mere spectators in the global politics of the Anthropocene.

Notes

1   Jiabao Wen, "Speech by H.E. Wen Jiabao, Premier of the State Council of the People's Republic of China," accessed October 29, 2016, http://www.chinamission.be/eng/sthd/t101949.htm.

2   Ye Zicheng, *Inside China's Grand Strategy: The Perspective from the People's Republic*, edited by Guoli Liu Ph.D and Steven I. Levine (Lexington, KY: University Press of Kentucky, 2010).

3   Commission of the European Communities, "Europe and Asia: A Strategic Framework for Enhanced Partnerships," April 9, 2001, accessed September 2, 2016, http://eur-lex.europa.eu/legal-content/EN/TXT/PDF/?uri=CELEX:52001DC0469&from=EN.

4   European Commission, "A Long Term Policy for China-Europe Relations," 1995, accessed September 10, 2016, eur-lex.europa.eu/legal-content/EN/TXT/PDF/?uri=C ELEX:52001DC0469&from=EN.

5   "The EU's Relations with China – Overview," accessed April 2004, http://www.europarl.europa.eu/meetdocs/2004_2009/documents/fd/d-ch2004092803/d-ch2004092803en.pdf.

6   D. Scott, "China and the EU: A Strategic Axis for the Twenty-First Century?" *International Relations* 21, no. 1 (March 1, 2007): 23–45; Feng Zhongping and Huang Jing, "China's Strategic Partnership Diplomacy," June 27, 2014, http://papers.ssrn.com/sol3/papers.cfm?abstract_id=2459948.

7   Chen Zhimin, "Results, Regrets and Reinvention: Premier Wen's Last China-EU Summit," *European Strategy*, no. 6 (October 2012), http://fride.org/descarga/PB_6_Last_China_EU_summit.pdf. "China's Policy Paper on the EU: Deepen the China-EU Comprehensive Strategic Partnership for Mutual Benefit and Win-Win Cooperation," accessed October 29, 2016, http://www.fmprc.gov.cn/mfa_eng/wjdt_665385/wjzcs/t1143406.shtml;"China's Policy Paper on EU," accessed October 29, 2016, http://www.chinamission.be/eng/zywj/zywd/t1227623.htm.

8   Francis G. Snyder, *The European Union and China, 1949-2008 Basic Documents and Commentary* (Oxford; Portland, OR.: Hart, 2009), 491;"China's Policy Paper on the EU."

9   "Speech by H.E. Wen Jiabao, Premier of the State Council of the People's Republic of China."

10 "Speech by H.E. Wen Jiabao, Premier of the State Council of the People's Republic of China."

11 Chen Zhimin, "Results, Regrets and Reinvention: Premier Wen's Last China-EU Summit."

12 David L. Shambaugh, *China's Future* (Cambridge, UK: Polity, 2016), 130.

13 The US and the EU are also negotiating the TTIP; *Commission of the European Communities*, "Questions and Answers (TTIP) – Trade," accessed October 30, 2016, http://ec.europa.eu/trade/policy/in-focus/ttip/about-ttip/questions-and-answers/.

14 European Union, "EU-China Summit Postponed - European Union Statement," accessed October 29, 2016, http://archive-ue2008.fr/PFUE/lang/en/accueil/PFUE-11_2008/PFUE-26.11.2008/Declaration_UE_Report_Sommet.html; Sebastian Bersick, "EU-China Relations in Times of Crisis," *EurActiv.com*, October 28, 2011, http://www.euractiv.com/section/global-europe/opinion/eu-china-relations-in-times-of-crisis/.

15 For the complexities of these attempts see Daniel W. Drezner, "Bad Debts: Assessing China's Financial Influence in Great Power Politics," *International Security* 34, no. 2 (Fall 2009): 7–45.

16 As Greece's Deputy Minister of Labor and Social Welfare, I participated in EU meetings where member-states' policies to protect the working population and the real economy were the major topic of discussion after the 2008 crisis. All countries were concerned about job losses and, depending on the nature of their economies, deployed varying programs to stabilize the situation, sharing best practices with each other.

17 "China to Keep Investing in Euro Zone Debt: China Central Bank," *Reuters*, February 15, 2012, http://www.reuters.com/article/us-china-europe-idUSTRE81E07J20120215.

18 Jonathan Holslag, "The Elusive Axis: Assessing the EU-China Strategic Partnership," *JCMS: Journal of Common Market Studies* 49, no. 2 (March 2011): 293–313.

19   Holslag, "The Elusive Axis: Assessing the EU-China Strategic Partnership."

20   European Commission, "China – Trade," accessed October 30, 2016, http://ec.europa.eu/trade/policy/countries-and-regions/countries/china/."Facts   and   figures   on EU-China trade," *European Commission-Trade*, March 2014, http://trade.ec.europa.eu/doclib/docs/2009/september/tradoc_144591.pdf.

21   European Commission-Directorate-General for Trade, "European Union, Trade in goods with China,", June 21, 2016, accessed October 30, 2016, http://trade.ec.europa.eu/doclib/docs/2006/september/tradoc_113366.pdf.

22   European Commission, "China – Trade," accessed September 26, 2016, http://ec.europa.eu/trade/policy/countries-and-regions/countries/china/.

23   "European Union, Trade in goods with China."

24   Nicola Casarini, "The Evolution of the EU-China Relationship: From Constructive Engagement to Strategic Partnership," *Institute for Security Studies, European Union*, October 2006.
      France and Germany both proposed the lifting of the embargo of arms sales in 2003 but met with staunch opposition from various quarters. The governments of Sweden and Denmark did not wish to oppose the lifting of the ban but their parliaments strongly opposed that measure. A variety of reasons led to the maintenance of the embargo, including the fact that in 2005 China passed the anti-cessation law. Other reactions came from the Taiwan lobby, the perceived lack of progress on human rights and US opposition to a change in policy. According to the Financial Times, Japan has become worried that the Brexit vote will allow the UK to effectively undermine the EU embargo which has yet to be lifted.Robin Harding, "Japan Fears Brexit Blow to EU Arms Embargo on China," *Financial Times*, July 4, 2016, https://www.ft.com/content/219af680-41c6-11e6-b22f-79eb4891c97d.

25   Daniela Vincenti, "EU Lawmakers Reject Granting China the Market Economy Status," *EurActiv.com*, May 12, 2016, https://www.euractiv.com/section/trade-society/news/eu-lawmakers-reject-granting-china-the-market-economy-status/.
      In an attempt to pre-empt the EC decision that was likely to grant market economy status to China, the European Parliament voted overwhelmingly against such a development. They urged the European Commission to pay closer attention to EU industry concerns, trade unions, and stakeholders especially because overproduction capacity in China is leading to very cheap imports. Already, the EU has 37 anti-dumping measures in force which if Market Economy Status (MES) were to be passed would become completely ineffective. At the time of writing this has become a topic of heated debate. Both in Washington, D.C. and among many EU governments there is a growing fear that if China were to be granted MES it would open the floodgates for cheap imports. The WTO Protocol to which anti-dumping laws are tied, expires in December of 2016, and until then the EU commission needs to strike a compromise given that MES is one of China's top political/economic aspirations resulting from its accession to the WTO. "Brussels Prepares Market Economy Compromise for China," *Financial Times*, accessed October 30, 2016, https://www.ft.com/content/9412fe0a-4dca-11e6-8172-e39ecd3b86fc.

26   Zhaokui Fengh, "What Are China's Core Interests?" *China-US Focus*, accessed October 30, 2016, http://www.chinausfocus.com/foreign-policy/what-are-chinas-core-interests-2.

27   China's definition of core interests may be getting broader to encompass more issues including sustainable development. Caitlin Campbell et al., "China's 'core Interests' and the East China Sea," *US-China Economic and Security Review Commission Staff Research Backgrounder*, May 10 (2013); Edward Wong, "Security Law Suggests a Broadening of China's 'Core Interests,'" *The New York Times*, July 2, 2015, http://www.nytimes.com/2015/07/03/world/asia/security-law-suggests-a-broadening-of-chinas-core-interests.html. See: Sophia Kalantzakos, *China and the Geopolitics of Rare Earths*, (New York: Oxford University Press, 2017).

28   Jisi Wang, "China's Search for a Grand Strategy," *Foreign Affairs*, (March- April 2011): 68–79, https://www.foreignaffairs.com/articles/china/2011-02-20/chinas-search-grand-strategy.

29   B. J. Murphy, "The Whole Party Should Take the Overall Interest Into Account and Push the Economy Forward," *The Selected Works of Deng Xiaoping*, February 25, 2013, https://dengxiaopingworks.wordpress.com/2013/02/25/the-whole-party-should-take-the-overall-interest-into-account-and-push-the-economy-forward/.

30   B. J. Murphy, "Use the Intellectual Resources of Other Countries and Open Wider to the Outside World," *The Selected Works of Deng Xiaoping*, March 8, 2013, https://dengxiaopingworks.wordpress.com/2013/03/08/use-the-intellectual-resources-of-other-countries-and-open-wider-to-the-outside-world/.

31   Paul Malone, "Trans-Pacific Partnership Agreement Seems Doomed," *The Sydney Morning Herald*, October 27, 2016, http://www.smh.com.au/comment/transpacific-part-nership-agreement-seems-doomed-20161027-gscd4x.html.Ben Chapman, "TTIP Trade Deal Could Re-launched Under a Different Name, Say EU Ministers," *The Independent*, September 23, 2016, http://www.independent.co.uk/news/business/news/ttip-latest-eu-deal-dead-must-be-relaunched-transparency-say-ministers-a7325276.html.

32   "EU-Canada Sign Long-Delayed Trade Deal," VOA, accessed October 31, 2016, http://www.voanews.com/a/eu-canada-sign-long-delayed-trade-agreement/3571928.html.

33   "China's Image," *Pew Research Center's Global Attitudes Project*, July 14, 2014, http://www.pewglobal.org/2014/07/14/chapter-2-chinas-image/.

34   "China's Image."

35   Richard Wike, Bruce Stokes, and Jacob Poushter, "Views of China and the Global Balance of Power," *Pew Research Center's Global Attitudes Project*, June 23, 2015, http://www.pewglobal.org/2015/06/23/2-views-of-china-and-the-global-balance-of-power/.

36   The Chinese stock-market had crashed in the summer of 2015 leading to a dramatic intervention from Beijing to avoid the contagion from spreading and aiming to stabilize the market flux. See Charles Riley and Sophia Yan, "China's Stock Market Crash … in 2 Minutes," *CNNMoney*, July 9, 2015, http://money.cnn.com/2015/07/09/invest-ing/china-crash-in-two-minutes/index.html; Riley and Yan,"China's Stock Market Crashes—Again," *The Economist*, January 4, 2016, http://www.economist.com/news/business-and-finance/21685146-chinas-stocks-and-currency-start-2016-big-tumbles-chinas-stockmarket;

        Chao Deng, Anjani Trivedi and Mark Magnier, "Why China's Market Fell So Much," *Wall Street Journal*, January 5, 2016, sec. Markets, http://www.wsj.com/articles/china-market-plunge-has-investors-wondering-about-more-turmoil-1451919595.

37   Jiao Wu, "Xi's Trip Builds Bridge to Europe," Chinadaily, accessed November 2, 2016, http://www.chinadaily.com.cn/world/2014xivisiteu/2014-04/01/content_17398123.htm.

38   Nicholas Stern, *The Economics of Climate Change: The Executive Summary of the Stern Review*, vol. 2012, November 5, 2010, http://www.hm-treasury.gov.uk/d/CLOSED_SHORT_executive_summary.pdf.

39   "The 10th Five-Year Plan (2001–2005)," accessed December 10, 2016, http://www.gov.cn/english/2006-04/05/content_245624.htm.

40   *Global Times*, "China Enters into Post-Coal Growth Era: Scholars," accessed November 2, 2016, http://www.globaltimes.cn/content/996517.shtml.

41   Damian Carrington, "China's Coal-Burning in Significant Decline, Figures Show," *The Guardian*, January 19, 2016, sec. Environment, https://www.theguardian.com/environment/2016/jan/19/chinas-coal-burning-in-significant-decline-figures-show.

42   "China's Position and Comment on COP 15," accessed November 2, 2016, http://dk.china-embassy.org/eng/ztbd/tqbh/t646842.htm.

43   "China's Position and Comment on COP 15."

44 Dale Jamieson, *Reason in a Dark Time: Why the Struggle Against Climate Change Failed – and What It Means for Our Future*, 1st edition (Oxford; New York: Oxford University Press, 2014), 56-59.

45 James Kanter, "E.U. Blames Others for 'Great Failure' on Climate," *The New York Times*, December 22, 2009, http://www.nytimes.com/2009/12/23/world/europe/23iht-climate.html.

46 European Commission, "EU Imposes Definitive Measures on Chinese Solar Panels, Confirms Undertaking with Chinese Solar Panel Exporters - Trade," accessed November 2, 2016, http://trade.ec.europa.eu/doclib/press/index.cfm?id=996.

47 Madeleine Cuff, "European Commission Extends Minimum Prices for Chinese Solar Panels," *Business Green*, December 8, 2015, http://www.businessgreen.com/bg/news/2438108/european-commission-extends-minimum-prices-for-chinese-solar-panels; "European Trade Groups Call for End to Duties on Solar Panels," *Hong Kong Means Business*, accessed November 2, 2016, http://hkmb.hktdc.com/en/1X0A6TWP.

48 EU ProSun, "Trade Distortions – Overcapacity," accessed November 2, 2016, http://www.prosun.org/en/fair-competition/trade-distortions/overcapacity.html.

49 European Commission, "EU and China: Strengthening Ties between the World's Largest Emission Trading Systems in 2017," November 23, 2016, http://ec.europa.eu/clima/news/articles/news_2016102001_en.

50 The US does not have a federal ETS scheme. A proposed cap and trade program failed in Congress in 2011. It does however have two CO2 emissions trading schemes: the Regional Greenhouse Gas Initiative (RGGI), covering nine states in the northeast, and a program in California.

Regional Greenhouse Gas Initiative (RGGI) CO2 Budget Trading Program, "Home Page," accessed November 2, 2016, https://www.rggi.org/;"California Cap and Trade | Center for Climate and Energy Solutions," accessed November 2, 2016, http://www.c2es.org/us-states-regions/key-legislation/california-cap-trade.

51 "EU and China: Strengthening Ties between the World's Largest Emission Trading Systems in 2017."

52 Daniel Bodansky, "The Copenhagen Climate Change Conference: A Postmortem," *American Journal of International Law* 104, no. 2 (2010): 230–40.

53 Paul Kennedy, ed., *Grand Strategies in War and Peace*, Reprint edition (New Haven: Yale University Press, 1992), 5.

54 Chen Li and Lucy Xu, "Chinese Enthusiasm and American Cynicism Over the 'New Type of Great Power Relations,'" *Brookings*, November 30, 2001, https://www.brookings.edu/opinions/chinese-enthusiasm-and-american-cynicism-over-the-new-type-of-great-power-relations/.

55 Stig Stenslie and Chen Gang, "Xi Jinping's Grand Strategy: From vision to implementation," in Robert S. Ross and Jo Inge Bekkevold, eds., *China in the Era of Xi Jinping: Domestic and Foreign Policy Challenges* (Washington, DC: Georgetown University Press, 2016), 121–123.

56 Will Ripley and Eimi Yamamitsu, "Assertive Japan Poised to Abandon 70 Years of Pacifism," *CNN*, accessed September 29, 2016, http://www.cnn.com/2015/09/16/asia/japan-military-constitution/index.html; Justin McCurry, "Japan Stokes Tensions with China over Plan to Buy Disputed Islands," *The Guardian*, September 5, 2012, sec. World news, https://www.theguardian.com/world/2012/sep/05/japan-china-disputed-islands; Sheila Smith, "Will Japanese Change Their Constitution?" *Forbes*, accessed October 2, 2016, http://www.forbes.com/sites/sheilaasmith/2016/07/07/japans-constitution/.

57 Katie Hunt and Vivian Kam CNN, "China: South China Sea Island Building 'Almost Complete,'" *CNN*, accessed September 25, 2016, http://www.cnn.com/2015/06/17/asia/china-south-china-sea-land-reclamation/index.html; Jesse Johnson, "China, Russia to Carry out Joint Military Drills in South China Sea," *The Japan Times Online*,

July 29, 2016, http://www.japantimes.co.jp/news/2016/07/29/asia-pacific/china-rus-sia-carry-joint-military-drills-south-china-sea/; Norman P. Aquino and Reo Calonzo, "Duterte Seeks Arms From China, Ends Joint Patrols With U.S.," *Bloomberg.com*, September 13, 2016, http://www.bloomberg.com/news/articles/2016-09-13/duterte-courts-china-for-weapons-ends-joint-patrols-with-u-s; Reuters with CNBC.com, "International Court Strikes down China's Territorial Claim," *CNBC*, July 12, 2016, http://www.cnbc.com/2016/07/12/tensions-in-south-china-sea-to-persist-even-after-court-ruling.html.

58   Fiona Harvey, Tom Phillips and Alan Yuhas, "Breakthrough as US and China Agree to Ratify Paris Climate Deal," *The Guardian*, September 3, 2016, sec. Environment, https://www.theguardian.com/environment/2016/sep/03/breakthrough-us-china-agree-ratify-paris-climate-change-deal.

59   Jean Chemnick, "U.S. and China Formally Commit to Paris Climate Accord," *Scientific American*, accessed November 1, 2016, https://www.scientificamerican.com/article/u-s-and-china-formally-commit-to-paris-climate-accord/.

60   Chemnick, "U.S. and China Formally Commit to Paris Climate Accord."

61   Julie Davis Hirschfeld, Mark Landler, and Coral Davenport, "Obama on Climate Change: The Trends Are 'Terrifying,'" *The New York Times*, September 8, 2016, http://www.nytimes.com/2016/09/08/us/politics/obama-climate-change.html.

62   "Ministers Approve EU Ratification of Paris Agreement - European Commission," accessed November 1, 2016, http://ec.europa.eu/clima/news/articles/news_2016 093001_en.htm.

63   "Ministers Approve EU Ratification of Paris Agreement."

64   REN21, "Renewables 2016: Global Status Report," accessed October 1, 2016, http://www.ren21.net/wp-content/uploads/2016/06/GSR_2016_Full_Report.pdf.

65   Jinping Xi, "Full Text of President Xi's Speech at Opening Ceremony of Paris Climate Summit – World" Chinadaily, accessed November 1, 2016, http://www.chinadaily.com.cn/world/XiattendsParisclimateconference/2015-12/01/content_22592469.htm.

66   European Commission, "International Climate Finance," accessed November 1, 2016, http://ec.europa.eu/clima/policies/international/finance/index_en.htm.

67   European Commission, "International Climate Finance."

68   It would have been hard for the EU to project its own strength as a superpower because of the fact that it is not one country nor a federation of states but "an organi-zation spanning policy areas, from climate, environment and health to external rela-tions and security, justice and migration." From "The EU in Brief," *Europa*, June 16, 2016, https://europa.eu/european-union/about-eu/eu-in-brief_en.

Bibliography

Aquino, Norman P., and Reo Calonzo. "Duterte Seeks Arms From China, Ends Joint Patrols With U.S." *Bloomberg.com*, September 13, 2016. http://www.bloomberg.com/news/articles/2016-09-13/duterte-courts-china-for-weapons-ends-joint-patrols-with-u-s.

Beesley, Arthur. "Brussels Prepares Market Economy Compromise for China." *Financial Times*. Accessed October 30, 2016. https://www.ft.com/content/9412fe0a-4dca-11e6-8172-e39ecd3b86fc.

Bersick, Sebastian. "EU-China Relations in Times of Crisis." *EurActiv.com*, October 28, 2011. http://www.euractiv.com/section/global-europe/opinion/eu-china-relations-in-times-of-crisis/.

Bodansky, Daniel. "The Copenhagen Climate Change Conference: A Postmortem." *American Journal of International Law* 104, no. 2 (2010): 230–40.

Brown, Kerry, ed. The EU-China Relationship: European Perspectives: A Manual for Policy Makers. Hackensack, NJ: Imperial College Press, 2015.

Campbell, Caitlin, Ethan Meick, Kimberly Hsu, and Craig Murray. "China's 'core Interests' and the East China Sea." *US-China Economic and Security Review Commission Staff Research Backgrounder, May* 10 (2013).

Carrington, Damian. "China's Coal-Burning in Significant Decline, Figures Show." *The Guardian*, January 19, 2016, sec. Environment. https://www.theguardian.com/environment/2016/jan/19/chinas-coal-burning-in-significant-decline-figures-show.

Casarini, Nicola. "The Evolution of the EU-China Relationship: From Constructive Engagement to Strategic Partnership." *Institute for Security Studies, European Union*, October 2006.

Center for Climate and Energy Solutions. "California Cap and Trade." Accessed November 2, 2016. http://www.c2es.org/us-states-regions/key-legislation/california-cap-trade.

Chapman, Ben. "TTIP Trade Deal Could Re-Launched Under a Different Name, Say EU Ministers" *The Independent*, September 23, 2016. http://www.independent.co.uk/news/business/news/ttip-latest-eu-deal-dead-must-be-relaunched-transparency-say-ministers-a7325276.html.

Chemnick, Jean. "U.S. and China Formally Commit to Paris Climate Accord." *Scientific American*. Accessed November 1, 2016. https://www.scientificamerican.com/article/u-s-and-china-formally-commit-to-paris-climate-accord/.

Commission of the European Communities. "Europe and Asia: A Strategic Framework for Enhanced Partnerships," April 9, 2001. http://eur-lex.europa.eu/legal-content/EN/TXT/PDF/?uri=CELEX:52001DC0469&from=EN.

Cuff, Madeleine. "European Commission Extends Minimum Prices for Chinese Solar Panels." *Business Green*, December 8, 2015. http://www.businessgreen.com/bg/news/2438108/european-commission-extends-minimum-prices-for-chinese-solar-panels.

Davis, Julie Hirschfeld, Mark Landler and Coral Davenport. "Obama on Climate Change: The Trends Are 'Terrifying.'" *The New York Times*, September 8, 2016. http://www.nytimes.com/2016/09/08/us/politics/obama-climate-change.html.

Deng, Chao, Anjani Trivedi, and Mark Magnier. "Why China's Market Fell So Much." *Wall Street Journal*, January 5, 2016, sec. Markets. http://www.wsj.com/articles/china-market-plunge-has-investors-wondering-about-more-turmoil-1451919595.

Drezner, Daniel W. "Bad Debts: Assessing China's Financial Influence in Great Power Politics." *International Security* 34, no. 2 (Fall 2009): 7–45.

Embassy of the People's Republic of China in Denmark. "China's Position and Comment on COP 15." Accessed November 2, 2016. http://dk.china-embassy.org/eng/ztbd/tqbh/t646842.htm.

European Commission. "A Long Term Policy for China-Europe Relations." European Commission, 1995. eur-lex.europa.eu/legal-content/EN/TXT/PDF/?uri=CELEX:52001DC0469&from=EN.

European Commission. "China – Trade." Accessed September 26, 2016. http://ec.europa.eu/trade/policy/countries-and-regions/countries/china/.

European Commission. "China - Trade - European Commission." Accessed October 30, 2016. http://ec.europa.eu/trade/policy/countries-and-regions/countries/china/.

European Commission. "EU and China: Strengthening Ties between the World's Largest Emission Trading Systems in 2017." Accessed November 1, 2016. http://ec.europa.eu/clima/news/articles/news_2016102001_en.htm.

European Commission. "EU Imposes Definitive Measures on Chinese Solar Panels, Confirms Undertaking with Chinese Solar Panel Exporters – Trade" Accessed November 2, 2016. http://trade.ec.europa.eu/doclib/press/index.cfm?id=996.

European Commission. "Ministers Approve EU Ratification of Paris Agreement." Accessed November 1, 2016. http://ec.europa.eu/clima/news/articles/news_2016093001_en.htm.

European Commission. "Facts and figures on EU-China trade." March 2014. http://trade.ec.europa.eu/doclib/docs/2009/september/tradoc_144591.pdf.

European Commission. "International Climate Finance." Accessed November 1, 2016. http://ec.europa.eu/clima/policies/international/finance/index_en.htm.

European Commission. "Questions and Answers (TTIP) – Trade." Accessed October 30, 2016. http://ec.europa.eu/trade/policy/in-focus/ttip/about-ttip/questions-and-answers/.

EU ProSun. "Trade Distortions – Overcapacity." Accessed November 2, 2016. http://www.prosun.org/en/fair-competition/trade-distortions/overcapacity.html.

European Union. "The EU in Brief." *Europa, the Official EU Website*, June 16, 2016. https://europa.eu/european-union/about-eu/eu-in-brief_en.

European Union. "EU-China Summit Postponed – European Union Statement." Accessed October 29, 2016. http://archive-ue2008.fr/PFUE/lang/en/accueil/PFUE-11_2008/PFUE-26.11.2008/Declaration_UE_Report_Sommet.html

Feng, Zhaokui. "What Are China's Core Interests?" *China-US Focus*. Accessed October 30, 2016. http://www.chinausfocus.com/foreign-policy/what-are-chinas-core-interests-2.

Global times. "China Enters into Post-Coal Growth Era: Scholars." Accessed November 2, 2016. http://www.globaltimes.cn/content/996517.shtml.

Harding, Robin. "Japan Fears Brexit Blow to EU Arms Embargo on China." *Financial Times*, July 4, 2016. https://www.ft.com/content/219af680-41c6-11e6-b22f-79eb4891c97d.

Harvey, Fiona, Tom Phillips, and Alan Yuhas. "Breakthrough as US and China Agree to Ratify Paris Climate Deal." *The Guardian*, September 3, 2016, sec. Environment. https://www.theguardian.com/environment/2016/sep/03/breakthrough-us-china-agree-ratify-paris-climate-change-deal.

Hirschfeld Davis, Julie, Mark Landler, and Coral Davenport. "Obama on Climate Change: The Trends Are 'Terrifying.'" *The New York Times*, September 8, 2016. http://www.nytimes.com/2016/09/08/us/politics/obama-climate-change.html.

HKTDC Research. "European Trade Groups Call for End to Duties on Solar Panels." *Hong Kong Means Business.* Accessed November 2, 2016. http://hkmb.hktdc.com/en/1X0A6TWP.

Holslag, Jonathan. "The Elusive Axis: Assessing the EU-China Strategic Partnership." *JCMS: Journal of Common Market Studies* 49, no. 2 (March 2011): 293–313. doi:10.1111/j.1468-5965.2010.02121.x.

Hunt, Katie, and Vivian Kam. "China: South China Sea Island Building 'Almost Complete.'" *CNN*. Accessed September 25, 2016. http://www.cnn.com/2015/06/17/asia/china-south-china-sea-land-reclamation/index.html.

Jamieson, Dale. *Reason in a Dark Time: Why the Struggle Against Climate Change Failed and What It Means for Our Future.* 1st edition. Oxford; New York: Oxford University Press, 2014.

Johnson, Jesse. "China, Russia to Carry out Joint Military Drills in South China Sea." *The Japan Times Online*, July 29, 2016. http://www.japantimes.co.jp/news/2016/07/29/asia-pacific/china-russia-carry-joint-military-drills-south-china-sea/.

Kanter, James. "E.U. Blames Others for 'Great Failure' on Climate." *The New York Times*, December 22, 2009. http://www.nytimes.com/2009/12/23/world/europe/23iht-climate.html.

Kennedy, Paul, ed. *Grand Strategies in War and Peace.* Reprint edition. New Haven: Yale University Press, 1992.

Li, Cheng, and Lucy Xu. "Chinese Enthusiasm and American Cynicism Over the 'New Type of Great Power Relations.'" *Brookings*, November 30, 2001. https://www.brookings.edu/opinions/chinese-enthusiasm-and-american-cynicism-over-the-new-type-of-great-power-relations/.

McCurry, Justin. "Japan Stokes Tensions with China over Plan to Buy Disputed Islands." *The Guardian*, September 5, 2012, sec. World news. https://www.theguardian.com/world/2012/sep/05/japan-china-disputed-islands.

Malone, Paul. "Trans-Pacific Partnership Agreement Seems Doomed." *The Sydney Morning Herald*, October 27, 2016. http://www.smh.com.au/comment/transpacific-partnership-agreement-seems-doomed-20161027-gscd4x.html.

Ministry of Foreign Affairs of the People's Republic of China. "China's Policy Paper on the EU: Deepen the China-EU Comprehensive Strategic Partnership for Mutual Benefit and Win-Win Cooperation." Accessed October 29, 2016. http://www.fmprc.gov.cn/mfa_eng/wjdt_665385/wjzcs/t1143406.shtml.

Mission of the People's Republic of China to the European Union. "China's Policy Paper on EU." Accessed October 29, 2016. http://www.chinamission.be/eng/zywj/zywd/t1227623.htm.

Murphy, B. J. "The Whole Party Should Take the Overall Interest Into Account and Push the Economy Forward." *The Selected Works of Deng Xiaoping*, February 25, 2013. https://dengxiaopingworks.wordpress.com/2013/02/25/the-whole-party-should-take-the-overall-interest-into-account-and-push-the-economy-forward/.

Murphy, B. J. "Use the Intellectual Resources of Other Countries and Open Wider to the Outside World." *The Selected Works of Deng Xiaoping*, March 8, 2013. https://dengxiaopingworks.wordpress.com/2013/03/08/use-the-intellectual-resources-of-other-countries-and-open-wider-to-the-outside-world/.

Pew Research Center. "Chapter 2: China's Image." *Pew Research Center's Global Attitudes Project*, July 14, 2014. http://www.pewglobal.org/2014/07/14/chapter-2-chinas-image/.

Regional Greenhouse Gas Initiative (RGGI) CO2 Budget Trading Program. "Home Page." Accessed November 2, 2016. https://www.rggi.org/.

REN21. "Renewables 2016: Global Status Report." Accessed October 1, 2016. http://www.ren21.net/wp-content/uploads/2016/06/GSR_2016_Full_Report.pdf.

Reuters with CNBC. "International Court Strikes down China's Territorial Claim." *CNBC*, July 12, 2016. http://www.cnbc.com/2016/07/12/tensions-in-south-china-sea-to-persist-even-after-court-ruling.html.

Ripley, Will, and Eimi Yamamitsu. "Assertive Japan Poised to Abandon 70 Years of Pacifism." *CNN*. Accessed September 29, 2016. http://www.cnn.com/2015/09/16/asia/japan-military-constitution/index.html.

Ross, Robert S., and Jo Inge Bekkevold, eds. *China in the Era of Xi Jinping: Domestic and Foreign Policy Challenges*. Washington, DC: Georgetown University Press, 2016.

Scott, D. "China and the EU: A Strategic Axis for the Twenty-First Century?" *International Relations* 21, no. 1 (March 1, 2007): 23–45.

Shambaugh, David L. *China's Future*. Cambridge, UK: Polity, 2016.

Smith, Sheila. "Will Japanese Change Their Constitution?" *Forbes*. Accessed October 2, 2016. http://www.forbes.com/sites/sheilaasmith/2016/07/07/japans-constitution/.

Snyder, Francis G. *The European Union and China, 1949–2008 Basic Documents and Commentary*. Oxford; Portland, OR: Hart, 2009.

Stern, Nicholas. *The Economics of Climate Change: The Executive Summary of the Stern Review*. Vol. 2012. November 5, 2010. http://www.hm-treasury.gov.uk/d/CLOSED_SHORT_executive_summary.pdf.

The Economist. "China's Stockmarket Crashes—Again." *The Economist*, January 4, 2016. http://www.economist.com/news/business-and-finance/21685146-chinas-stocks-and-currency-start-2016-big-tumbles-chinas-stockmarket.

Vincenti, Daniela. "EU Lawmakers Reject Granting China the Market Economy Status." *EurActiv.com*, May 12, 2016. https://www.euractiv.com/section/trade-society/news/eu-lawmakers-reject-granting-china-the-market-economy-status/.

VOA. "EU-Canada Sign Long-Delayed Trade Deal." *VOA. Accessed October 31, 2016.* http://www.voanews.com/a/eu-canada-sign-long-delayed-trade-agreement/3571928.html.

Wang, Aileen, and Nick Edwards. "China to Keep Investing in Euro Zone Debt: China Central Bank." *Reuters*, February 15, 2012. http://www.reuters.com/article/us-china-europe-idUSTRE81E07J20120215.

Wang, Jisi. "China's Search for a Grand Strategy." *Foreign Affairs*, February 20, 2011. https://www.foreignaffairs.com/articles/china/2011-02-20/chinas-search-grand-strategy.

Wen, Jiabao. "Speech by H.E. Wen Jiabao, Premier of the State Council of the People's Republic of China." Accessed October 29, 2016. http://www.chinamission.be/eng/sthd/t101949.htm.

Wike, Richard, Bruce Stokes, and Jacob Poushter. "Views of China and the Global Balance of Power." *Pew Research Center's Global Attitudes Project*, June 23, 2015. http://www.pewglobal.org/2015/06/23/2-views-of-china-and-the-global-balance-of-power/.

Wong, Edward. "Security Law Suggests a Broadening of China's 'Core Interests.'" *The New York Times*, July 2, 2015. http://www.nytimes.com/2015/07/03/world/asia/security-law-suggests-a-broadening-of-chinas-core-interests.html.

Wu, Jiao. "Xi's Trip Builds Bridge to Europe." Accessed November 2, 2016. http://www.chinadaily.com.cn/world/2014xivisiteu/2014-04/01/content_17398123.htm.

Xi, Jinping. "Full Text of President Xi's Speech at Opening Ceremony of Paris Climate Summit - World - Chinadaily.com.cn." Accessed November 1, 2016. http://www.chinadaily.com.cn/world/XiattendsParisclimateconference/2015-12/01/content_22592469.htm.

Yan, Sophia and Charles Riley. "China's Stock Market Crash … in 2 Minutes." *CNNMoney*, July 9, 2015. http://money.cnn.com/2015/07/09/investing/china-crash-in-two-minutes/index.html.

Zhimin, Chen. "Results, Regrets and Reinvention: Premier Wen's Last China-EU Summit." *European Strategy*, no. 6 (October 2012). http://fride.org/descarga/PB_6_Last_China_EU_summit.pdf

Zicheng, Ye. *Inside China's Grand Strategy: The Perspective from the People's Republic.* Edited by Guoli Liu and Steven I. Levine. Lexington, KY: University Press of Kentucky, 2010.

Zhongping, Feng and Jing, Huang, "China's Strategic Partnership Diplomacy." SSRN, June 27, 2014. http://papers.ssrn.com/sol3/papers.cfm?abstract_id=2459948.

6 Networks of states to spur hope and change

It was never a good idea to sacrifice the importance of climate action on the pyre of the US–China rivalry. The United States (US) continues to vacillate between climate action and climate skepticism, and US–China relations, even at their best, have been plagued by underlying suspicion and possibilities of geopolitical tension. Furthermore, the leadership that Barrack Obama projected to the world with respect to the US position on climate did not correspond to the political realities of Washington, D.C.

The new US president, Donald Trump, moreover, espouses an outlook that is the polar opposite of his predecessor. In order to "make America great again,"[1] Trump for instance, has promised to reinvigorate the coal industry. Though coal's decline is mainly a result of the US shale gas revolution, as a candidate Donald Trump blamed the Obama administration's clean energy agenda for coal's fortunes. Other political developments also spell a retreat from the Obama action plan on climate. There are expected budget cuts for the EPA reminiscent of the Reagan and George W. Bush years of deregulation and dramatic program reduction. Moreover, statements questioning the scientific validity of climate change, a triumphant dominance of both House and Senate by the Republican Party and an expressed preference for US isolation are not encouraging signs for international climate leadership by the US. Even if in practice the new administration does not opt for such a dramatic repositioning, US credibility will have effectively been shattered. All in all there is no longer any realistic possibility that the US will lead the fight in the climate crisis. Fears are already rampant that with the US out of the picture, other nations can and will now choose to pull back from their commitments to the planet and their citizens.[2]

Perhaps all is not lost, however. As I have argued throughout, there is a better and more effective alternative. The European Union (EU) and China should jointly take on the leadership role on global climate action, more urgently because the fight against the climate crisis is not only a battle to reduce emissions through energy alternatives. There are wider challenges ahead for cities, agriculture, production, health, mass migration flows, ecologies, and more importantly, the earth's system. Dealing with the climate crisis is but one of the many extraordinary difficulties facing the international community in the "Anthropocene."

The new human epoch that has replaced the Holocene was given the name "Anthropocene" by Nobel Laureate Paul J. Crutzen and Eugene F. Stoermer in 2000,[3] to explain the notion that "in today's world and for the foreseeable future, what is happening on Earth is strongly determined by what humans do."[4] In the past, other scholars, such as Antonio Stoppani in 1873, had pointed to the transformative nature of human activity on the planet.[5]

> It is not enough to consider earth under the impetus of telluric forces anymore: a new force reigns here; ancient nature distorts itself, almost flees under the heel of this new nature. We are only at the beginning of the new era; still, how deep is man's footprint on earth already! Man has been in possession of it for only a short time ... yet ... How many events already bear the trace of this absolute dominion.[6]

More recently, Bruno Latour has argued that,

> If geologists themselves, rather stolid and serious types, see humanity as a force of the same amplitude, as volcanoes or even of plate tectonics, one thing is now certain – we have no hope whatsoever – no hope in the future than we had in the past – of seeing a definitive distinction between science and politics.[7]

Paul J. Crutzen in 2002 used telling figures to underscore the effect of human impact on the planet: "The methane-producing cattle population has risen to 1.4 billion. About 30–50% of the planet's land surface is exploited by humans ... More than half of all accessible fresh water is used by mankind."[8] He also described the frightening increases in our energy use, sixteen fold since the twentieth century, producing staggering amounts of atmospheric sulphur dioxide emissions and greenhouse gases (GHG). Even so the developing world has still not fully joined the ranks of the developed countries that had been primarily responsible for the current footprint.[9] Moreover, population is projected to reach nine billion by the middle of the twenty-first century, up from three billion[10] in 1960.

The Anthropocene itself has provoked heated debates.[11] Scholars, for instance, have differed in their estimation about when the Anthropocene "officially" began. Crutzen and Stoermer argued that the beginning of the Anthropocene can be dated to the late eighteenth century, coinciding with the onset of the age of steam and the beginning of industrialization. In time, Crutzen made adjustments to acknowledge that humanity's transformative impact was a result of activities of 25 percent of the world population.[12] After working with historian John McNeill,[13] he argued that "only beyond the mid-20th century is there clear evidence for fundamental shifts in the state and functioning of the Earth System that are beyond the range of Holocene and driven by human activities,"[14] that is to say, during the period of the Great Acceleration. Others, like William Ruddiman, placed the beginning of the Anthropocene in the pre-industrial age, citing human development of agriculture as the first force of change.[15] Some scholars have gone even farther back in time attempting to connect the Anthropocene to the mastery of fire.[16] Historical periodization aside, there are other foci such as "the role played by human societies in altering the earth's biosphere," proposed by Smith and Zeder. This shifts the focus from the changes themselves to humanity's capacity to make these changes.

The debate later took on a more political bent challenging the notion about whether or not critiques of capitalism were any longer sufficient to "address questions of human history once the crisis of climate change has been acknowledged."[17] Dipesh Chakrabarty, who opened this discussion more widely, argued that, "Whatever our socioeconomic and technological choices, whatever the rights we wish to celebrate as our freedom, we cannot afford to destabilize conditions (such as the temperature zone in which the planet exists) that work like boundary parameters of human existence."[18] Although critiques of political systems which lead to economic and social injustices, capitalism in particular, continue to hold significance, Chakrabarty seems to suggest that a new double perspective may now be required, the mix of "the immiscible chronologies of capital and species history."[19]

A considerable backlash greeted Crutzen and Stoermer's declaration that a new world of possibilities opens up from the moment that we fully understand our transition into the Anthropocene because global research and global engineering would lead to global solutions for sustainable environmental management. Critics stormed back that there could not be a universal one-size fits all solution to the planet's predicament given the unequal distribution of resources, funding and development. In fact, they argued, even the mere suggestion that a global push of collaboration and good will might pave the way forward, subsumed the political inequalities that have been forged by a predominant political ideology. Clearly, this kind of elevation of social processes to the geological scale created a series of new challenges to our existing notions of the relationships between humans and the environment. Chakrabarty pointed out that the notion of the Anthropocene signaled "the collapse of the age-old humanist distinction between natural history and human history."[20] The rapidity of change of the social, political and physical parameters defining the world will require new forms of inquiry and the birth of new ideas and a new vocabulary that allows us to better label and understand it. Clearly, humanity is faced with changing circumstances directly resulting from its own actions and not from natural causes. As Simon Dalby, moreover, eloquently reminds us, the Anthropocene requires a different type of reaction to that linear human response to danger, or to an imminent catastrophe. "The point about the Anthropocene," he writes, "is that it is the next time, not the end time, and hence focusing on making the future, rather than responding to danger, has to be the pedagogic priority."[21]

This heated debate over the implications of the Anthropocene suggests that a world responding to the climate crisis as a largely technological and managerial problem will not be sufficient in this new geological era because as Hamilton points out "the Anthropocene concerns human impacts on the Earth System."[22] The advent of the Anthropocene has thereby raised a host of pressing and daunting problems requiring action and robust leadership moving forward. In searching for possible configurations that might produce effective results in response to these complex challenges, some scholars have shifted their attention from the wider global stage to regional scales of environmental governance. Others have been taking a closer look at the web of both private and public actors that, through different configurations, have offered alternatives to climate and environmental governance.[23] While numerous stakeholders and institutions will inevitably weigh in on the challenges ahead, states will, nevertheless, continue to play a central role.

This is because states render structure to politics and the economy, provide the legal framework and maintain economic and administrative instruments at their disposal. As Duit, Feindt and Meadowcroft argue,

> States stand at the juncture of domestic and international political order. They remain the most powerful human mechanism for collective action that can compel obedience and redistribute resources. And it is not just that states actually wield power, but also that they are understood to embody legitimate authority.[24]

Given the importance of states as actors not only within their own boundaries, but even more so as the principal actors in international affairs, it follows that leadership in the Anthropocene will originate from them. States will need to make efforts at domestic transformation in response to the new epoch and contribute to global institutional redesign and transformation that will be necessary moving forward. This of course does not preclude the contributions and significance of other entities including local government, civil society and the business community. Their mobilization will certainly influence, compliment or even oppose the decision-making of state actors who ultimately are the ones that negotiate treaties and agreements at a global level.

Throughout this book, I have argued that an EU–China partnership offers the best chance to streamline efforts and achieve concrete results first in global emission reductions but simultaneously across a wide range of other issues that require sustainable policies for future development. Together they represent a population of 1.8 billion and constitute two of the strongest economic actors on the world stage. Through their systems of soft diplomacy and the cultivation of ties throughout the developing world, they are currently the best placed to influence a number of other states in order for them to honor their commitments and accelerate to a low carbon economy.

There are, of course, considerable political hurdles to overcome. The relationship between India and China, for instance, brings with it opportunities but geopolitical difficulties as well. Both countries are latecomers to industrialization, making their process of urbanization and industrialization highly material and energy intensive. Both are ancient civilizations bearing the wounds of past imperial conquests. As part of their industrialization process, both have also become the manufacturing facilities of the developed world, thereby carrying emissions that would have otherwise belonged to developed nations. Moreover, they are collectively home to over one-third of the world's population, accounting for 2.3 billion people that aspire to join the middle class. China and India have different political systems. Their relationship is, furthermore, burdened by an unresolved territorial dispute along their Himalayan border[25] as well as by India's decision to continue hosting a Tibetan government in exile that is considered a separatist movement by China. Both nations are concerned with the affairs of the region. India is particularly worried about China's South East Asia policy. China, meanwhile, faces security concerns over its dependence on India's sea routes by which its trade and energy pass on a daily basis. While both countries continue to grow, there is an underlying concern that if the development gap between them widens considerably or if there is social and political instability in one of the two nations, then geopolitical rivalry between them will also heighten in response to domestic weakness.

That is not to say that India and China do not share some important similar challenges. Securing access to energy supplies and other natural resources including water, for instance, are common shared concerns. This allows them to pursue cooperation in an effort to build sustainable practices into the development process. Making use of economic and technological complementarities is one way to avoid unnecessary duplication. As energy security remains a high priority for both, renewable energy can be an area of cooperation between them. China and India, furthermore, participate in the G20, the BRICS, BASIC and G77+China which gives them ample room to interact and pursue collaborative solutions.

With respect to the intergovernmental negotiations on climate, India's initial approach was particularly contrarian. In 1991, Agarwal and Narain argued that, "the idea that India and China must share the blame for heating up the earth and destabilising its climate … is an excellent example of environmental colonialism."[26] Over time India's position evolved and by COP 21 in Paris it had become more amenable. Still, while both the US (under Obama) and the EU had made previous separate overtures to draw India toward a more binding commitment to decarbonization, India had not responded in the same way as China. President Obama, for instance, reached out to India as part of his climate diplomacy agenda and during his visit to New Delhi in January of 2015 offered a proposal similar to the one he had agreed on with China. In this case, however, the result was different. The Indian government did not agree to a cap on emissions, for instance.[27]

The EU had also turned its attention to India as part of its international effort to convince the most advanced of the developing countries to begin reducing their emissions "by 15 to 30 percent below business as usual."[28] Initially, the EU had been focused on ensuring cooperation of the developed nations to help achieve an effective and lasting international regime on climate. After 2005, however, its attention turned to those nations that were growing rapidly. The objective was to secure their commitment to limit their emissions growth as part of the global climate agreement. In 2005, the EU signed the "India–EU Initiative on Clean Development and Climate Change."[29] Although the proposal was similar to the EU's agreement with China, the end result was less ambitious. There remained an underlying suspicion toward the EU that was perhaps perceived as trying to dictate the terms of India's economic growth. Moreover, there appeared to be a disconnect between EU goals of emission cutting in a continent where citizens' basic needs were already satisfied, and India's, where millions of people still had no access to energy. In India, poverty reduction and development remained the top priorities, and the equity framework continues to form the basis for the development of its climate politics. Moreover, India has forwarded the notion of "co-benefits" by which actions on climate produce both development results and climate gains.[30]

Although the EU and the US may not have achieved their aims, in May 2015 during President Xi's visit to India a joint statement affirmed that a bilateral partnership on climate change would be mutually beneficial. The two nations reaffirmed their commitment to "common but differentiated responsibilities" *vis-à-vis* the climate crisis, and their communiqué included wording about cooperation on sustainable development. India and China had cooperated on the climate before, especially earlier when the developing world was pitted squarely against the developed nations.[31] Early on, as has been noted elsewhere, developing countries, especially the largest of them, were particularly insistent on pursuing their national development unobstructed, given the level of poverty and lack of infrastructure available in their regions. After Paris, all parties now have a legally binding obligation to prepare, communicate and maintain a nationally determined mitigation contribution. This marks a significant shift because, prior to COP 21, only some countries had mitigation commitments. By Paris, countries like India and China, because of their size and overall emissions, were no longer able to avoid taking on a level of global responsibility with respect to global emission outputs. For climate action to work, every country was asked to do its share. Accordingly, striking the right balance with a country like India will be critical for both global emission reductions and in response to the wider challenges of the Anthropocene.

Another geopolitical concern for both the EU and China is the changing role of Russia because it is seeking to redefine its place on the world stage. Once a superpower, Russia's global influence diminished following the collapse of the Soviet Union and the Warsaw pact. Nonetheless, its aspirations to regain some of its old power, prestige and influence make it a particular concern to global stability. Furthermore, Russia is one of the biggest exporters of fossil fuels, especially to China and Europe, and as such, has a critical role to play in both climate talks and in responding to other challenges in the Anthropocene. The current status of the EU–Russia relationship is difficult after the events in the Ukraine and the sanctions that have been placed on Russia by both the US and the EU. Increasingly, however, the Russia–China axis is strengthening on a number of fronts. First, the two nations are collaborating in terms of security by holding joint military exercises. Second, with respect to trade, China is already Russia's largest trading partner, with trade among them fluctuating at around $80 – 90 billion in combined export and import volume in 2014 and 2015.[32] Third, energy cooperation is rising with the two countries having signed major oil and gas export agreements since

2009, which promise to bring in fossil fuels from Russia to China. Agreements in the energy sector relieve some of Russia's dependence on European exports and offer them a lucrative alternative market. They simultaneously help reduce China's dependence on oil deliveries via the Malacca Strait and diversify their fossil fuel imports away from the Middle East. At present, China imports approximately 550,000 barrels of oil per day from Russia, and this is set to increase as the Eastern Siberia–Pacific Ocean oil pipeline will be linked to Northeast China in 2017. The pipeline linking Siberia's Chayandinskoye oil and gas field to China comes online in 2018.[33]

In Paris, Russia joined the rest the community of nations that submitted Intended Nationally Determined Contributions (INDC) for emission reductions and President Putin declared that "the quality of life of all people on this planet depends on … our ability to resolve the problem of climate."[34] Moscow submitted an official climate plan on May 31, 2015 in advance of COP 21. Critics of Moscow's INDC plan were quick to point out that emissions are already way below 1990 levels and in fact the way that the plan was structured left considerable room for an increase in emissions. The INDCs also led to some controversy that remains to be clarified over Russia's use of forests as sinkholes for emissions. China and Europe can influence Russia to incorporate sustainable planning practices given its heavy reliance on fossil fuels and its growing vulnerability to climate change that will affect agricultural production[35] and water availability. The melting of the permafrost, for instance, could alter, some argue, river patterns affecting Stavropol and Krasnodar which have been at the center of Russia's agricultural production belt.

Geopolitical considerations, of course, are not limited to bilateral relations within the region. China, India and Russia in combination, and their individual economic and geopolitical aspirations, also influence events. China worries about a renewed US–India cooperation.[36] This also worries Russia. India too looks at the China–Russia partnership as a threat to its role and its security in the region. Nonetheless, all three nations have shared interests as members of the BRICS that allow them to jointly agree on some issues. On April 19, 2016 for instance, China, India and Russia reaffirmed in a Joint Communiqué their commitment to implementing the 2030 Agenda for Sustainable Development and its Sustainable Development Goals (SDGs) as well as the Paris Agreement on climate change.[37] While respecting each nation's individual choice in terms of social systems and chosen paths to development, they met in Moscow to demonstrate their cooperative desire to work together on global and regional issues. Moreover, all three are founding members of the Asian Infrastructure Investment Bank (AIIB), a Chinese initiative and rising alternative to the World Bank.

Particularly interesting is the AIIB Energy Strategy Issue Report of 2016 that is a proposal for developing sustainable energy in Asia. The AIIB's strategy aims to "accompany clients as they develop energy infrastructure to meet their energy needs and achieve their economic development and poverty reduction goals during the global transition towards an efficient and less intensive energy mix."[38] The proposed objective for energy sustainability is to secure access to "adequate and reliable supplies of environmentally and socially acceptable forms of energy at competitive prices without compromising the energy needs of future generations."[39] The energy needs of Asia are rapidly increasing, and the reliance on fossil fuels is heavier than in other regions. This is why the AIIB has opened up this issue for discussion among its members, factoring in the climate crisis as part of the wider conversation of energy availability. In addition, a working paper was published in 2016 that discusses investment in climate change action.[40] From the outset, this report notes that, in the coming years, as Asian countries develop their infrastructure in energy and transport, their decisions will impact the world's collective response to the climate crisis. This is why the AIIB—as a new multilateral development bank—has the opportunity to establish "a new approach to infrastructure investment that prioritizes renewable energy, climate resilience and sustainable development."[41] Furthermore, the report itself looks to China as the founder of the AIIB and as its largest shareholder to lead in the transition to renewables by helping to "expand markets for renewable energy, and change the narrative around the emphasis of China's overseas investments as one focused on clean sustainable development, rather than resource extraction."[42]

Hurdles and opportunities are not limited to major countries that will play a significant role in the global fight to tackle the climate crisis and address the more comprehensive challenges of the Anthropocene. Collaboration of states large and small will be necessary. China and the EU both have longstanding ties and interests across the developing world. They have built diplomatic and institutional ties and have provided considerable technical and financial aid to countries around the globe. Moreover, through investment and trade they have cultivated strong economic relationships on the ground. They have launched a number of climate initiatives and projects for mitigation, adaptation and sustainability. Together, they bring to bear considerable influence in Africa and Latin America and can lead by example. A brief overview of their respective initiatives and networks in both continents may help highlight existing opportunities that both actors can jointly or separately pursue to achieve greater effect moving forward.

Much has been written about China's relationship with the developing world, especially with respect to Africa and Latin America. Following the Cold War and the end of the rivalries for strategic spheres of influence, it had been hoped that a new era in North–South relations would dawn, marking a shift from military confrontation to policies of poverty alleviation and development. This kind of shift did not occur but, rather, it seemed that Africa in particular was being largely overlooked.[43] The period of renewed neglect coincided with China's years of rapid economic development. The PRC's initial interaction in these regions had been brief and opportunistic. It was part of its period of export of both radical politics and weapons needed for hard cash. It was also a period during which China sought to gain its seat at the UN, a goal that it accomplished with the help of many newly independent African states in 1971. Following Mao's era, however, the PRC turned its focus to domestic development. China's pace and scope of economic growth was astonishing and because of that, it once again turned its attention to the developing world no longer through the prism of ideology but through one of a more practical nature. It made use of its previous networks, which it revived to begin re-engaging in search of markets for its goods, energy to power its industry and natural resources to promote its growth. To achieve these goals, China began to deepen its political and diplomatic collaboration with states across the developing world. It sought to construct its relationship based on equality and mutual respect and promised to produce win–win results of mutual benefit with respect to its budding economic relations. Over the years, investments in both Africa and Latin America have soared. China has in fact helped many African countries to develop important sectors such as the oil industry, securing in turn beneficial deals and trade relations. It has provided low interest loans for the construction of infrastructure as well as billions in development aid. Its growing influence has alarmed many of its competitors that have increasingly criticized China for some of its most controversial ties with African nations. Its policy of "non-interference" in the domestic affairs of its partners, especially in those that have egregiously violated human rights, has been a source of contention. Nonetheless, China's trade with African states hit the $300 billion mark in 2015,[44] and its relationships across the globe continue to deepen and evolve. Due to its size and impact, local criticism has also begun to grow, and China needs to adjust its strategy to maintain its good standing. Climate cooperation, sustainability initiatives and adjustment to the Anthropocene offer ample opportunities for renewed collaborations.

In 2014, the Chinese government issued its second white paper outlining the philosophy and the kinds of initiatives that were funded through China's foreign aid program. Asia and Africa were the major recipients of China's foreign assistance. To promote the realization of the Millennium Development Goals, China directed most of its assistance to low income developing countries. From 2010–2012 the PRC appropriated $14.1 billion in grants, interest free loans and concessional loans (i.e., for the manufacturing of large and medium-sized infrastructure projects with economic and social benefits, etc.) Moreover, according to China's White Paper, the PRC provided assistance to "121 countries, including 30 in Asia, 51 in Africa, nine in Oceania, 19 in Latin America and the Caribbean, and 12 in Europe. China also provided assistance to regional organizations such as the African Union (AU)."[45]

Farther afield, China has sought to cultivate relations with countries in both the Caribbean and Latin America. In 2008, the PRC issued its first policy paper on the region. In 2014, a comprehensive and cooperative partnership featuring equality, mutual benefit and common development was announced. High-level exchanges and political dialogues have followed in trade, investment, finance and increasingly close cultural and people-to-people exchanges. There has been growing coordination in international affairs and the Forum of China and the Community of Latin American and Caribbean States (China–CELAC Forum) was established to provide a new platform for cooperation. Environmental protection, climate change and disaster reduction are among the areas where cooperation is being pursued, especially under the *United Nations Framework*

Convention on Climate Change (UNFCCC) and other relevant mechanisms. In its stated intentions China has included the promotion of the Paris Agreement on climate, continuing to adhere to the principles of equity, common but differentiated responsibilities and respective capabilities. Moreover, the PRC works closely with Latin American and Caribbean countries in support of the 2030 Agenda to "improve global partnerships, strengthen the main channel status of North-South cooperation, and urge developed countries to fulfill their commitments on official development assistance, while placing importance on the role of South-South cooperation and trilateral cooperation."[46]

China's global initiatives have increasingly grown in scope and breadth. Among its most recent are China's decision to set-up a separate South–South Cooperation fund in 2014. Xie Zhenhua, China's special representative on climate change, said it would be based on principles of "mutual respect, justice, shared benefit and practicality and efficiency; and that other nations, bilateral and multinational bodies and the private sector are all welcome to participate and promote the investment in the green and low-carbon sectors worldwide."[47] At the UN in November of 2015, moreover, President Xi announced that the China South–South Climate Cooperation Fund would provide $3.1 billion to help developing countries tackle climate change.[48] Already in 2011, China had launched a three-year climate change cooperation project with the goal of offering the least developed countries, the small island countries and a few African countries support to tackle climate change. The PRC has additionally signed Memorandums of Understanding (MOU) with more than ten countries such as Grenada, Ethiopia, Maldives, Samoa and Uganda and has provided them assistance through energy-saving and low carbon products and capacity-building trainings.[49]

Turning to EU relations with the developing world, they are burdened by the negative historical experience of colonialism. Although this legacy has not faded in many nations that experienced its effects, nonetheless, today EU ties and networks across the developing world are extensive, diverse and growing in strength. Through trade, political collaboration, soft diplomacy and aid support, the EU has launched a number of initiatives for education, health, economic development, poverty alleviation, institution building and climate. A brief overview of the EU's outreach to the developing world indicates the importance that the EU places not only on climate but in providing aid and technical assistance to the most vulnerable of nations. This is meant to demonstrate Europe's commitment to the eradication of global poverty and the transition to a sustainable development model within the changing parameters of the climate crisis and the Anthropocene. According to EU data, the EU and its member-states together constitute the world's largest aid donors. In 2013, they provided more than half of public aid or "official development assistance" together spending €56.5 billion to help countries fight poverty.[50] The EU, moreover, has built a wide network of 139 delegations and offices around the world. In addition, the EU is the largest contributor of climate finance to developing countries and is increasingly integrating climate change into its broader development strategy.[51] Through the Global Climate Change Alliance (GCCA) initiative, the EU provides technical and financial support to developing countries to integrate climate change into their development policies and budgets, and to implement projects that address climate change on the ground. The GCCA is also a platform for dialogue and exchange of experience.[52]

With respect to the UN Green Climate Fund (GCF), the EU and its member states have pledged nearly half of the fund's resources: $4.7 billion. By 2020, at least 20 percent of the EU budget will be spent on climate action, and at least €14 billion of public grants will support activities in developing countries between 2014 and 2020.

In 2005, the European Commission (EC) published a communication entitled "Winning the Battle Against Climate Change," which called for stronger cooperation with third world countries to tackle the climate crisis. The EU has since formed a number of partnerships around the world, has initiated dialogues and has interacted with a number of regional groupings on environment and climate change issues. Regional groupings with which the EU collaborates are African, Caribbean and Pacific (ACP) countries, Asia Europe Meeting (ASEM), the Association of South East Asian Nations (ASEAN), the Gulf Cooperation Council (GCC), Latin American and Caribbean (LAC) countries and the Organization of the Petroleum Exporting Countries (OPEC). EU relations with the African continent have a long history and have been particularly singled out for further and deeper cooperation.[53] The EU has furthermore formed Economic Partnership Agreements (EPAs) on trade and development with Africa, Caribbean and Pacific (ACP) partners. Moreover, ACP countries represent more than 5 percent of EU imports and exports.[54] In 2014, EU exports to Africa stood at €153 billion. Imports from Africa for that year consisted predominantly of energy products (mainly crude oil) and amounted to €91.5 billion, representing 59 percent of total African imports by EU–28.[55]

African countries as well, after 2005 have raised their profile in climate negotiations by increasingly speaking in one voice to draw attention to their particular concerns and vulnerabilities. Rapprochement between the African countries and the EU especially grew after Durban in 2011. Multilateral negotiations have taken place between their respective institutions, and meetings at ministerial level were convened to address divergences and to share their overall positions ahead of multilateral climate negotiations. Such meetings took place, for instance, both ahead of the Warsaw and Lima COP meetings in 2013 and 2014 respectively. Development cooperation frameworks have not only supported dialogues, but also the implementation of adaptation and mitigation measures for African countries.[56]

The Joint Africa–EU Strategy (JAES) signed in 2007,[57] moreover, made climate change a priority area of cooperation. Expectations ran high, and they achieved a better understanding of the actors' positions at climate talks that allowed for better coordination. Examples include ClimDev–Africa, a JAES-sponsored program that provides climate information and analytical support. In this case, the particular program has contributed to better policy formulation for projects such as the Great Green Wall for the Sahara[58] and the Sahel Initiative (GGWSSI),[59] that aim to reverse land degradation and desertification in both the Sahel and the Sahara. It is an adaptation initiative supporting local communities faced with the impacts of climate change to help boost their food security.[60] Nonetheless, there is significant room for improvement so that the discussions translate into concrete outcomes. Tondel et al, argue that some of the most pronounced reasons for which the JAES has not been as effective as it might are due to

> a cumbersome institutional structure and inefficient policy processes that discouraged stakeholders; weak linkages between the consultative, technical structure and both decision-making and implementing bodies; the ambiguous mandate of the consultative structure with respect to the initiatives supposedly overseen by the JAES; and above all a deficit of political support on both sides.[61]

In any event, the institutional structure does exist and strong historical and cultural ties which the EU shares with the African continent, along with the high levels of aid and assistance, offer a sound base for the deepening of the working relationship.

The EU has also developed a number of policies and financial instruments by which to build up its ties with Latin American countries and its cooperation on climate change. The Regional Program for Latin America for the period 2014–2020 has a budget of €925 million. It is broken down into two components, the first one with a budget of €805 million funds initiatives that reinforce the capacity of states to effectively ensure security conditions conducive for inclusive development (€70 million); good governance, accountability and social equity (€42 million); inclusive and sustainable growth for human development (€215 million); environmental sustainability and climate change (€300 million); higher education (€163 million) and support measures (€15million). The second component with a budget of €120 million is a sub-regional program for Central America that focuses on regional economic integration (€40 million); security and rule of law (€40 million); climate change and disaster management (€35 million); support measures (€5 million).[62]

Moreover, since 2008 the EU has launched a Euroclima program for Latin American countries that

> facilitates the integration of climate change mitigation and adaptation strategies and measures into Latin American public development policies and plans at national and (sub) regional levels. During the period of 2014–2016 the EU contribution reached €11.450.000 out of a total of €12.587.500.[63]

With Brazil, in particular, the EU launched a strategic partnership in 2007, recognizing its growing importance both as a global economic player and within the Americas.[64] According to an EU Commission Report of 2007,

Based on powerful historical and cultural links, the EU enjoys broad relations with Brazil. Over the last few years Brazil has emerged as a champion of the developing world in the UN and at the WTO. The EU and Brazil share core values and interests, including respect for the rule of law and human rights, concern about climate change and the pursuit of economic growth and social justice at home and abroad. Brazil is a vital ally for the EU in addressing these and other challenges in international fora.[65]

The EU also has a strategic partnership with Mexico. The two actors collaborate in a number of areas that include working towards "societies where production and consumption are in balance with the planet's resources. The EU and Mexico are leaders in their commitments to dealing with climate change."[66]

Today, the EU boasts 10 "strategic partnerships" and China close to 50 that it has established (mostly) since the early 2000s, giving evidence of the latter's embrace of globalization and multidimensional diplomacy.[67] While the previous list of initiatives and projects launched around the world is not comprehensive but indicative, it is clear that both the EU and China are well placed to offer assistance, guidance, incentives and exchange best practices with the most vulnerable of nations, but also with those that are on a strong trajectory of growth so that they avoid the pitfalls of past transitions to more highly industrialized economies.

All things being equal, the biggest hurdle that EU–China leadership will face may come from the US because their partnership would spell a considerable and potentially unwelcome geopolitical shift. It is difficult at this time to predict what kind of reaction an EU–China leadership role may provoke from a US under the presidency of Donald Trump. It is safe to say, however, that US climate leadership will certainly not be in the offing; not in the way that the Obama administration had sought to frame the issue and pursue a climate agenda. As president, Donald Trump will seek some early victories on issues that will prove his consistency on some of his most publicized campaign promises. He will also reach out selectively to friends and foes, rivals and individual nations, to strike up bilateral deals because that would be consistent with his "'business" approach to policymaking. Certainly, the high unpredictability of his presidency allows for instability and insecurity to spread through the international system, especially if the US moves more squarely into the isolationist camp.

With respect to climate, it is not that the US under Trump will exponentially increase its carbon emissions. Too many changes have already happened on the ground that have led to the use of natural gas versus coal in power production, that have increased fuel efficiency in transport and that have allowed for renewable energy to take off. US states and cities are also playing a more decisive role in how they prepare their adaptation and mitigation plans to deal with the impacts of the climate crisis. Public consciousness will also affect policies on the ground. Countless US businesses, moreover, have grown to accept the reality of climate change and are taking measures to cope with new risks and disruptions that it may provoke. Appreciating consumer concern but also the needs of their bottom line, they are conserving resources and applying energy efficiency measures to reduce costs and reduce emissions. Indicative of business support for climate action was Bill Gates' announcement on December 13, 2016 that he would head a new fund called Breakthrough Energy Ventures that will increase investments in energy-related technologies. The Gates announcement came after Trump's appointment of climate skeptic Scott Pruitt to head the EPA.[68] Nonetheless, while the probability of the US leading the world in tackling the climate crisis is highly unlikely, it may become more obstructionist at the intergovernmental level, once again aiming to disrupt meaningful negotiation.[69] The US security establishment will certainly not like the building of stronger political ties between the EU and China, especially given their vast network of friends and partners across the developing world. This kind of meaningful strategic partnership will go against the Asia Pivot and the belief that Europe's alignment with US interests is a foregone conclusion. Complications will undoubtedly arise as the US, under new leadership, begins to unveil its international agenda. Nonetheless, the world is already in flux. There are significant realignments taking place across the globe; ongoing conflicts and failed states are becoming the new normal, ultra-conservative forces are on the rise in Europe, anti-globalization is reaching a new peak and mass population movement is a rising concern. While all these challenges seem overwhelming, none of the obstacles they pose are insurmountable if the EU and China take the lead on the climate and the wider transition into the Anthropocene and make it their main narrative. In any event, as things stand now and given the urgency of the climate crisis and the global challenges ahead, this partnership may offer the world a glimmer of hope moving into the future.

Notes

1   "SHOW YOUR SUPPORT FOR DONALD J. TRUMP," accessed March 15, 2017, https://www.donaldjtrump.com; "How Trump Came up with His Slogan 'Make America Great Again,'" *Business Insider*, accessed March 15, 2017, http://www.businessinsider.com/trump-make-america-great-again-slogan-history-2017-1.
2   John Vidal and Oliver Milman, "Paris Climate Deal Thrown into Uncertainty by US Election Result," *The Guardian*, November 9, 2016, sec. Environment, https://www.theguardian.com/environment/2016/nov/09/us-election-result-throws-paris-climate-deal-into-uncertainty.
3   Paul J. Crutzen and Eugene F. Stoermer, "The Anthropocene," *Global Change Newsletter*, no. 41 (May 2000): 17–18.
4   Crutzen and Stoermer, "The Anthropocene."
5   Etienne Turpin and Valeria Federighi, "A New Element, a New Force, a New Input: Antonio Stoppani's Anthropozoic," 2012, http://ro.uow.edu.au/eispapers/2986/.
6   Turpin and Federighi, "Antonio Stoppani's Anthropozoic."
7   Bruno Latour, *An Inquiry into Modes of Existence: An Anthropology of the Moderns*, translated by Catherine Porter, 1st edition (Cambridge, Massachusetts: Harvard University Press, 2013), 9.
8   Paul J. Crutzen, "Geology of Mankind," *Nature* 415, no. 6867 (January 3, 2002): 23–23.
9   Crutzen, "Geology of Mankind."

10 US Census Bureau Demographic Internet Staff, "International Programs, International Data Base: World Population: 1950-2050," accessed November 5, 2016, https://www.census.gov/population/international/data/idb/worldpopgraph.php.

11 For a comprehensive analysis of the ongoing debates see Jeremy Davies, *The Birth of the Anthropocene* (Oakland, California: University of California Press, 2016), 41-68.

12 Crutzen, "Geology of Mankind."

13 Will Steffen, Paul J. Crutzen, and John R. McNeill, "The Anthropocene: Are Humans Now Overwhelming the Great Forces of Nature," *AMBIO: A Journal of the Human Environment* 36, no. 8 (2007): 614–621.

14 Will Steffen et al., "The Trajectory of the Anthropocene: The Great Acceleration," *The Anthropocene Review*, January 16, 2015.

15 William F. Ruddiman, "The Anthropogenic Greenhouse Era Began Thousands of Years Ago," *Climatic Change* 61, no. 3 (2003): 261–293.

16 Andrew Y. Glikson and Colin Groves, *Climate, Fire and Human Evolution*, vol. 10, *Modern Approaches in Solid Earth Sciences* (New York: Springer International Publishing, 2016), http://link.springer.com/10.1007/978-3-319-22512-8.

17 Dipesh Chakrabarty, "The Climate of History: Four Theses," *Critical Inquiry* 35, no. 2 (2009): 197–222.

18 Chakrabarty, "The Climate of History: Four Theses," 197–222.

19 Chakrabarty, "The Climate of History: Four Theses," 197–222.

20 Chakrabarty, "The Climate of History: Four Theses," 197–222.

21 Elizabeth Johnson et al., "After the Anthropocene: Politics and Geographic Inquiry for a New Epoch," *ResearchGate* 38, no. 3 (May 15, 2014): 439–56.

22 Clive Hamilton, "Getting the Anthropocene so Wrong," *The Anthropocene Review* 2, no. 2 (August 1, 2015): 102–7.

23 Diarmuid Torney, "Bilateral Climate Cooperation: The EU's Relations with China and India," *Global Environmental Politics* 15, no. 1 (December 5, 2014): 105–22.

24 A. Duit, P.H. Feindt and J. Meadowcroft, "Greening Leviathan: The Rise of the Environmental State?" *Environmental Politics* 25, no. 1 (02 2016): 1–23.

25 "India-China Border Dispute," accessed December 1, 2016, http://www.globalsecurity.org/military/world/war/india-china_conflicts.htm; Katherine Richards, "China-India: An Analysis of the Himalayan Territorial Dispute," 2015, http://www.defence.gov.au/ADC/Publications/IndoPac/Richards%20final%20IPSD%20paper.pdf.

26 Anil Agarwal and Sunita Narain, *Global Warming in an Unequal World: A case of Environmental Colonialism*, (New Delhi: Center for Science and Environment, 1991), http://cseindia.org/challenge_balance/readings/GlobalWarming%20Book.pdf.

27 Pan Jiahua, "Working Together Towards an Ecologically Civilized World: A Chinese Perspective," in Kanti Bajpai, Jing Huang, and Kishore Mahbubani, *China-India Relations: Cooperation and Conflict* (London; New York: Routledge, 2016), 93–107.

28 Diarmuid Torney, *European Climate Leadership in Question: Policies toward China and India* (Cambridge, MA: MIT Press, 2015), 133.

29 European Commission, "India," *Climate Action*, November 23, 2016, http://ec.europa.eu/clima/policies/international/cooperation/india_en.

30 Navroz K. Dubash, "The Politics of Climate Change in India: Narratives of Equity and Co-benefits," *Wiley Interdisciplinary Reviews: Climate Change* 4, no. 3 (2013): 191–201; Netherlands Environmental Assessment Agency (PBL), "Co-Benefits of Climate Policy," 2009, http://www.unep.org/transport/gfei/autotool/understanding_the_problem/Netherlands%20Environment%20Agency.pdf.

31 Dhanasree Jayaram, "A Shift in the Agenda for China and India: Geopolitical Implications for Future Climate Governance," *Carbon & Climate Law Review* 9, no. 3 (2015): 219–30.

32 Sara Hsu, "Is A Russia-China Economic Alliance On The Horizon?" *Forbes*, accessed December 1, 2016, http://www.forbes.com/sites/sarahsu/2016/11/07/is-a-russia-

china-economic-alliance-on-the-horizon/; TASS, "Trade Between Russia, China Could Reach $90bln by 2016," *Russia Beyond The Headlines*, August 12, 2016, http://rbth.com/news/2016/08/12/trade-between-russia-china-could-reach-90bln-by-2016_620425.

33 Isabel Gorst, "Russia – Espo: Asia's Gain, Europe's Pain," *Financial Times*, accessed December 1, 2016, http://blogs.ft.com/beyond-brics/2014/02/19/russia-espo-asias-gain-europes-pain/; Aibing Guo, "CNPC to Start Laying Second China-Russia Oil Pipeline in June," *Bloomberg.com*, accessed December 1, 2016, https://www.bloomberg.com/news/articles/2016-05-12/cnpc-to-start-laying-second-china-russia-oil-pipeline-in-june-io48uk3h;"Chayandinskoye Field," accessed December 1, 2016, http://www.gazprom.com/about/production/projects/deposits/chayandinskoye/.

34 Quentin Buckholz, "Russia and Climate Change: A Looming Threat," *The Diplomat*, accessed December 1, 2016, http://thediplomat.com/2016/02/russia-and-climate-change-a-looming-threat/.

35 Although some scholars have indicated that climate change may allow for increases in crop production in the North, something that may initially appear advantageous for Russia, it is not entirely clear what the overall changes will be and how they will end up impacting food production overall as weather patterns will lead to more droughts and floods and impact water availability, which is vital to agricultural production. Nikolai Dronin and Andrei Kirilenko, "Climate Change and Food Stress in Russia: What If the Market Transforms as It Did during the Past Century?" *Climatic Change* 86, no. 1–2 (January 1, 2008): 123–50.

36 Andrew Korybko, "The Threat To Russia and China From India's New Pro-US Realignment," *The Duran*, May 7, 2016, http://theduran.com/threat-russia-china-indias-new-pro-us-realignment/.

37 IISD Reporting Services, "China, India, Russia Reaffirm Commitment to SDGs, Climate Change," accessed December 1, 2016, http://sdg.iisd.org/news/china-india-russia-reaffirm-commitment-to-sdgs-climate-change/.

38 "AIIB Energy Strategy: Sustainable Energy for Asia" (October 2016), http://www.aiib.org/en/news-events/news/2016_download/aiib-strategy-sustainable-energy-for-asia-issues-note-for-discussion.pdf.

39 "AIIB Energy Strategy: Sustainable Energy for Asia."

40 Darius Nassiry and Smita Nakhooda, "The AIIB and Investment in Action on Climate Change," 2016, https://www.odi.org/sites/odi.org.uk/files/resource-documents/10441.pdf.

41 Nassiry and Nakhooda, "The AIIB and Investment in Action on Climate Change."

42 Nassiry and Nakhooda, "The AIIB and Investment in Action on Climate Change."

43 Joshua Eisenman, Eric Heginbotham and Derek Mitchell, eds., *China and the Developing World: Beijing's Strategy for the Twenty-First Century* (Armonk, N.Y: Routledge, 2015).

44 "China-Africa Trade Approaches $300 Billion in 2015," *Chinadaily*, accessed December 3, 2016, http://www.chinadaily.com.cn/business/2015-11/10/content_22417707.htm.

45 "China 2nd White Paper on Foreign Aid 2014," *Information Office of the State Council*, July 2014, http://ssc.undp.org/content/dam/ssc/dgspaces/China/files/China%202nd%20White%20Paper%20on%20Foreign%20Aid%202014.pdf.

46 "China 2nd White Paper on Foreign Aid 2014."

47 Hongqiao Liu, "China Pledges US$20 Million a Year to Its New South-South Cooperation Fund," *China Dialogue*, accessed December 1, 2016, https://www.chinadialogue.net/blog/7596-China-pledges-US-2-million-a-year-to-its-new-South-South-Cooperation-Fund/en.

48 Martin Khor, "Opinion: China's New South-South Funds – a Global Game Changer?" *Inter Press Service*, accessed December 1, 2016, http://www.ipsnews.

net/2015/11/opinion-chinas-new-south-south-funds-a-global-game-changer/; "China South-South Climate Cooperation Fund Benefits Developing Countries," *Chinadaily*, accessed December 1, 2016, http://www.chinadaily.com.cn/world/Xiat tendsParisclimateconference/2015-11/30/content_22557413.htm.

49   "China South-South Climate Cooperation Fund Benefits Developing Countries."

50   "EU Development Aid | European Year for Development," accessed December 2, 2016, https://europa.eu/eyd2015/en/content/eu-development-aid.

51   European Commission, "International Climate Finance," accessed November 1, 2016, https://ec.europa.eu/clima/policies/international/finance/index_en.htm.

52   "International Climate Finance."

53   European Commission, "Climate Change Cooperation with Non-EU Countries," accessed November 7, 2016, https://ec.europa.eu/clima/policies/international/coop-eration/index_en.htm.

54   European Commission, "Economic Partnerships - Trade," accessed December 2, 2016, http://ec.europa.eu/trade/policy/countries-and-regions/development/economic-part-nerships/.

55   "Africa-EU - Key Statistical Indicators - Statistics Explained," accessed December 2, 2016, http://ec.europa.eu/eurostat/statistics-explained/index.php/Africa-EU_-_key_statistical_indicators.

56   Fabien Tondel, Hanne Knaepen, and Lesley-Anne van Wyk, "Africa and Europe Combatting Climate Change," 2015, http://www.climdev-africa.org/sites/default/files/files/DP177-Africa-Europe-Combatting-Climate-Change-May-2015.pdf.

57   "FACTSHEET – EU-Africa Relations," *General Secretariat of the Council*, 2014, http://www.consilium.europa.eu/uedocs/cms_data/docs/pressdata/en/ec/141975.pdf.

58   Great Green Wall for the Sahara and the Sahel Initiative (GGWSSI), "Home Page" accessed December 2, 2016, http://www.greatgreenwallinitiative.org/.

59   "What Is the Great Green Wall?" accessed December 2, 2016, http://www.greatgreen-wallinitiative.org/what-great-green-wall.

60   Fabien Tondel, Hanne Knaepen, and Lesley-Anne van Wyk, "Africa and Europe Combatting Climate Change," 2015, http://www.climdev-africa.org/sites/default/files/files/DP177-Africa-Europe-Combatting-Climate-Change-May-2015.pdf.

61   Tondel, Knaepen, and Van Wyk, "Africa and Europe Combatting Climate Change."

62   European Commission, "Latin America - Regional Cooperation - Funding," *International Cooperation and Development*, accessed December 2, 2016, https://ec.europa.eu/europeaid/regions/latin-america/euroclima_en.

63   European Commission, "Latin America – EUROCLIMA – Climate Change Regional Cooperation Programme - International Cooperation and Development," *International Cooperation and Development*, accessed December 2, 2016, https://ec.europa.eu/europeaid/regions/latin-america/euroclima_en.

64   Commission of the European Communities, "Towards an EU-Brazil Strategic Partnership," COM (2007) 281 Final, May 30, 2007, http://eur-lex.europa.eu/legal-content/EN/TXT/PDF/?uri=CELEX:52007DC0281&from=EN; Secretariat EU-Brasil, "EU-Brazil Strategic Partnership Three Years on: Proposals to Foster Economic and Business Cooperation," accessed December 2, 2016, http://www.eubrasil.eu/en/2011/07/28/eu-brazil-strategic-partnership-three-years-on-proposals-to-foster-eco-nomic-and-business-cooperation/.

65   "Towards an EU-Brazil Strategic Partnership."

66   European Union External Action Service (EEAS), "Projects in Mexico," *EEAS*, accessed December 2, 2016, /delegations/mexico/14898/projects-in-mexico_en.

67   EPRS Library, "EU Strategic Partnerships with Third Countries," *European Parliamentary Research Service Blog*, accessed October 2, 2012, https://epthinktank.eu/2012/10/02/eu-strategic-partnerships-with-third-countries/.Zhongping and Jing, "China's Strategic Partnership Diplomacy."

68   Jon Sharman, "Bill Gates Announces a $1bn Fund for Clean Energy Technology," *The Independent*, December 12, 2016, http://www.independent.co.uk/news/people/bill-gates-clean-energy-investment-fund-climate-change-a7469201.html.
69   Steven Mufson and Juliet Eilperin, "Trump Transition Team for Energy Department Seeks Names of Employees Involved in Climate Meetings," *Washington Post*, accessed December 10, 2016, https://www.washingtonpost.com/news/energy-environment/wp/2016/12/09/trump-transition-team-for-energy-department-seeks-names-of-employees-involved-in-climate-meetings/.

Bibliography

Agarwal, Anil, and Sunita Narain. *Global Warming in an Unequal World: A Case of Environmental Colonialism*. New Delhi: Center for Science and Environment, 1990. http://cseindia.org/challenge_balance/readings/GlobalWarming%20Book.pdf.

AIIB. "AIIB Energy Strategy: Sustainable Energy for Asia." AIIB, October 2016. http://euweb.aiib.org/uploadfile/2016/1013/20161013092936280.pdf.

Bajpai, Kanti, Jing Huang, and Kishore Mahbubani. *China-India Relations: Cooperation and Conflict*. London; New York: Routledge, 2015.

Buckholz, Quentin. "Russia and Climate Change: A Looming Threat." *The Diplomat*. Accessed December 1, 2016. http://thediplomat.com/2016/02/russia-and-climate-change-a-looming-threat/.

Chakrabarty, Dipesh. "The Climate of History: Four Theses." *Critical Inquiry* 35, no. 2 (2009): 197–222.

Chinadaily. "China South-South Climate Cooperation Fund Benefits Developing Countries" Accessed December 1, 2016. http://www.chinadaily.com.cn/world/XiattendsParisclimateconference/2015-11/30/content_22557413.htm.

Chinadaily. "China-Africa Trade Approaches $300 Billion in 2015." Accessed December 3, 2016. http://www.chinadaily.com.cn/business/2015-11/10/content_22417707.htm.

Commission of the European Communities. "Towards an EU-Brazil Strategic Partnership." COM (2007) 281 Final, May 30, 2007. http://eur-lex.europa.eu/legal-content/EN/TXT/PDF/?uri=CELEX:52007DC0281&from=EN.

Crutzen, Paul J. "Geology of Mankind." *Nature* 415, no. 6867 (January 3, 2002): 23–23. doi:10.1038/415023a.

Crutzen, Paul J., and Eugene F. Stoermer. "The Anthropocene." *Global Change Newsletter*, no. 41 (May 2000): 17–18.

Davies, Jeremy. *The Birth of the Anthropocene*. Oakland, California: University of California Press, 2016.

Dronin, Nikolai, and Andrei Kirilenko. "Climate Change and Food Stress in Russia: What If the Market Transforms as It Did during the Past Century?" *Climatic Change* 86, no. 1–2 (January 1, 2008): 123–50.

Dubash, Navroz K. "The Politics of Climate Change in India: Narratives of Equity and Cobenefits." *Wiley Interdisciplinary Reviews: Climate Change* 4, no. 3 (2013): 191–201.

Duit, A., P.h. Feindt and J. Meadowcroft. "Greening Leviathan: The Rise of the Environmental State?" *Environmental Politics* 25, no. 1 (02 2016): 1–23.

Eisenman, Joshua, Eric Heginbotham and Derek Mitchell, eds. *China and the Developing World: Beijing's Strategy for the Twenty-First Century*. Armonk, N.Y: Routledge, 2015.

EU–Brazil, Secretariat. "EU-Brazil Strategic Partnership Three Years on: Proposals to Foster Economic and Business Cooperation." Accessed December 2, 2016. http://www.eubrasil.

eu/en/2011/07/28/eu-brazil-strategic-partnership-three-years-on-proposals-to-foster-economic-and-business-cooperation/.

European Commisssion. "Climate Change Cooperation with Non-EU Countries." Accessed November 7, 2016. https://ec.europa.eu/clima/policies/international/cooperation/index_en.htm.

European Commission. "Economic Partnerships – Trade – European Commission." Accessed December 2, 2016. http://ec.europa.eu/trade/policy/countries-and-regions/development/economic-partnerships/.

European Union. "European Year for Development – EU Development Aid." *Europa.* Accessed December 2, 2016. https://europa.eu/eyd2015/en/content/eu-development-aid.

European Commission. "International Climate Finance." Accessed November 1, 2016. https://ec.europa.eu/clima/policies/international/finance/index_en.htm.

European Commission. "India." November 23, 2016. http://ec.europa.eu/clima/policies/international/cooperation/india_en.

European Commission. "Latin America – EUROCLIMA – Climate Change Regional Cooperation Programme." *International Cooperation and Development.* Accessed December 2, 2016. https://ec.europa.eu/europeaid/regions/latin-america/euroclima_en.

"European Commission. "Latin America – Regional Cooperation – Funding." *International Cooperation and Development.* Accessed December 2, 2016. /europeaid/regions/latin-america/latin-america-regional-programmes-eu-funding_en.

European Union External Action Service (EEAS). "Projects in Mexico." *EEAS.* Accessed December 2, 2016. https://eeas.europa.eu/headquarters/headquarters-homepage_en/14898/Projects%20in%20Mexico

Eurostat. "Africa-EU – Key Statistical Indicators." Accessed December 2, 2016. http://ec.europa.eu/eurostat/statistics-explained/index.php/Africa-EU_-_key_statistical_indicators.

Gazprom. "Chayandinskoye Field." Accessed December 1, 2016. http://www.gazprom.com/about/production/projects/deposits/chayandinskoye/.

General Secretariat of the Council. "FACTSHEET – EU-Africa Relations," 2014. *General Secretariat of the Council.* http://www.consilium.europa.eu/uedocs/cms_data/docs/pressdata/en/ec/141975.pdf.

Glikson, Andrew Y., and Colin Groves. *Climate, Fire and Human Evolution.* Vol. 10. *Modern Approaches in Solid Earth Sciences.* New York: Springer International Publishing, 2016. http://link.springer.com/10.1007/978-3-319-22512-8.

Global Security. "India-China Border Dispute." Accessed December 1, 2016. http://www.globalsecurity.org/military/world/war/india-china_conflicts.htm.

Gorst, Isabel. "Russia – Espo: Asia's Gain, Europe's Pain." *Financial Times.* Accessed December 1, 2016. http://blogs.ft.com/beyond-brics/2014/02/19/russia-espo-asias-gain-europes-pain/.

Great Green Wall for the Sahara and the Sahel Initiative (GGWSSI). "Home Page." Accessed December 2, 2016. http://www.greatgreenwallinitiative.org/.

Guo, Aibing. "CNPC to Start Laying Second China-Russia Oil Pipeline in June." *Bloomberg.com.* Accessed December 1, 2016. https://www.bloomberg.com/news/articles/2016-05-12/cnpc-to-start-laying-second-china-russia-oil-pipeline-in-june-io48uk3h.

Hamilton, Clive. "Getting the Anthropocene so Wrong." *The Anthropocene Review* 2, no. 2 (August 1, 2015): 102–7.

Hsu, Sara. "Is A Russia-China Economic Alliance On The Horizon?" *Forbes.* Accessed December 1, 2016. http://www.forbes.com/sites/sarahsu/2016/11/07/is-a-russia-china-economic-alliance-on-the-horizon/.

IISD Reporting Services. "China, India, Russia Reaffirm Commitment to SDGs, Climate Change." Accessed December 1, 2016. http://sdg.iisd.org/news/china-india-russia-reaffirm-commitment-to-sdgs-climate-change/.Information Office of the State Council. "China 2nd White Paper on Foreign Aid 2014," July 2014. http://ssc.undp.org/content/dam/ssc/dgspaces/China/files/China%202nd%20White%20Paper%20on%20Foreign%20Aid%202014.pdf.

Jayaram, Dhanasree. "A Shift in the Agenda for China and India: Geopolitical Implications for Future Climate Governance." *Carbon & Climate Law Review* 9, no. 3 (2015): 219–30.

Johnson, Elizabeth, Harlan Morehouse, Simon Dalby, Jessi Lehman, Sara Nelson, Rory Rowan, Stephanie Wakefield, and Kathryn Yusoff. "After the Anthropocene: Politics and Geographic Inquiry for a New Epoch." *ResearchGate* 38, no. 3 (May 15, 2014): 439–56.

Khor, Martin. "Opinion: China's New South-South Funds – a Global Game Changer?" *Inter Press* Service. Accessed December 1, 2016. http://www.ipsnews.net/2015/11/opinion-chinas-new-south-south-funds-a-global-game-changer/.

Korybko, Andrew. "The Threat To Russia and China From India's New Pro-US Realignment." *The Duran*, May 7, 2016. http://theduran.com/threat-russia-china-indias-new-pro-us-realignment/.

Latour, Bruno. *An Inquiry into Modes of Existence: An Anthropology of the Moderns.* Translated by Catherine Porter. 1st edition. Cambridge, Massachusetts: Harvard University Press, 2013.

Liu, Hongqiao. "China Pledges US$20 Million a Year to Its New South-South Cooperation Fund." Accessed December 1, 2016. https://www.chinadialogue.net/blog/7596-China-pledges-US-2-million-a-year-to-its-new-South-South-Cooperation-Fund/en.

Ministry of Foreign Affairs of the People's Republic of China. "China's Policy Paper on Latin America and the Caribbean." Accessed December 2, 2016. http://www.fmprc.gov.cn/mfa_eng/zxxx_662805/t1418254.shtml.

Möllers, Nina. "'A Huge Variety of Possibilities': Interview with Nobel Laureate Paul Crutzen on His Life, His Career in Research, and His Views on the Anthropocene Idea | Environment & Society Portal." Accessed December 9, 2016. http://www.environmentandsociety.org/exhibitions/anthropocene/huge-variety-possibilities-interview-nobel-laureate-paul-crutzen-his-life.

Mufson, Steven and Juliet Eilperin. "Trump Transition Team for Energy Department Seeks Names of Employees Involved in Climate Meetings." *Washington Post.* Accessed December 10, 2016. https://www.washingtonpost.com/news/energy-environment/wp/2016/12/09/trump-transition-team-for-energy-department-seeks-names-of-employees-involved-in-climate-meetings/.

Nassiry, Darius, and Smita Nakhooda. "The AIIB and Investment in Action on Climate Change," 2016. https://www.odi.org/sites/odi.org.uk/files/resource-documents/10441.pdf.

Netherlands Environmental Assessment Agency (PBL). "Co-Benefits of Climate Policy," 2009. http://www.unep.org/transport/gfei/autotool/understanding_the_problem/Netherlands%20Environment%20Agency.pdf.

Richards, Katherine. "China-India: An Analysis of the Himalayan Territorial Dispute," 2015. http://www.defence.gov.au/ADC/Publications/IndoPac/Richards%20final%20IPSD%20paper.pdf.

Ruddiman, William F. "The Anthropogenic Greenhouse Era Began Thousands of Years Ago." *Climatic Change* 61, no. 3 (2003): 261–293.

Sharman, Jon. "Bill Gates Announces a $1bn Fund for Clean Energy Technology." *The Independent*, December 12, 2016. http://www.independent.co.uk/news/people/bill-gates-clean-energy-investment-fund-climate-change-a7469201.html.

Steffen, Will, Wendy Broadgate, Lisa Deutsch, Owen Gaffney, and Cornelia Ludwig. "The Trajectory of the Anthropocene: The Great Acceleration." *The Anthropocene Review*, January 16, 2015.

Steffen, Will, Paul J. Crutzen, and John R. McNeill. "The Anthropocene: Are Humans Now Overwhelming the Great Forces of Nature." *AMBIO: A Journal of the Human Environment* 36, no. 8 (2007): 614–621.

TASS. "Trade between Russia, China Could Reach $90bln by 2016." *Russia Beyond The Headlines*, August 12, 2016. http://rbth.com/news/2016/08/12/trade-between-russia-china-could-reach-90bln-by-2016_620425.

Tondel, Fabien, Hanne Knaepen, and Lesley-Anne van Wyk. "Africa and Europe Combatting Climate Change," 2015. http://www.climdev-africa.org/sites/default/files/files/DP177-Africa-Europe-Combatting-Climate-Change-May-2015.pdf.

Torney, Diarmuid. "Bilateral Climate Cooperation: The EU's Relations with China and India." *Global Environmental Politics* 15, no. 1 (December 5, 2014): 105–22.

Torney, Diarmuid. *European Climate Leadership in Question: Policies toward China and India.* Cambridge, MA: MIT Press, 2015. http://www.jstor.org/stable/j.ctt16f98z9.

Turpin, Etienne, and Valeria Federighi. "A New Element, a New Force, a New Input: Antonio Stoppani's Anthropozoic," 2012. http://ro.uow.edu.au/eispapers/2986/.

US Census Bureau, Demographic Internet Staff. "International Programs, International Data Base." Accessed November 5, 2016. https://www.census.gov/population/international/data/idb/worldpopgraph.php.

Vidal, John, and Oliver Milman. "Paris Climate Deal Thrown into Uncertainty by US Election Result." *The Guardian*, November 9, 2016, sec. Environment. https://www.theguardian.com/environment/2016/nov/09/us-election-result-throws-paris-climate-deal-into-uncertainty.

Index

For Product Safety Concerns and Information please contact our EU
representative GPSR@taylorandfrancis.com
Taylor & Francis Verlag GmbH, Kaufingerstraße 24, 80331 München, Germany